The Key of David

by Patrice Horn Bates

TRILOGY

The Key of David

Trilogy Christian Publishers A Wholly Owned Subsidiary of Trinity Broadcasting Network

2442 Michelle Drive Tustin, CA 92780

Cover design by: Natalee Dunning

For information about special discounts for bulk purchases, please contact Trilogy Christian Publishing.

Manufactured in the United States of America

10 9 8 7 6 5 4 3 2 1

Library of Congress Cataloging-in-Publication Data is available.

ISBN: 978-1-63769-478-7
E-ISBN: 978-1-63769-479-4

This book is dedicated to the memory of—

Ordained Ministers Sylvia Thompson,
Irene Farley,
&
Pastor David Berkheimer;

Also,
to Bennie, Julianne, Gerrah,
our families & many friends in Christ
who have prayed, counseled,
and encouraged me in the Lord.

Thank you and may God richly bless you.

Special thanks for Sandy Wagner's editorial contribution.

*All Scripture references are taken from the
New King James Version of the Bible,
unless otherwise cited.*

TABLE OF CONTENTS

INTRODUCTION

"And the hunger and the seeking shall not be denied, sayeth God. For I have called thee in a specific way, and thou shalt surely enter into it," began a prophetic word from Sylvia Thompson on January 29, 1986. Sylvia prophesied in the King James vernacular. She also said, "Patrice, there's not one experience that comes your way that God is not going to use to bless someone else." At the time, I had no idea a book would be part of this prophecy's fulfillment, but it is because *The Key of David* is a compilation of testimony and teaching. Testimony of the many times Jesus has shown Himself mighty on my behalf and teaching of what I have learned as a result.

Some people never question God as to why things happen, not me. In John 16:12, Jesus said, "I still have many things to say to you, but you cannot bear them now." Regarding certain biblical truths, my heart would have been forever closed had I not walked through the account you are about to read. At age twenty, my life took an unexpected, alarming turn. I questioned the Lord about what was happening, and in time, He answered. Through divine appointments, Jesus connected me with people who offered hope and help. He also occasionally revealed angelic and demonic beings, scenarios, and structures hidden behind the veil of the natural realm, strengthening my understanding and appreciation of Scripture.

In the day-to-day, it's usually tyranny of the urgent that corners the lion's share of our time, but there is inconceivably more at stake than our temporal needs, desires, and comfort. As human beings, we have an unsearchable amount to gain and an unthinkable amount to lose, all hinging on our relationship with God the Father through His Son, Jesus. Some Christians have no desire to go further than

1

salvation, but there is a great deal more available in Christ. Not more important but required for success in certain situations. We can know what is happening behind the scenes and, more notably, do something about it. Indeed, "… in all these things we are more than conquerors through Him who loved us" (Romans 8:37). In the following pages, may you discover or strengthen the scriptural tools, weapons, and keys Holy Spirit has anointed and appointed for *your* triumph in Jesus Christ—shout! For the Lord has given us the victory!

For His glory,
Patrice

WHY ME?

I wasn't raised in a strictly religious home, going to church only occasionally as a child with my mom. I accepted Jesus as my Savior at age eleven at Little Cypress Baptist Church in Orange, Texas, following with water baptism because a dear friend reached out to me. She invited me to church on Sundays and Friday night football fellowships. But I had loved the Lord since I was little, thanks to my mom's faithfulness to take me to Vacation Bible School at First Baptist Church several years before. Because of this influence, I cannot remember a time in my life when I did not love or think of the Lord.

My early years seemed to be blessed with favor and promise, although my parents weren't wealthy. They worked and provided me with everything I could physically or emotionally need. As a preteen, my church involvement was limited; my mom tried to get my dad to attend, but it didn't happen. She became discouraged and, as a result, did not attend much herself. Although in dad's later years, he gave his heart to Christ and was baptized at Magnolia Springs Methodist Church (sprinkling) and again in a friend's swimming pool (dunking—just covering the baptismal bases) and had a supernatural encounter with God after his heart surgery in 1984. While still recuperating and praying in our living room, the Lord touched him. He felt an overwhelming sensation of peace and raised his hands to the Lord. The only thing wrong with that, he said, was it didn't last long enough! He shared this with me much later with tears in his eyes and said he was no longer afraid of death.

People probably shouldn't discuss religion or politics at gatherings but talking about the Lord with my mother's family was always an exciting topic at get-togethers. Sometimes the conversation would end with someone becoming angry when others didn't agree with his or her opinion. Still, I knew God was important to them, and every time these spiritual discussions took place my heart was greatly stirred. My mom's family loved the Lord but was also fearful of going overboard with religion. She had two brothers who were tormented most of their adult lives, and in both instances, erroneous religious beliefs seemed to be the root of their problems. Our hearts grieved for them; my grandmother and family prayed diligently, and my uncles received times of respite but never obtained complete deliverance. At one point, I asked the Lord if He would use me to help them and people like them because I believed God had their answers, even if those answers didn't come as quickly or permanently as we all prayed for.

There was faith in my mother's family, but I didn't realize how worldly most of us were until I began reading the Bible myself. My mom and dad occasionally went out dancing and drinking when I was small and were a normal couple, except for the occasional heated arguments they had, which greatly distressed me. Not ironically, partying became an enjoyable activity as a teenager. That generational thing took root in my heart and when I reached the legal age of eighteen during my high school senior year, having an occasional drink or beer came to be the norm, and "going out" was a weekend priority. I still thought of myself as a Christian; I didn't think I was hurting anyone or myself, but I inadvertently opened spiritual doors to the enemy through some of these activities.

From my baptism until my late teens, my walk with the Lord was sporadic, and I had little, although some, insight into the effect or boundaries of the spirit realm. I attribute this to the fact I had indeed accepted Christ and received water baptism when I was eleven; therefore, the Holy Spirit was resident in my spirit even if I didn't recognize His work at the time. I often felt the need to be closer to God, so several times I made a New Year's resolution to read the Scriptures through in one year. But usually, after about two weeks, I would fall off the wagon and neglect my Bible. Something would happen to get me fired up again, and for a short time, I tried but simply did not have the motivation to stay with a dedicated Christian walk. I was a baby, double-minded Christian. I believed in Jesus, but I also enjoyed the world.

In 1975, I graduated from Little Cypress-Mauriceville High School and started attending Stephen F. Austin State University in Nacogdoches, Texas. I was listening to popular but spiritually detrimental music, going dancing, drinking alcohol, and attending movies that pushed the envelope, unknowingly giving the enemy legal ground to oppress and control areas of my soul. The more I fed on this worldly diet, the less sensitivity and desire I felt for the things of God. First John 2:15 says, "Do not love the world or the things in the world. If anyone loves the world, the love of the Father is not in him." I was walking the fence, wanting to have my cake and eat it too. Wanting to avoid hell, but not wanting to miss the fun either.

But God. While attending SFA, a Christian outreach group sponsored a gathering on campus to enlighten students of lyrics in hard rock music, among other things. It was frightening because a song I was familiar with contained a phrase saying, "the soul I took from you was not even missed." I repented (or told the Lord I was sorry—my concept of repentance), but then I would slip back into the same old same old. One time my friend, Jim, sitting beside me in geology class, wrote on his paper, "Patrice is on another religious kick!" Others could recognize I was living a yo-yo Christian life, and deep inside, I knew it, too. I needed more than just self-determination or willpower to live for Christ. I needed the supernatural Holy Spirit baptism that only Jesus gives.

The problem began when I was around twenty. It was as though something got hold of my mind and would not let it go. Thoughts I didn't want to think kept coming and troubling me almost continuously. I struggled to pull my thinking away from these disturbing words and scenarios and attempted assertively, but quite unsuccessfully, to redirect my thoughts. Prayer helped, but the thoughts returned.

What I am describing sounds somewhat like obsessive-compulsive disorder, which is an anxiety disorder characterized by intrusive thoughts, producing uneasiness, anxiety, fear, and worry.[1] It became apparent something like what my uncles experienced was now happening to me, but I didn't say anything to anyone. They had gotten little relief, so how was I going to get relief and—more importantly —release? I had prayed for *them,* so why was God allowing this torment into *my* life? I eventually understood that my sin, my ancestor's sin, wounds from sin and deception operating through my flesh, the world, and the demonic network, combined to fulfill conditions necessary for the enemy to construct a stronghold in my mind.

According to the International OCD Foundation, estimates are about one in one hundred or between two to three million adults in the United States currently have OCD.[2] Not discrediting professional findings, I have come to believe that OCD (among a multitude of disorders attributed to the mental faculties) is the world's label to address seemingly psychological symptoms from a natural standpoint, unaware or disbelieving the possibility of spiritual influences. First Corinthians 2:14 says, "But the natural man does not receive the things of the Spirit of God, for they are foolishness to him; nor can he know them, because they are spiritually discerned." Although this Scripture is speaking of recognizing the moving and dealings of God in the context it is written, it also reveals parallel truth of how the enemy works undercover in the unseen realm with a multitude of vexations due to human beings' lack of spiritual discernment. If we don't know what we're dealing with, we can't do anything about it. Hosea 4:6 says, "My people are destroyed for lack of knowledge." I later learned it was fear these thoughts produced that gave the enemy legal ground to continue injecting them into my mind. Once I became secure in the knowledge these thoughts did not originate with me but were from the pit, and my relationship with Christ was intact, I could resist the enemy with unquestionably more success.

If you or someone you know has experienced something like this, hopefully, this book will bless you. If not, the spiritual principles (particularly the main subject) set forth may help you overcome obstacles to your freedom in Christ. It's my prayer this information will assist in fulfilling Jesus' mission to "preach deliverance to the captives and set at liberty those who are oppressed" (Luke 4:18). May you glean from precious revelation the Lord has bestowed; understanding which has the potential to take you to the next level in your walk with Him. It did in my life, and God is no respecter of persons (Acts 10:34).

It was not until my friend, Elaine, brought me to a prayer meeting when I was twenty-six that I began to get relief from the constant mental assault. During college and early marriage, I was still living very much in the world. However, the enemy's attacks against my mind motivated me to get serious about my walk with the Lord, so I turned to the only spiritual authority I was familiar with. At this point, I had been married four years to my husband, Bennie, and had our first child. I was reading my Bible and attending North Orange Baptist Church regularly, thinking "getting with the program" should help with the troubling thoughts. While these are good and necessary disciplines every Christian should observe and do, surprisingly, reading my Bible and going to church did not bring relief. I was headed in the right direction, which is vitally important, but I didn't grasp my sin had opened spiritual doors that could not be closed by becoming more involved in church. I accepted Jesus as my Savior but didn't consider what it meant to make Him my Lord. "Lord," as it is mostly used in the New Testament, is from the word "kurios" (Strong's Exhaustive Concordance[3] Greek, #2962), which means "supreme in authority." Many people call Jesus Lord, but He is *not* the supreme authority in their lives, which means He is not their Lord. I was one of those people until He kindly revealed the truth.

The prayer meeting at Community Church in Orange, Texas, was held in October 1983. This was approximately six months after I quit my job to be a stay-at-home mom. About a year before that, the Lord began dealing with me about my occupation in radio sales and production to come home because I had to put Julianne, our daughter, in daycare while I worked. One day while praying, the Lord whispered, "There's something you're putting ahead of Me." I said, "What, Lord?" As I went through the list of people and obligations in my life, when I got to my job, I could see red flashing lights in my mind. My first thought was, "If I quit my job, all our 'stuff' will get repossessed. I can't do that." I was torn because of our daughter, but I liked working for KOGT, the local radio station, and it paid well. Then the Lord said, "Come home and be a wife and mother and seek ye first the kingdom of God." I didn't recognize He spoke a portion of Matthew 6:33, but I certainly prayed about what I felt He was calling me to do, and for nine months, didn't do it.

After praying and talking it over with my husband, I finally obeyed the Lord and told my boss I was resigning. It felt like a heavy burden lifted off me. Ironically, after fretting and worrying, I now couldn't wait to come home. There was no way of knowing all God was up to, but since I felt such an increase of peace, I thought, *I must be on the right track.* Colossians 3:15 says, "And let the peace of God rule in your hearts, to which also you were called in one body, and be thankful." The Greek word for "rule" here is "brabeuo,"[4] meaning "to arbitrate or to umpire." Like the umpire in a baseball game, the peace of God in our heart can substantiate a correct choice, while the absence of it can be a warning. God is Jehovah Shalom,[5] which means "The Lord is peace." The peace He gives can be a confirmation we are in His will or our prayers are answered. It's difficult to appreciate this blessed peace until we have been in the throes of turmoil. It's truly a little "peace" of heaven on Earth.

The Wednesday morning Bible Study was a full gospel first for me (except for a visit to a Pentecostal church years before). I was in the company of people who understood and practiced spiritual warfare. These people prayed together and out loud! They praised God and took authority over the devil. From the time I had recommitted to attending church as an adult, I had been praying the Lord would connect me with people who felt about Him as I did; people who got excited about the things of God, and at last, He had.

I had been mainly exposed to the doctrine and teaching of the Baptist church, and it served a meaningful purpose in my life. Through the Baptist church, I received Jesus as my Savior and water baptism; I received teaching that strengthened and reinforced my understanding of the death, burial, and resurrection of Christ, which is foundational to all other Christian doctrines. I still had mental bondage, but I was growing spiritually. First Peter 2:2 says when we desire the pure milk of the Word—reading the Bible, listening to and meditating on it—our spirit man will grow. Just like a baby grows when fed the sustenance of milk, our spirits grow when fed the Word of God. Nearly the entire sixth chapter of the book of John deals with the spiritual nourishment found in the Scriptures and in Christ.[6] While I attended the Baptist church, God strengthened my foundation in Christ; my spirit man was fed. But in that denominational setting, nothing was taught about the spiritual weapons I needed to ascertain the freedom Jesus has given us.[7]

While working for KOGT, I began watching the 700 Club on TV when I came home for lunch. Listening to Pat Robertson talk about the power of the Holy Spirit prepared my heart for the ministry I would receive through the Wednesday meetings and beyond. As Pat spoke about the supernatural power of God, faith was building in my heart in a new way. To my recollection, I never consciously heard the voice nor experienced the power of God before the Miss Beaumont pageant in 1976 and New Year's Eve, 1981, when I was five months pregnant with Julianne. As Bennie and I prepared to go to a friend's house for the evening, something happened that greatly upset me. Without even thinking, I asked the Holy Spirit to give me strength and—*zing!* He gave it to me. The distress immediately left my mind and body. I was amazed that God could and would answer my prayer so quickly and powerfully.

I had another brush with His supernatural intervention about three and a half years later after our second daughter, Gerrah, was born. I had become ill with food poisoning causing vomiting and diarrhea. For days, I prayed for God to heal me but became weaker and dehydrated. Bennie called my physician, Dr. Rogers, who had me admitted to Orange Memorial Hospital. The IV and meds worked beautifully, and within twenty-four hours, I was well enough to go home. Thirty minutes after the removal of the IV, I felt weakness seeping back into my body. I was alarmed but kept my mouth shut and hoped for a miracle. By bedtime, the nausea had become intense; I didn't know what else to do but pray, so I said, "Lord Jesus, if you have heard any of my prayers, please settle my stomach and let me go to sleep." Instantly, my stomach stopped churning and began to settle, like Jesus calming the storm in Matthew 8:26. I drifted off to sleep, but not before telling Him, "Thank you."

The next day, my body was still recovering from the trauma it had been through the past week, but I didn't throw up again. The supernatural release of God's peace into my spirit and the supernatural settling of my stomach taught me God is still in the miracle-working business. Ephesians 3:20 says that He is "able to do exceedingly abundantly above all that we ask or think, according to the power that works in us." Whatever our highest aspiration is, God can do astronomically more, and He does it by the power of the Holy Spirit resident in every heart where Christ lives.

Because of the 700 Club and Elaine, God connected me to people who understood the power of Jesus Christ and the authority He has given His followers; the only way to effectively deal with demons and have real and lasting success. And it was becoming clearer I was dealing with the demonic. My friend Vicki tells of a vision where she stood before the Lord Jesus, and He said to her, "I proclaim liberty to you!" When the Lord spoke those words to her, things she didn't realize were hanging onto her began to fall off. In the spirit, she saw demonic beings with claws attached to her body in the stomach area, release her and fall each time the Lord spoke. The Lord spoke four times, each time disabling another demon. We all deal with demonic influence, deception, and bondage, but most of the time demons are hidden and well-disguised; without supernatural revelation and intervention, they can and will remain concealed and entrenched in people's lives during their entire existence on Earth. But it doesn't have to be that way because Jesus is *the way* to truth, deliverance, and freedom!

Psalm 34:8 says, "O taste and see that the Lord is good, blessed is the man who trusts in Him!" Finding myself in a full Gospel meeting where the power of God flowed was exciting; a good place to ask for help, so I asked for prayer about the distressing thoughts. Up to now, I hid my struggle, not telling anyone for fear of what they would think. But I was desperate; I had nowhere to turn because I had never heard anyone discuss these things. Our anointed teacher addressed the enemy and told him to "pack up his tools and go home." I soon learned every true believer in Christ has been given the key of authority over the devil's power. Jesus told His disciples in Luke 10:19, "Behold, I give you the authority to trample on serpents and scorpions and over all the power of the enemy..."[8] but many Christians lack or ignore this revelation. A great resource on this subject is Kenneth E. Hagin's book entitled, *The Believer's Authority.*[9] I began to experience a measure of release through the power and authority of Christ that these ladies prayed and walked in immediately.

This happened before Prozac and other anti-depressants of the late '80s and early '90s. If I had known those medications were available, I might have gone to the doctor for a prescription. But even in my naiveté, I knew these attacks were demonic and needed to know why the enemy was able to harass me. I didn't know how he was doing it; I didn't feel depressed, but I did know something was awry in my thought processes. And taking medicine to get rid of symptoms wouldn't deal with him or any root causes. This is not criticism of anyone taking medication to keep their emotional or mental balance. God can and does use physician's, pharmacist's, psychologist's, and other professional's skills. He gave them their abilities, and every good and perfect gift is from Him.[10] Chemical or hormonal imbalances are factual; as women, hormones wane as we age or cause physical problems at any point in life, significantly affecting thought patterns, mood, and outlook. Not to mention the whole gamut of physical problems that assail the human body, including the brain (Note: if you are on medication, *do not* stop taking it without consulting your physician).

However, the Bible states that demons are real, too. They are not a mindless, mysterious "dark side of the force," although they operate under Satan's malevolent authority, aligning themselves in opposition to the plans and purposes of our holy Creator. Demons are individual spirit beings who usually work with other demons to mislead, pervert, corrupt, and destroy anyone or anything they possibly can. They are knowledgeable (Ezekiel 28:12), organized (Ephesians 6:12), destructive (Mark 9:18), deceptive (2 Corinthians 11:14), they communicate (Mark 1:24), are evil (Luke 8:2), and can inhabit living organisms (Luke 8:30). Our eyes may not see them, but we can observe their effect and influence on people, events, and the atmosphere. In Strong's Concordance, the word "devils"[11] occurs four times in the Old Testament and fifty times in the New Testament; the singular word "devil" doesn't appear even once in the Old Testament![12] Jesus, the Light of the World, tore off the enemy's covers and exposed the hidden works of Satan, who supervises his entire evil empire under the concealment of spiritual darkness and has been doing so since man first believed his lies and sinned.

A great deal of Jesus' ministry was devoted to freeing those who were oppressed or possessed by demons. I had read it; now I needed answers. What sin or event took place that opened the door to demonic assault? My reasoning was, "If the enemy can find a way in, there's a way to kick him out!" But how can we cast something out when we aren't even sure what it is? We look to Jesus, the author, and finisher of our faith (Hebrews 12:2). My deliverance was not instantaneous but has come in steps as the Lord has little by little revealed the lies of the enemy and helped me replace those lies with the truth of His Word; word replacement therapy. Some revelation has come from Him as a "rhema"[13]word spoken directly to my spirit or through the Scriptures (it "jumps" out), and He has ministered to me through teachings and ministries of others in the Body of Christ who understand the spiritual "rules of engagement." But God is not limited to those in the Body of Christ; He can speak to us out of the mouths of babes and even the unsaved. If He can use a donkey (Numbers 22:28), He can use anyone or anything to communicate with us.

In our quest for freedom in Christ, everything we receive as truth must line up with His Word. Many people have gotten off track with a "revelation" that was not scriptural. God's Word, the Holy Bible, is our road map and plumb line; it gives direction and keeps us balanced. God will never tell us to do something the Bible specifically defines as sin. Psalm 119:160a says, "The entirety of Your word is truth..." and we interpret the Scriptures through other Scriptures. Consequently, every revelation we receive must be measured against the authority of the Bible.

Before I understood spiritual warfare, the battle in my thought life wore me down; over time, I worried that God was angry, and I questioned my salvation. Although I knew the Bible says God is love (1 John 4:8), I wondered how He could still love me. If I understood what was happening, I could have spoken to the enemy, saying, "Jesus said, 'All that the Father gives Me will come to me and the one who comes to Me I will by no means cast out,' in John 6:37; in Hebrews 13:5, 'I will never leave you or forsake you,' and Romans 8:38, 39 says nothing shall separate me from God's love, so leave now devil!" We must read our Bibles, for to use the Word effectively, we first become familiar with it and commit it to memory, so Holy Spirit can retrieve and anoint it in times of need. Indeed, the sword of the Spirit, which is the Word of God, is the only offensive weapon in the Christian's armor in Ephesians 6:10–17, and it works. But there is also another...

Even if we're not a spiritual dynamo, the Lord isn't restricted by our insufficiency and can use other people who are sensitive and obedient to the Spirit. While working for KOGT, I met Lillian, who had done a painting for NOBC that hung in the entryway. As we talked and shared our faith in the Lord, she felt impressed to tell me how much Jesus loved me. She discerned that I was burdened, yet she couldn't know the full extent of my concerns. Her words were comforting, reinforcing my resolve to continue trusting in the love and faithfulness of God. When the enemy has spun a web of lies in our mind, one word from God may enable us to cut ourselves free; or possibly use His Word like a searchlight, unraveling that web one thought at a time. Eventually, the truth and light of God's Word overtake the lies and darkness of Satan, freeing us in areas we don't even realize we are bound. Thank God for Lillian's sensitivity and kindness to share God's Word with me that day; it came at a time I seriously needed it, a Kairos, or divinely timed moment. It's not cliché to tell someone God loves them; it flows from His heart through ours to them, and it *will* impact them because God's Word is *alive!*[14]

That Wednesday meeting was my first real opportunity to receive help, though my issue was difficult to talk about. Second Corinthians 3:17 says, "Now the Lord is the Spirit, and where the Spirit of the Lord is, there is liberty." I believe it was the flowing, unconditional love of God freeing me enough to ask for prayer. And what prayer! The faith these women demonstrated in believing God for deliverance, healing, and miracles was like nothing I had ever seen; the very atmosphere was charged with the tangible presence of God. Full Gospel churches have recognized and operated in the perceptible presence of God for years; the Scriptures bear witness this spiritual phenomenon is discernibly real.[15]

Years before this, I was told there was nothing substantial to the spiritual frenzy that "holy roller" churches were famous for; they were just getting worked up and babbling (speaking in tongues). We laughed at some of the things that reportedly went on in Pentecostal gatherings (please forgive me). Nevertheless, suffering, be it physical, emotional, mental, or spiritual, tends to supply an entrance to anything that offers hope. I was not entirely familiar with the full Gospel, but I read the Bible and knew that Hebrews 13:8 declares

Jesus Christ is the same yesterday, today, and forever. If that's true, then Jesus' deliverance ministry is relevant for today and, specifically, for me. Jesus said, "All things are possible to him who believes" (Mark 9:23), and I believed God could help me, but it took time and preparation for supernatural ministry due to previously held beliefs.

The enemy has duped large numbers of Christians regarding the fullness and power of the Holy Spirit, but that's changing for those who desire healing, deliverance, and power to do "greater things" Jesus spoke of in John 14:12. I was skeptical, but now I understand the spirit realm is not only real; it controls just about everything in the natural![16] Many of our seemingly unanswered prayers have been blocked by demonic beings occupying legal ground that we, our ancestors, or occupants of our region have unwittingly given them through sin, ignorance, and rebellion regarding God's spiritual laws.

Ira Milligan, in *The Anatomy of a Scorpion,* writes,

> Yielding to iniquity constitutes an agreement or covenant. Amos 3:3 states, "Can two walk together except they be agreed?" Like a vow, an agreement is the same as a covenant or contract. A covenant can be entered into by word or deed and is perpetually binding until it is annulled, fulfilled, or forgiven.[17]

The enemy seeks a place of agreement in our thoughts or actions, giving him legally granted access to exercise a measure of control in our lives. Knowing, speaking, and living the Word of God is necessary to extricate ourselves from his entanglements and lay claim to the freedom, blessings, and benefits we possess as Christians.

After I received prayer for the unwanted thoughts, I was asked if I wanted to receive the baptism of the Holy Spirit. I said yes, not realizing the magnitude of the impact it would have upon my life. They laid hands on me and prayed, asking Jesus to fill me, and as the minister said, "Lord, let the joy come out!" I literally felt a bubble of joy rise from within my spirit. I could not contain it; it was like air bubbles coming to the water's surface. It burst out of my mouth with praise unto the Lord, and then, as they encouraged me, I began to speak words I did not recognize. This was "tongues" as spoken of in the book of Acts[18] and in 1 Corinthians.[19] It did sort of sound like babbling but had been accompanied with unmistakable joy and peace, prompting me to step out and trust God.

The Holy Spirit's baptism is life-changing—and all for the better! I already had Jesus in my heart, but now the certainty of His presence became much more real, all to the enemy's chagrin. Nevertheless, when leaving the meeting, the enemy launched a counterattack. It's a given that Satan doesn't want us saved, but he sure doesn't want us receiving power that can be used against *him*. In Acts 1:8, Jesus said, "you shall receive power when the Holy Spirit has come upon you," and it's true! There is at least a three-fold impartation given with the baptism of the Holy Spirit, each portion releasing overflow of God's Spirit in your life, bringing supernatural understanding, ability, and utterance as the Lord wills. It's no wonder when God gives us something that adversely impacts the kingdom of darkness, our adversary will attempt to wrestle God's truth from our hearts.[20]

The enemy mostly speaks to us in first person singular, so we won't recognize an evil spirit masquerading as our own thoughts. Thoughts that sound like, "Was that really God? Did that really happen? What would so-and-so think if he/she heard me speaking in tongues?" This is usually accompanied by feelings of uneasiness. Depending on the amount and fortification of strongholds in our mind prior to the God encounter—salvation, Holy Spirit baptism, healing, deliverance, or financial blessing, the more determined the enemy will be to talk us out of our miracle or harvest (Matthew 13:19–23). But don't give up! Become strong in Bible knowledge and understanding. The more truth we know, the more we can counter-attack those doubting, fearful thoughts, neutralizing their effect.

The power of God is available to all who are in covenant with Him, whether it comes easily or if we must press in through fasting and prayer. The enemy knows he is already defeated, but he is going to fight us in our spiritual progression until *we* know he is and

against the demonic when spoken in faith as a member of God's family. And we are members of His family when we receive the salvation that Jesus alone provides. Attempting to use these weapons without a viable relationship with Christ may not prove successful. Remember the seven sons of Sceva in Acts 19:13–16. When trying to cast out demons without being in the right relationship with God through Jesus, they got a colossal whipping!

By ourselves, we cannot defeat the devil nor recognize his deceptions. Before Lucifer (Satan's original name) fell from his place in heaven, he was one of the highest order of angels God created.[23] Michael the Archangel alone may be his match in the spirit realm.[24] But for those who have Jesus Christ, greater is He who is in us than he who is in the world (1 John 4:4), and He has provided everything we need to become more than conquerors. Jesus is not a created being like Satan. He is the Son of God, and He is on our side! Once we realize Jesus alone is the Way, the truth, and the life, and Victor over sin, self, and Satan, we must align ourselves with Him and His purposes through repentance, the new birth, and the baptism of the Holy Spirit. Then our journey can become an adventure.

Friend, serving God is *not* boring! Knowing the Lord is the greatest honor in life; His sacrifice is incalculable and amazing to me. Jesus paid for our eternal salvation from a devil's hell, our healing physically, emotionally, mentally, and for our deliverance from fear, torment, and everything that brings bondage. This freedom He freely gives us, but it is through revelation, faith, and action (or obedience) that His power is made manifest in our lives. Yes, the devil may have an agenda, but don't overlook the second part of John 10:10, which is Jesus' mission statement: "...I have come that they (you and I) may have life and that they may have it more abundantly." Jesus, though the power of the Holy Spirit, has equipped us to fight, and win, the good fight of faith.

WHY JESUS?

Just as there are battles in the natural that we feel and observe with our physical senses, there are battles in the spirit realm, but these are only discerned by spiritual means. Those means may be accessed legally via a relationship with God through Jesus Christ or illegally through Satan's devices. The former is revelation and life; the latter is deception and death. Many people think dabbling in witchcraft or other forms of the occult to attain mystical knowledge is harmless, thanks to our culture's definition of entertainment. And there are those whom the enemy has duped into thinking Satan's devices are a means for receiving what they want in life, but the Bible is indisputably clear concerning the penalty for such activities.[25]

Deuteronomy 18:10–12 states that taking part in such things as child sacrifice (which is like abortion), witchcraft, sorcery, fortune-telling, spiritism, and consulting the dead are "abominations to the Lord." An abomination is a disgusting, revolting, shamefully wicked thing. Although God offers forgiveness and deliverance to those who have participated in such activities, or any other sin, those attempting to access the spirit realm apart from God must tap into demonic power, which is in alliance with the occult and is extremely dangerous. But hey, just living a life without God is also extremely dangerous because, without His sovereign protection, our life can end at any moment, and we must then give an account of how we lived our life on Earth (Romans 14:12).

We are going to live forever—either in a state of eternal life or eternal death.[26] Hebrews 9:27 says, "...it is appointed for men to die once, but after this, the judgment." Some think death is like going to sleep because it appears that way from the outside looking on. But the Word reveals there is a quickening of the spirit upon separation from the body (1 Peter 3:18), whereby our spirit and soul immediately proceed to the destination we have prepared for—either life with God, which is only possible through Christ,[27] or separation from Him in hell's abode until the Great White Throne Judgment, culminating in the lake of fire for those whose names are not written in the Book of Life.[28] Physical death isn't the end of our existence; it's the beginning of how we will spend eternity.

When I was young, I wondered why hearing from God, like other people claimed, seemed so difficult. And I had lots of questions. Even though I read the Bible (sporadically), I would talk to Him when I walked, asking things like, "Why don't you just shout from heaven and make your wishes clearer?" Clearly, even after reading the Word, I was still oblivious to much of what He had spoken and revealed, what He has done and is doing as we speak. I was thankful He had answered many of my prayers, but I only knew Him by His acts of kindness and not so much His ways.

I remember coming home from Kirbyville, Texas, with my dad one day, gazing out the car window. Surrounded by tall, green, southeast Texas piney woods, my dad said, "I don't know how anyone can see the beauty of this world and not believe there is a God." I totally agreed but didn't realize the depth of his statement, nor what he spoke was scriptural. Romans 1:20 says, "For since the creation of the world His invisible attributes are clearly seen, being understood by the things that are made, even His eternal power and Godhead (divine nature), so that they are without excuse." When I am blessed to see the brilliance of a rainbow's spectrum, towering thunderheads with the sun's rays dancing through them, the majesty of a black sky filled with stars, the vastness of an ocean, or the incalculable array of incredible creatures on Earth, I am in awe of God's creative knowledge, wisdom, and power. And yet, all these things are only the backdrop for who He made them. It's astounding that He loves us regardless of all we have done, continue and neglect to do, and take for granted.

The Scriptures declare God created humanity for fellowship with Himself. Revelation 4:11 (KJV) says, "Thou art worthy, O Lord, to receive glory and honor and power: for Thou hast created all things, and for Thy pleasure they are and were created." It brings pleasure to God to know us, and He wants us to know Him, not just know about Him. I know some things about the President of the United States, but I don't know him personally. However, I do know the King of Kings, and He has revealed in His Word that He is seeking even more than fellowship with us. Jesus said in John 17:21, "...that they all may be one, as You, Father, are in Me, and I in You; that they also may be one in Us, that the world may believe that You sent Me." God is seeking union, which means "to become one" and Jesus has made that possible. There's just one not-so-little problem.

Because He is Creator, God alone has the right to define what's right and wrong in His creation. He originally created all things in perfection, but the world no longer exists in that perfect state. And He has revealed what has prevented us from really knowing Him. That thing, that "problem" He says is wrong He calls sin, or unrighteousness (1 John 5:17)—un-right-ness; not right. Sin is an offense to God. Feelings of offense are unpleasant. Now multiply that by over 107 billion (the number of people that ever lived according to the Population Reference Bureau as of this writing).

The apostle Paul, in Romans, says we have all sinned and fallen short of God's glory (verse 3:23). We try to be good, but our sin causes us to fall short or miss the mark every time, and we are unable to attain true revelation of or fellowship with the Lord. Romans 6:23 says the wages (payment) of our sin is death. If we never recognize our sinful state and continue doing things that God has declared unrighteous, the result, or reward, can only be death. It's not what God wants, but our sin puts us on automatic pilot toward destruction, and we must make a course correction to find the path of life. That course correction is called repentance.

The prophet Isaiah wrote, "But your iniquities (perversity) have separated you from your God, and your sins have hidden His face from you..." verse 59:2. Even when people seek after God, without dealing with the sin element in their hearts, a barrier remains. Ezekiel's words, recorded over 600 years prior to Jesus' ministry, are remarkably like what Paul said in Romans. Ezekiel 18:20 says, "the soul who sins shall die." Because of sin, physical death for all of us is certain, except for those who are supernaturally changed in the rapture.[29] That's because we've all sinned, but death in this life is only the beginning of human beings' eternal existence.

However, God didn't leave us hopeless in an everlasting state of separation from Himself. Before we got into this mess, He already had a plan. Revelation 13:8 says the Lamb, who is Jesus Christ, was slain from the foundation of the world. Jesus now offers us the gift of eternal life made possible through His own sacrificial death, burial, and resurrection.[30] To believe and receive that gift or to reject it is a choice God requires each of us to make. Therefore, Jesus commissioned the Church to preach the Gospel to all nations (Matthew 28:19–20). Jesus Himself is the key to eternal life; indeed, He holds and is the Key for everything in existence! Colossians 1:16–17 says,

> For by Him (Jesus) all things were created that are in heaven and that are on Earth, visible and invisible, whether thrones or dominions or principalities (rulers) or powers. All things were created through Him and for Him. And He is before all things, and in Him all things consist.

Jesus of Nazareth, the Messiah, has opened the door to heaven, and all mankind is invited to come into His Kingdom. It doesn't matter how terrible a sinner you think you are or someone else is. God loves you; He wants you. He loves everyone—no exceptions. The call has gone forth that *whosoever*[31] will hearken to His invitation and follow Him can come and be part of His kingdom now and forever.

Choosing to accept the Lord's indescribable gift is the best decision we will ever make, even if we are met with opposition. When we believe the Bible and make the course correction (repent, think differently), turning from a life of sin and self-seeking, then believing in and accepting Jesus as our Savior, we enter a personal relationship with Father God through His Son and become part of His family. John 1:12 says, "But as many as received Him, to them He gave the right to become children of God, to those who believe in His name." The relationship was God's desire from the beginning, but sin impeded that from happening. Consequently, God Himself provided the way for us through the cross, the flesh, and the blood of Jesus. Because the "life is in the blood" (Leviticus 17:11), when we receive Jesus, He also receives us into Himself. His lifeblood then washes away our sin and simultaneously grafts us into His body, which is the Church.

There is much to be gained through a relationship with God: joy, peace, health, protection, wisdom, fulfillment, fellowship, and eternal life, although there will be persecution (Mark 10:29–30). But any persecution we endure will never rival man's worst nightmare: hell, and eternal separation from all that is good. Bill Wiese's book, *23 Minutes in Hell*, gives a vivid and scriptural account of what hell may be like. Kenneth E. Hagin's mini-book, *I Went to Hell*, tells of his dying, going to hell, and conversion experience. Friend, nobody wants to end up in hell, and it's not God's will that any should spend eternity there. He didn't create hell's prison and the second death in the lake of fire for humans; He created them for Satan and his fallen angels (Matthew 25:41). However, that is all that's left for those who reject or ignore Jesus Christ, the only way of escape from a world set on a collision course with God's judgment by the first created man, Adam.

Jesus said, "I am the way, the truth, and the life. No one comes to the Father except through Me"[32] (John 14:6). If there was any pathway to God other than through Christ, that would make Jesus a liar. It would mean He died a humiliating, excruciating, bloody death in vain. But Jesus isn't a liar, and He didn't die in vain. He died for you and me. "For God so loved the world, that He gave His only begotten Son, that whosoever believes in Him, should not perish, but have everlasting life" (John 3:16). Why would He pay such an exorbitant price to save us puny little humans from eternal separation from God? Because He loves us, and He loves His Father that much. Sinful flesh could never abide in the presence of the great and Holy God, Jehovah (1 Corinthians 15:50), but He miraculously desires our fellowship, so His Word made flesh created a way for us to come into His presence through Jesus' supreme, atoning sacrifice.

And Jesus was the only man in history qualified to make that sacrifice.[33] He was the first Person born of the Spirit because God was His Father (Luke 1:35). Although He was fully God, He was also fully man, capable of sin but never sinning the entire thirty-three and a half years He walked the Earth. Because the rest of us are descendants of Adam, we're all born with an inclination to sin, passed down from generation to generation because of his and Eve's original disobedience (Romans 5:12). Therefore, God Himself intervened in humanity to do away with sin altogether by sending His own Son in the *likeness* of sinful flesh (Romans 8:3).

Jesus, who is the last Adam[34] and eternally existent as the second Person of the Godhead (1 John 5:7), revealed the nature of His pre-human existence in Matthew 12:34. The first part of this Scripture is a rebuke to the Pharisees, but a principle is concealed in the second part, "...out of the abundance of the heart the mouth speaks." Jesus is "The Word of God." God spoke everything into existence (Genesis 1:3–25) through His Word, who is Jesus.[35] Jesus resided in the very heart of God and went forth to do His will every time God spoke. Ultimately, He made His entrance into humanity as the Word of God clothed with human flesh. Jesus was born, He lived, and He died without yielding to sin's temptation even once, and then offered Himself as payment for our sin, obtaining eternal redemption for all who would call on His name in faith. This redemption, this gift of eternal life, is free, but it's not cheap; and the high price God paid for our salvation is not something to be lightly esteemed.

Without the revelation of Scripture, people tend to accept the world's preconceived notions about spiritual matters that are diametrically opposed to what the Bible reveals as truth. We cannot be saved by osmosis (just being around other Christians), becoming a member of the local church, or doing good deeds. To enter the kingdom of God, which is the sphere of being saved, or salvation itself, according to Jesus, "you must be born again." He said this to Nicodemus, a Pharisee and member of the Sanhedrin, three times: John 3:3, 5, and 7. To understand why Jesus said this, we must first examine man's creation.

In Genesis, chapter two, the Bible reveals Adam was originally created with life in his spirit; he and Eve could have lived forever in the ideal condition God created them, but when presented with a choice in chapter three, they decided to believe the serpent over what God had spoken and disobey the only command God gave them: not to eat the fruit of the tree of knowledge of good and evil, for if they did, on that day they would surely die. When they chose to disobey and eat, they sinned. Immediately their union with the Holy One was severed, and they "fell from grace," meaning they lost their original, spiritual connection to God.

Although Adam and Eve's bodies and souls didn't instantly die, their spirits did. The Bible does not mention Adam's spirit specifically; it says that "the Lord God formed man of the dust of the ground, and breathed into his nostrils the breath of life, and man became a living soul" (Genesis 2:7, KJV). It was more than air blown into Adam's nostrils. The word "breath" is translated from the Hebrew word, "neshamah,"[36] which can mean "a puff, divine inspiration, soul *or* spirit." Since God told them on the day they ate of the tree of knowledge of good and evil, they would die (Genesis 2:17), and God is not a man that He should lie;[37] when they sinned, something died. By process of elimination, we see it was not their body, because Adam lived to be 930 years old; it was not their soul (comprised of the intellect, emotions, and will), because they could still think, feel, and make choices; it had to be their spirit. God reveals through this devastating event that the real person, our very core, is the spirit man.

Some believe because Adam lived to be nearly a thousand years old, he did indeed die on the day he sinned—by counting his years in "God days." Second Peter 3:8 says, "But, beloved, do not forget this one thing, that with the Lord one day is a thousand years, and a thousand years as one day." However, this view doesn't consider the realm of Adam's human spirit, and it wouldn't be until the appearance of Christ that revelation concerning these matters would be released. Adam's body probably began the process of deterioration immediately, but slowly, after he sinned, taking much time for physical death to manifest. This may be due to the vibrancy and residue of his original perfect, created state.

Bible understanding is built in levels; as we move forward with revelation we have, the Holy Spirit through the Word adds to this understanding by incorporating parallel truths and principles, creating deeper, fuller meaning. The entirety of truth can be comprehended as layers of corresponding truth incorporated into the original thought (Psalm 119:160). This process is disclosed in Isaiah 28:10, "For precept must be upon precept, precept upon precept, line upon line, line upon line, here a little, there a little." Some truths mentioned in the Old Testament are brought into clearer, more accurate meaning in the New Testament. It's been said, "the New is in the Old concealed, and the Old is in the New revealed." Hence, we know from 1 Thessalonians 5:23 and Hebrews 4:12 that man is a tripartite, or three-part being. He is essentially a spirit who possesses a soul and lives in a body with all three parts interconnected.

Adam and Eve's disobedience to God was sin. Sin is "to break the law of God; to offend."[38] Man's sin broke or fractured, his union with the source of his life, the living God, who is holy.[39] Holy means pure, clean, and set apart. Adam took one bite of the forbidden fruit, and instantly the life-giving force God alone supplied to his and Eve's spirits was cut off. Like a branch cut from a tree no longer has access to the life-sustaining nutrients the tree supplies, their spirits were separated from God, and separation from God is death. Adam and Eve's spirits didn't disintegrate; they were still existent, but in a darkened, empty state, void of the previous internal light and presence of God.[40]

Physical death eventually followed because the sin principle had been set in motion, though many years passed before Adam and Eve experienced bodily death. Because sin took life from Adam's spirit, fellowship with God could only be restored through the sacrifice of another life. Before the sin, Adam and Eve enjoyed union with God because their spirits were infused with His Holy Spirit's breath of life. After the sin, God Himself demonstrated the righteousness His holiness demands *and* the mercy He longs to extend by clothing Adam and Eve's naked bodies with skin from an animal He obviously sacrificed on their behalf (Genesis 3:21). His righteous judgment is clearly seen in the "eye for an eye" principle in Exodus 21:24.[41] But His mercy is revealed in Genesis 22 when God provided Abraham a substitutionary ram to sacrifice in place of Isaac, pointing to the superior sacrifice He would finally make through His own Son.

In like manner, other spiritual leaders to whom God revealed Himself also offered blood sacrifices—Abel, Noah, Isaac, Jacob, and Moses.[42] Approximately 2500 years after man's fall, God, through Moses, instituted the Levitical priesthood in the nation of Israel, where various animals were specified by God for sacrificial offerings.[43] A foreshadowing of what would come, the sacrifice of animals could never cleanse mankind, for these creatures were a lower order; it would require a sinless Man to accomplish this. Because animals aren't made in God's image, nor given revelation of God's holiness, they aren't capable of sin. However, God honored these sacrifices, and in so doing, He "passed over" (Exodus 12:27) man's sin to continue to work to bring about the Great Exchange—His life for ours through the Person of Jesus.

There were other notable factors that took place in the garden, where sin initially contaminated humanity. The serpent (Satan in disguise) deceived Eve, telling her she wouldn't die if she ate the fruit of the tree of knowledge—lie—she and Adam *did* die spiritually. He told her that her eyes would be *opened,* and she would be like God, *knowing* good and evil (Genesis 3:1–5). Scripture does not totally refute this statement (Genesis 3:22). Herein lies the insidiousness of deception. What he implied in saying her eyes would be opened was that God had withheld something good from her, something she needed to be like Him. The Hebrew word for "*opened*" in verse 5 is "paqach,"[44] meaning "to open (the senses; especially the eyes)" and "*knowing*" is "yada,"[45] meaning "to ascertain (learn, discover) by seeing." God is an invisible Spirit Being (Colossians 1:15), but the serpent implied Eve would be like God if she lived life through her senses, especially her eyesight, instead of spiritual discernment.

That snake knew she and Adam were already like God, created in His image, and possessed the Spirit of Life. And though God the Father knows about sin, sin doesn't originate in Him, nor is He tempted by it (James 1:13). But if the serpent convinced them to choose sin, its entrance through their disobedience would cut their lifeline to God *and* darken their understanding by removing the spiritual light or covering their relationship with God innately provided. Psalm 104:2 says, "Who cover Yourself with light as with a garment." God is light, and His clothing is light. In Him is no darkness at all (1 John 1:5). It stands to reason that Adam and Eve were also clothed with light, which may have emanated from their spirit. When sin came in, the light went out, and they saw their nakedness.

The shame of no longer being clothed with God's light propelled them into making their own coverings, which happened to be the proverbial fig leaf. Without God's provision, Adam and Eve were still spiritually naked even though managing to somewhat cover themselves physically. With the severing of their relationship with God, their spiritual understanding was no longer operational. False religion is like the fig leaf cover-up: it doesn't deal with the issues of the heart; it's an outside decoration or set of rules—a placebo—to deal with the inadequacy we feel inside. It may provide a temporary *feeling* of security, but it is a false security.

Before coming to Jesus, we may not realize it, but down inside, we know something is lacking, or we wouldn't constantly try to fill the void in our hearts. Some fill it with sinful pleasures that last for a season, which they must repeat and increase only to find themselves, and others they have influenced ushered to the precipice of eternal destruction. Many are deceived into thinking all roads lead to heaven; I'm okay, you're okay, don't knock my religion, and I won't knock yours, with some busying themselves with religious activities and good works. But Isaiah 64:6 says, "All our righteousnesses are like filthy rags." Even our good intentions are tainted with selfishness thanks to the fruit of the tree of knowledge of good and evil,[46]nurturing a spiritual uncleanness inherent to man's sin. Without the Word and Holy Spirit's revelation, our spiritual malady cannot be resolved.

Good deeds cannot pay for sin, nor can they offset or undo sins we have committed. Without the shedding of blood, there is no remission (freedom) from sin (Hebrews 9:22), so God Himself set the precedent in the garden of Eden by making the first sacrifice on behalf of Adam and Eve, then clothing them with tunics of animal skin instead of fig leaves, which represented their own works. With this action, we see man is totally incapable of restoring his lost relationship with God; we are utterly dependent upon Him. False religion says clean yourself up, work hard, do things our way, and you will then be acceptable to God; a "works" religion. If a "works" religion was sufficient to please God, so would a fig leaf. Good works *do* have their place in the lives of Christians. Ephesians 2:10 says, "For we are His workmanship, created in Christ Jesus for good works, which God prepared beforehand that we should walk in them." However, Ephesians 2:8–9 make it crystal clear that *no one* can earn salvation brownie points with God.[47]

Adam and Eve were oblivious to the magnitude of what was at stake when they sinned. Through that fatal transaction, the enemy usurped the authority God had originally given to them, which was probably Satan's motivation all along. Before the fall, in Genesis 1:26–28, God blessed Adam and Eve and told them to increase in the Earth, subdue it and have dominion over all living things. Adam basically handed his authority over to the enemy by yielding to his suggestion to disobey God, and the enemy has been in control of the world systems ever since,[48] his ultimate goal ending in complete world domination (you can almost hear an evil laugh with that statement).

However, Satan's stint as "the god of this age" and the "prince of the power of the air"[49] is running out because he doesn't own the Earth—God does. Through Jesus Christ, God judged and pronounced sentence on the enemy,[50] but the full manifestation of judgment won't come to fruition until the end of existence as we know it. Revelation 20:10 says, "The devil, who deceived them, was cast into the lake of fire and brimstone where the beast and the false prophet are. And they will be tormented day and night forever and ever." After this will come the judgment of mankind (Revelation 20:11–15), who followed Satan's example and "did it their way."

Because of Adam's transgression, sin infiltrated humanity and has passed down from generation to generation; no one is exempt. Everyone in Adam's posterity is born with the propensity to sin, and it's just a matter of time before we do. King David recognized mankind's malfunction and wrote twice in Psalm 14, "There is none who does good." His son, Solomon, said, "For there is not a just man on earth who does good and does not sin" (Ecclesiastes 7:20). And the apostle Paul quoted David in Romans 3:10, "There is none righteous, no, not one." Therefore, God created another race born of the Spirit, a race not characterized by rituals and outward appearances but by truth and love flowing through forgiven, regenerated hearts, starting with Jesus. Jesus took our punishment for sin, and now the forgiveness, love, and power of God flows through Him to all who genuinely believe.

Although Jesus was and is eternally existent as the Word of God, He was also the first Person born of the Spirit through the human vessel of Mary. The angel Gabriel, who announced Christ's birth, told her, "The Holy Spirit will come upon you, and the power of the Highest will overshadow you; therefore, also that Holy One who is to be born will be called the Son of God," (Luke 1:35). This was to provide the sinless blood that would pay for sin, but also prepare the way for God to breathe the breath of life into man once again, "...that He (Jesus) might be firstborn among many brethren" (Romans 8:29b).

While Jesus didn't inherit Adam's proclivity toward sin, He was tempted in every area by Satan through the entrapments of the world: the lust of the flesh (carnal satisfaction), the lust of the eye (material possessions), and the pride of life (worldly significance).[51] During the forty days of fasting and temptation in the desert, He used the Word of God to vanquish Satan's every attempt to lure Him into using God's power for selfish reasons (Luke 4:1–14). Jesus never took the bait; He never sinned in thought, word, or deed. When He came forth from the days of testing, He began to demonstrate the love and power of God to all whose hearts were open to Him. Day by day, Jesus confirmed His victory over sin, self, and Satan by casting out devils, healing the sick, and performing miracles.

When time came to give His life on the cross, He steadfastly set His face to go to Jerusalem, knowing full well the enormity of the task that lay before Him. He was the object of mockery, rejection, and incredible physical pain, not to mention the spiritual oppression He must have endured. Probably every demon in existence gathered to see if He would use His power and authority to save Himself from death and bypass the cross, the only way man could ever be free of Satan's control. But He didn't. He chose you and me above Himself, and He gave His all. John 19:30 records Jesus' last words, "It is finished." The Greek word for "finished" here is "teleo,"[52] meaning "to end, i.e., complete, execute, conclude, discharge (a debt)—accomplish, make an end, expire, fill up, finish, go over, pay, perform." Jesus alone accomplished the work of reconciling man to God.[53]

God accepted Jesus' holy sacrifice for mankind, signified by the tearing of the veil in the Jewish temple[54] at the precise moment of Jesus' death. The veil separated the Holy of Holies, where God's presence manifested, from the rest of the temple, where priests performed their religious duties. Only the High Priest could go into the holy of holies once a year with the specified blood sacrifice for himself and the nation of Israel. When the veil was torn, it indicated the way into God's presence had been restored for all who would come to Him through the sacrifice of His Son. Hebrews 9:9 says gifts and sacrifices offered under the old covenant were symbolic, and they could not "make him who performed the service perfect in regard to the conscience." Verse 10 says these were "imposed until the time of reformation." The word for reformation is "diorthosis,"[55] meaning "to straighten thoroughly; rectification; the Messianic restoration." Only the blood of the sinless man, Jesus Christ, has the power to "cleanse your conscience from dead works to serve the living God" (Hebrews 9:14).

The event ratifying everything Jesus accomplished was the resurrection. Of all the purported "gods" this world has exalted, only Jesus has tasted death and overcome; and He is alive forevermore! God has "qualified us to be partakers of the inheritance of the saints in the light. He has delivered us from the power of darkness and translated us into the kingdom of the Son of His love, in Whom we have redemption through His blood, the forgiveness of sins" (Colossians 1:12–14).

At the culmination of Jesus' sacrifice, He bowed His head and gave up His spirit. Simultaneously, events of cataclysmic proportions were taking place in the spirit realm. In the natural, Jesus' blood was spilled on the ground and the cross, but in the spirit, Jesus would soon present and apply His blood to the mercy seat[56] of God in heaven. The sin of man would be forever atoned for, paid in full. Everything transpiring between Jesus' last breath on the cross and his initial appearance on resurrection morning sealed the deal. Jesus broke through the veil of death with a spirit unstained by sin, legally authorized to strip Satan of the authority Adam gave him. Days before His death, Jesus revealed a transfer of power in the spirit was about to occur. In John 12:31, He said, "Now is the judgment of this world; now the ruler of this world will be cast out." Then, Ephesians

4:9 corroborates Jesus' statement: "Now this, 'He ascended'—what does it mean but that He also first descended into the lower parts of the earth?" This was a purposeful, deliberate action on Jesus' part.

After His blood was shed, Jesus' descending was Satan's death knell. Hebrews 2:14–15 says,

> Inasmuch then as the children have partaken of flesh and blood, He Himself likewise shared in the same, that through death He might destroy him who had the power of death, that is, the devil, and release those who through fear of death were all their lifetime subject to bondage.

In Revelation 1:18, Jesus said, "I am He who lives, and was dead, and behold, I am alive forevermore. Amen. And I have the keys of Hades and of Death." Satan's authority was stripped from him, but also that of every demon in his hierarchy. Colossians 2:15 says Jesus, "having disarmed principalities and powers, made a public spectacle of them, triumphing over them in it."

Jesus descended into the depths of Earth to deal with the enemy but also release death's prisoners belonging to God through faith. In 1 Peter 3:18–19, the apostle wrote, "For Christ also suffered once for sins, the just for the unjust, that He might bring us to God, being put to death in the flesh, but made alive by the Spirit, by whom He also went and preached to the spirits in prison..." The word for preached is "kerusso,"[57] meaning "to herald (as a public crier), especially divine truth (the gospel); to proclaim." While Jesus' body lay in Joseph's tomb, His spirit descended into a portion of the underworld then known as "Abraham's bosom." The Lord describes this place in the parable of Lazarus, a beggar, and a rich man in Luke 16:19–31. Abraham's bosom was a separate but visible place from the rich man's location after his death. The rich man "lifted up his eyes and saw Abraham afar off, and Lazarus in his bosom." Abraham and Lazarus' resting place was peaceful and comforting, but not the rich man's. He was in a place of tremendous discomfort, tormented by flames and separated from Abraham by a great gulf that neither could cross (verses 23, 24).

Faithful believers in the Old Testament who followed the God of Abraham were assigned to this peaceful resting place upon death (except Enoch and Elijah, who didn't experience physical death but were both physically transported to heaven[58]). People who didn't believe in or follow the God of Abraham landed in the same place as the rich man in Jesus' parable—hell, literally. Jesus' arrival at Abraham's bosom heralded a soon departure to heaven for God's faithful, with some making an appearance on Earth before their total terrestrial exit. There were other resurrections besides Jesus' resurrection. Matthew 27:51–53 says the signs that accompanied Jesus' death were:

> The veil in the temple was torn in two from top to bottom; and the earth quaked, and the rocks were split, and the graves were opened; and many bodies of the saints who had fallen asleep were raised; and coming out of the graves after His resurrection, they went into the holy city and appeared to many.

Because Jesus gave His precious lifeblood, exonerating all who believe in Him of sin, He could legally release the Holy Spirit's life-sustaining power into the spirit of all who accept Him as Savior and Lord. Jesus' blood cleanses us from sin and prepares our spirit to receive the Holy Spirit. After the resurrection, but before Jesus' ascension, Jesus did something that parallels what God did in Genesis 2:7. John 20:22 says, "And when He had said this, He breathed on them (the disciples) and said to them, 'Receive the Holy Spirit.'" The disciples were, at that point, born again by receiving the Holy Spirit to permanently indwell their spirits because the righteous blood had been shed on mankind's behalf. Seventeen chapters earlier, when Jesus conversed with Nicodemus, He said, "You must be born again," speaking of the regeneration made available after His death, burial, and resurrection, to whoever repents of sin and believes in, or receives Him (John 1:12–13). Though Christ's blood hadn't been shed when He spoke to Nicodemus, His statement pointed to what must happen in every believer's life once His sacrifice was complete.

Jesus told His disciples,

> And I will pray the Father, and He will give you another Helper (Comforter), that He may abide with you forever, even the Spirit of truth, whom the world cannot receive, because it neither sees Him nor knows Him; but you know Him, for He dwells with you and will be in you.
>
> John 14:16–17

The Spirit was with them at this point because Jesus was with them. But after Jesus' blood was offered at Calvary, those who believed in Him were born again and became alive spiritually. The Spirit was then inside of them, just as Jesus said, restoring them and restoring us to the spiritual life that Adam and Eve originally enjoyed before the fall.

Without being born again, we cannot see, recognize, or enter the kingdom of God in this life or the next. Therefore, it is vitally important we undergo the new birth process while we can receive and act on this truth. Our own flesh nature, the world, and the enemy are constantly pressuring and pulling our soul to distract us from our greatest need: to be reconciled with God through faith in what He has done for us through His Son, Jesus, and allowing Him to work in our lives through His Spirit that others may see and be drawn to His goodness. If the enemy can distract us long enough, we will miss the opportunity to fulfill the very reason for our existence and relinquish all possibilities that could have been if we had only hearkened to His call to repent, believe, and receive.

Before Jesus made the new birth accessible, people of faith in biblical history could be temporarily filled with the Holy Spirit, or He briefly rested upon them, but this is different from being continually indwelt by the Spirit through the new birth. John the Baptist was filled with the Spirit even from his mother's womb (Luke 1:15), but Jesus said in Luke 7:28, "For I say to you, among those born of women there is not a greater prophet than John the Baptist; but he who is least in the kingdom of God is greater than he." John was the last and greatest Old Testament prophet according to Jesus, yet those born into God's kingdom give the least important person greater standing with God than what John had under the Old Covenant.

We are blessed to live in "the Church Age," or the dispensation of grace. We look back to Calvary, and by faith appropriate Jesus' death for ours, bridging the sin gap between God and ourselves. Before Jesus' sinless birth, life, death, burial, and resurrection, believers looked forward to God's salvation, though they weren't sure how this would be accomplished. Job said in verses 19:25–26, "For I know that my Redeemer lives, and He shall stand at last on the earth; and after my skin is destroyed (struck off), this I know, that in my flesh I shall see God." David wrote in Psalm 16:10, "For you will not leave my soul in Sheol (Hebrew; can be translated as grave, hell, pit, or abode of the dead), nor will You allow Your Holy One to see corruption" (a prophetic reference to the time frame of Jesus' death and resurrection). Solomon, the wisest man who ever lived except for Jesus, said in Ecclesiastes 3:11, "...He has put eternity in their (mankind's) hearts..." Also, Daniel 12:2 says, "...and many of those who sleep in the dust of the earth shall awake, some to everlasting life, some to shame and everlasting contempt."

After Jesus finished His Father's work, all who would believe in and follow Him thereafter would be born of the Spirit, just as He was. Genesis 1:11 reveals a principle of replication: "Then God said, 'Let the earth bring forth grass, the herb that yields seed, and the fruit tree that yields fruit according to its kind, whose seed is in itself, on the earth;' and it was so." Once Jesus' blood had been shed, He could legally release the Holy Spirit into the spirits of the faithful resting in Abraham's bosom just as He does for those who believe today. Those who cooperate with the Holy Spirit within will produce the fruit of the Spirit (Galatians 5:22–23), which, when manifest in the believer's life, plants seed of the Spirit in all he/she interacts with. As Christians submitted to Christ, we plant seeds in others by our actions, reactions, and words every day! But the flip side is also true—those not submitted to Christ (even though He may indwell their spirit) are sowing seed that will undoubtedly produce an unpleasant harvest.

Abraham's bosom was needed before Jesus' resurrection, but not now because believers go immediately into God's presence upon death.[59] Eternal salvation has been secured through Christ, but we must choose to trust Him before we die, and it's the most important decision we will ever make. For the Christian, to be absent from the body is to be present with the Lord, 2 Corinthians 5:8. Therefore, if you haven't made that decision, choose Jesus, and choose life. Your future with God depends on it, and it's a future you don't want to miss.

Jesus' triumph over sin, self, and Satan is also our triumph over the same if we believe in Him in faith. You can receive Him today if you recognize you are a sinner (the Bible says we all are)[60] in need of a Savior and turn from sin to Jesus, the one who paid the price of sin for the entire world. God bought the world to get the Church, the ones who would genuinely reciprocate His offer of forgiveness and eternal life. Incredibly, not everyone is going to accept the Lord's invitation, but it is still offered to every living soul, and I pray you have already accepted Jesus or will do so today.

Romans 10:9–10 says, "that if you confess with your mouth the Lord Jesus and believe in your heart that God has raised Him from the dead, you will be saved. For with the heart one believes to righteousness and with the mouth confession is made to salvation." When someone confesses faith in Christ and sincerely believes in Him, he/she will be saved or made whole in his relationship with God. His/her name is then written in the Book of Life (Revelation 20:12). Via the Holy Spirit, Jesus Himself comes into our hearts and makes it His home; our body and soul then become the tabernacle, or house, of God. We are "born again" by the Spirit of God, who breathes life into our spirit, which was dead through sin. This is only possible through Jesus' sinless blood, which washes our spirit-man and regenerates, or gives it life, by the power of His Holy Spirit (Titus 3:5).

Of all the keys that open doors in life, entering a saving relationship with Jesus is by far the most important key we can ever receive. Because without Him, everything is nothing. Whether we are rich or poor, in good health or suffering, intelligent or mentally challenged, stable or tormented, at some point in the not-so-distant future, we will face a holy God, and the only one qualified to vouch for us at that moment is Christ. Jesus said in Mark 8:36, "For what will it profit a man if he gains the whole world and loses his own soul?" Jesus, the one and only, sent by God to save the souls of men, is the only one who offers mankind the gift of eternal life.

JESUS IS LORD!

Can you imagine how ill-prepared our troops would be if America's armed forces dispensed with recruit training and placed enlistees immediately on the front lines of battle? They would be annihilated. It is no surprise, then, when men and women enlist in the US military, the first challenge they must surmount is what is commonly referred to as "boot camp." My friend Lisa's son, Ryan, was whisked off to boot camp to begin his initial indoctrination and instruction in military operations and procedures *immediately* after he was sworn in. And anyone who is serious about serving God will undergo a type of spiritual "boot camp" experience as well. Maybe not exactly like the one I went through but be "wise as a serpent" (Matthew 10:16) and understand our enemy's goal is to circumvent, if not completely shut down, our faith in God. Satan's wiles and ways go undetected by most of the church and nearly all the unsaved world. God says wake up! Yes, boot camp is tough and stretches people beyond what they think they can endure. But boot camp prepares us for the hazards and realities of war. Those who persevere can effectively deal with issues they were previously unable or unwilling to confront.

Don't wimp out on me here. Take courage! When we place our trust in the Lord Jesus, we place our trust in God Himself. Jesus said when we become His true follower, no one can snatch us out of His or His Father's hand (John 10:28, 29). But even Jesus experienced an initial period of testing. After His baptism and confirmation by the Father, He was led into the wilderness to be tempted for forty days by the devil.[61] And He won! Our personal boot camp may be much different, but we must be patient and know God is preparing us to overcome for His glory. Sylvia Thompson once told me,

"When the Lord is about to raise someone up, He doesn't just fling 'em out there; He trains 'em!" And part of our training is to become spiritually combat-ready.

The apostle Paul compared Christian discipleship to the life of a soldier. As faithful followers of Jesus, we may graduate from boot camp, but we will always be soldiers of the cross.[62] This is because the enemy of our soul is militant and committed in his efforts to derail our faith in God, cause us to stumble in our walk with Christ and spoil our spiritual fruit. All to discredit our claim as Christians. And he won't stop until he is bound by the angel of the Lord and cast into the bottomless pit (Revelation 20:1–3). Until then, he is aided and abetted by his armies of fallen angels and demons, the world systems and his inside ally, our flesh nature; all or any of which have a significant impact in bringing about the various trials humans endure. Not to mention generational curses and unwise choices the enemy seeks to enforce and bring to bear upon our lives. Therefore, it is imperative we understand God is for us and not against us, and there are basic truths we cannot ignore. Primarily of which, Jesus must be our Savior *and* Lord.

There are many people who say they are Christians, and yet their relationship with the Lord Jesus appears more like the purchase of a "fire insurance" policy from their neighborhood State Farm Agent or the receipt of a "get out of jail" card in the board game, Monopoly. No condemnation; I've been there. But when we say we believe, is it a matter of heart or just intellectual assent? Are we committed to Jesus for life or when it's convenient? James, the half-brother of Jesus, said in verse 2:19, "You believe that there is one God. You do well. Even the demons believe—and tremble!" An associate pastor at NOBC once said, "It is totally ludicrous for someone to say, 'Lord Jesus, please save my soul from hell, but just don't bug me for the next fifty years!'" Jesus desires a heart commitment and a willing vessel. James 2:20 says, "...faith without works is dead." If we truly accepted Jesus as our Savior and Lord, there should be fruit in our lives giving credibility to our statement of faith.

But even the most dedicated Christian is somewhat of a mixture. Have you ever heard the phrase, "Jesus is either Lord of all or not at all"? Indeed, He is Lord of all creation for "of Him and through Him and to Him are all things" (Romans 11:36). However, He will never force His lordship and rule on those who do not believe or want Him in their lives. He waits for each of us to cooperate with the Holy Spirit in bringing us to a personal commitment—when we exit our earth suit, it will become completely comforting or catastrophically clear that Jesus is who He says He is.[63] Is it possible for Jesus to be Lord of a human heart that is not totally submitted to Him? I thought mine was, even though I was not confident of altogether fulfilling that ideal. When the Lord showed me something about myself that was obscuring His rule in my heart, I was aghast. In my conscious mind, I had made Him Savior, and I thought, Lord. But remember, "Lord" means supreme authority.

Jesus will not force His lordship on anyone, and He will not force His lordship on the many compartments that comprise the soul and heart of man—some of which we may not be aware. No one knows everything inside his or her own soul, much less what's in someone else's. Who can remember everything he/she said or thought one month ago off the top of their head? What about everything we have ever been exposed to or happened to us along with the accompanying thought processes as a young adult, adolescent, or child? In the human heart exists the probability of unmet needs or desires; places where rejection, pride, condemnation, or unforgiveness of self or others is present, or fears (real or imagined) contending for control of the mind, emotions, and will. The subliminal presence of these elements might not affect us on a day-to-day basis but can be latent, applying pressure only when confronted with certain personal, environmental, or social conditions, producing undesirable thoughts, feelings, actions, and reactions.

Recognizing recuring anger or fear, destructive thinking patterns, unhealthy emotions, etc., is the first step in dealing with them. Seeking God for revelation concerning their origin (generational curse, sin, trauma, etc.) will help us understand if repenting of sin, forgiving others or ourselves (whatever the Word requires) should be done. Once the trap is exposed and disarmed, through Christ, we are in a position to loose ourselves from enemy claims and ask for restoration. Chester & Betsy Kylstra's book, *Restoring the Foundations*, outlines and details the four basic problem/ministry areas that can be investigated and acted upon, enabling us to experience freedom and "establish a firm foundation" under our Christian walk. These areas are 1. Sins of the Fathers and Resulting Curses, 2. Ungodly Beliefs, 3. Soul/Spirit Hurts, and 4. Demonic Oppression.[64] Another powerful resource is Katie Souza's CD set "Stay Un-Offendable," where she shares tools and strategies available in Christ regarding His ability and desire to heal and restore our souls and physical bodies.

We are all broken in some way, possessing wounded areas in our souls. Some are easily concealed; others cannot be hidden. The ongoing presence of unhealthy thought patterns, feelings, and mind-sets such as pride, perfectionism, fear, depression, rebellion, jealousy, insecurity, addiction, lust, covetousness, etc., are indicators that somewhere in our soul, strongholds exist where Jesus is not ruling. And where Jesus is not ruling, we are susceptible to negative influence and possibly bound, giving the enemy a foothold to launch his plan of action. Ephesians 4:27 says, "...nor give place to the devil." The Greek word for "place" here is "topos,"[65] which means "a spot (generally in space, but limited by occupancy); i.e., *location* (as in a position, home, tract, etc.)."

It may be obvious where Jesus is not ruling in our life, or we may need a word of knowledge to understand where the problem lies. Simply reading our Bible with an open heart may help diagnose our dilemma, for 2 Timothy 3:16 says, "All Scripture is given by inspiration of God, and is profitable for doctrine, for reproof, for correction, for instruction (training, discipline) in righteousness." Hebrews 4:12 says, "For the word of God is living and powerful, and sharper than any two-edged sword, piercing even to the division of soul and spirit, and of joints and marrow, and is a discerner of the thoughts and intents of the heart." His Word received is illumination, but strongholds sometimes require supernatural intervention with a Spirit-led counselor using the Word to help us peel off layers of deception. Cleansing Stream Ministries is another avenue of ministry whose purpose is to help participants break free from enemy entrapment. There, we find others dealing with issues not unlike our own, who desire to become stronger Christians; the Lord is working with us to provide insight as to where we may need healing, deliverance, and/or restoration.

Whatever the issue, and with our cooperation, Jesus can and will deliver our soul from captivity. Since He has defeated death on its own turf, all authority in heaven and on Earth has been committed to Him by the Father.[66] According to Hebrews 2:15, it is the fear of death that subjects mankind to bondage. The list of ways and means the enemy uses to enslave humans is practically inexhaustible, but Jesus is the Bondage Breaker. Because He gave His all, He now owns it all; the air we breathe, the molecules in the cells of our body, the money He allows us to make. He *can* set us free instantly, like the numerous deliverances recorded in Scripture. But I have found He usually uses a process, which helps us understand how we became ensnared, that we may not be deceived again. God created us as free moral agents. His desire is to work with us in cooperation; He will lead and guide but never force or manipulate. The enemy, on the other hand, works to gain a place (topos) of influence in our thought life to do just the opposite. He has no problem manipulating or pressuring people to do his bidding.

Unsaved people are, for the most part, ruled by the enemy, although they rarely, if ever, comprehend this. First John 5:19 says, "We know that we are of God, and the whole world lies under the sway of the wicked one." But as Christians, we are still a mixture. This is because man is a three-part being: spirit, soul, and body. When we sincerely repent, asking Jesus to forgive our sins and invite Him to live in our hearts, He does. His place of residence is our spirit, and when the Holy Spirit of Jesus is present in our human spirit, no demon can inhabit the same space. However, our soul (intellect, emotions, and will) is another matter entirely. Our minds must be renewed by reading and hearing God's Word, thereby enlightening our intellect and influencing our emotions and will. Our flesh, which is the lower nature of our soul, is not submitted to God (sometimes called "the old man") and must be crucified. We do this by choosing God's ways over our own, and there are daily, if not moment-to-moment, opportunities to "die to self."[67] Transforming our thinking into Bible truth and recognizing problems our flesh nature is causing, then working together with the Holy Spirit to bring every part of our being under the rule of Christ is called *sanctification*—and it is a life-long process.

Some problems will be recognized and dealt with when walking daily with the Lord through prayer, renewing our minds with the Word, and connecting with other Christians. However, other difficulties and deep-rooted issues will take discernment, power, and gifts of the Holy Spirit to dismantle enemy lies, strategies, and structures (strongholds) and bring that portion of our soul under the authority and protection of the Lord. Therefore, it is vitally important to allow the Holy Spirit to reveal areas of our lives where Jesus is not ruling. And each time He does, we have a choice to make. We can either humble ourselves under His mighty hand, dying to our own desires and, by the power of the Holy Spirit, enthrone the Lord in that area of our lives; or we can go another trip around the mountain, which is continuing to go through a similar set of circumstances until we understand the only way out is Jesus Christ and His will for our life in that area.

We must not become introspective, looking for everything that is wrong and coming under condemnation. Rather, may we see that, although the "inner space" of our soul and spirit is complex and ultimately unsearchable to carnal human understanding (psychology can only take us so far), when we submit to the lordship of Christ, He can lead us to freedom in Him, if we are willing. Proverbs 20:27 says, "The spirit of a man is the lamp of the Lord, searching all the inner depths (rooms of the belly) of his heart." The words most often used in the Old Testament to refer to the heart mean, "feelings, will, intellect, the center of anything; the most interior organ."[68] The heart of man is part of the soul nearest to our spirit; it is the seat of our emotions. Solomon, who is credited with writing almost all of Proverbs, recognized the light or presence of God visiting man's spirit could illuminate pockets of hurtful memories, selfish motives, wrong thinking, harbored resentment, judgments of others (the list could be endless) located in the depths of our soul. Only God's light, truth, and love can bring a release to the heart of man, and only if man will allow the Spirit of God to do so.

We, who are in covenant with God through Jesus Christ, have the awesome privilege and responsibility to allow Him to search our hearts through prayer, and that on a regular basis, that He may truly become our Lord. When we do, we experience greater freedom by cooperating with the Holy Spirit as He works to conform us to the image of Christ.[69] The more we think like, act like, and speak like Jesus, the more we can shut down the enemy's operations in our lives and in the lives of others. Satan fights tirelessly to lure us into snares, to deceive, discourage, humiliate, frighten, and wound our souls, all in the hope that we will "go with the world's flow," believe "this is just how I am" or "things will never change" and not press into God and receive all He has for us.

When we choose to serve the Living God, the enemy is going to oppose us. A friend of mine used to say he was just doing his job. Therefore, let us move forward comprehending how much Jesus loves us and in so doing strengthen our faith, cultivate a steadier spiritual walk, and bear precious fruit of the Spirit, which brings God great glory (John 15:8). Making Jesus our Lord is a journey that we will walk out the rest of our lives, one day at a time. But it is well worth it, so press on! The more He gets of you, the more you get of Him, and the best is yet to come...

So, have *you* made Jesus your Savior and Lord? If you have never received Jesus, or you would like to re-commit your life to Him, there is a simple prayer of invitation at the end of this chapter. But before that, please allow me to address something that many people wrestle with, whether they have had an authentic "born again" experience even though they have repented, believed, and asked Jesus to come into their hearts. In the first chapter of this book, I shared how I began to believe in the Lord Jesus when I was five or six years old and made a public profession of faith when I was eleven, following the Lord in water baptism; but it was not until I was forty-seven that I knew for sure I was born again. Up until that point, I believed from Scriptures like Romans 10:9–10 that I was, indeed, saved:

Matthew 10:32 (KJV), "Whosoever therefore shall confess Me before men, him will I confess also before my Father which is in heaven." Mark 16:16, "He who believes and is baptized will be saved; but he who does not believe will be condemned." John 1:12–13, "But as many as received Him to them He gave the right to become children of God, to those who believe in His name: who were born not of blood, nor of the will of the flesh, nor of the will of man, but of God." In John 10:9, Jesus said, "I am the door. If anyone enters by Me, he will be saved, and will go in and out and find pasture."

Acts 16:31, "Believe on the Lord Jesus Christ and you will be saved, you and your household." Romans 10:13, "For whoever calls upon the name of the Lord shall be saved" (also see Joel 2:32). First Corinthians 12:3, "...no one can say that Jesus is Lord except by the Holy Spirit." Second Corinthians 5:17, "Therefore, if anyone is in Christ, he is a new creation; old things have passed away; behold, all things have become new." Ephesians 2:8–9, "For by grace you have been saved through faith, and that not of yourselves, it is the gift of God, not of works, lest anyone should boast." Hebrews 7:25, "Therefore He is also able to save to the uttermost those who come to God through Him, since He ever lives to make intercession for them." Revelation 3:20, "Behold, I stand at the door and knock; If anyone hears My voice and opens the door, I will come in to him and dine with him, and he with Me."

I couldn't put my finger on a born-again "experience" per se, though I said the sinner's prayer many times, even after my baptism. From my water baptism in 1968, until God spoke to me at the Miss Beaumont pageant and the 1981 New Year's Eve experience, I didn't recognize any other godly supernatural occurrences in my life. However, I did attempt an out-of-body experience during college due to the psychology course I was taking. The book described and told the reader how such an experience is induced. I had no idea that was demonic and have long since repented and closed the door. Not all supernatural experiences are of God! I also made the mistake of going to see a fortune teller "for fun" and have also repented and closed that door as well. But moments of recognizable divine intervention began to occur after the December 31, 1981 incident, and I attribute that to my heart being opened to the supernatural ministry of the Holy Spirit through watching the 700 Club. The instantaneous healing of gastroenteritis, baptism of the Holy Spirit, deliverance from depression, etc., was to me, along with Scripture, a confirmation that I was saved. We walk by faith and not by sight (2 Corinthians 5:7).

However, I had a nagging something that seemed to be in my heart, not my thought life, where the distressing thoughts had occurred. It was as if I was holding something back from the Lord, but I wasn't sure just what it might be. In going to see Mel Gibson's *Passion of the Christ* in March of 2004, more clarity began to come. In the light of seeing for myself, in that movie, what Jesus endured because of my sin—the extent of His suffering—I began to feel that if I had to stand before Him right then and there, I would be ashamed. I didn't know exactly why I would feel ashamed because, in my understanding, I thought I had been doing (at least most of) the right things Scripture says we should all do. However, something was amiss. God was preparing my heart to receive the truth, but it would not be until three months later that the Holy Spirit would bring it all together.

On a Friday evening in June 2004, Bennie and I went to Spanky's restaurant for dinner. As it has occasionally happened, my appetite left me. The thought crossed my mind that I was going to need the power of the Holy Spirit the next day, so I decided to skip dinner that evening, wondering what was coming.[70] Saturday morning at 7 a.m. I got a phone call from my friend, Karen, who said that her daughter, Natalie, needed immediate prayer. I called another prayer warrior friend, Donna, and we took authority over the spirit of death, interceding for Natalie.

Later that afternoon, when I talked to Karen again, she told me Natalie had pulled through, but the Lord had led her into a deep intercession for the church. I told her I would also intercede, praying for revelation and strength. The following day was Sunday—Father's Day. When I got to church, Karen shared that she had been given a very strong word for Community Church. In this word, she said there was not a person in the room that didn't have some need for deliverance; this day was our heavenly Father's Day, and God wanted to search our hearts. I thought, *Okay, Lord. That's a good word. Amen.* I wasn't thinking about what I felt after seeing *The Passion of the Christ* (how quickly we forget!), and I was, at that moment, oblivious to the fact that *my* heart needed searching. Probably because I was, at that time, part of an intercessory prayer team, thinking I was doing all I could do.

When a prophetic word is given, it demands a response. Two days later, I was on my face in my living room begging God to search my heart. Psalm 139:23–24 says, "Search me, O God, and know my heart; try me, and know my anxieties; and see if there is any wicked way in me and lead me in the way everlasting." After waiting and crying out to Him for some time, the Lord gave me a vision, and it was a shocker. I saw *myself* sitting on the throne of my heart with "ministry" at my right side. I had idolized myself and made ministry an idol also! All this time, I thought Jesus was sitting on the throne of my heart. I told the Lord that if He didn't deliver me from myself, I didn't know what I was going to do because I had tried to "die to self" in the past, and apparently, I didn't completely understand what that meant. Then I knew—that little piece of my heart I had been holding onto, afraid to give it to Jesus out of fear that He would take it away, must be laid on the altar.

Back in the 80s, when I was in those full gospel meetings, a desire was birthed in me to preach and teach the Word of God as they did. Yes, I got some deliverance in those meetings and the baptism of the Holy Spirit. I also received prophecies and answered prayer, but up until I began attending those meetings, I still did not know what it was I was called to do with my life. I did pray about it (a little) as a teenager, but since I never heard specifically from the Lord, I chose the closest thing I could that seemed to fit my personality, which was a degree from Lamar University in Beaumont, Texas, in Mass Communications. In my carnal thinking, being seen and heard, along with serving the public, would maybe give my life some significance, but I knew even then I had not hit the sweet spot.

Many years prior to Father's Day 2004, and not long after I started attending the Wednesday morning meetings, I remember feeling my spirit joyfully rise as I listened to the preaching and teaching. And suddenly, it was crystal clear! I wanted to do exactly what my teacher was doing, and I told her so. She told me not to get the cart before the horse. In other words, I had a lot to learn, and she was right. And so, fast forward to Tuesday, June 22, 2004, a day that was quite sobering. God knows our hearts, and I had to face the fact that I may never preach or teach the Word in the capacity I had hoped, and if that is God's will, I must accept it and be thankful for what He has given me. I felt like Abraham laying Isaac down on the altar, but I also realized that even if I got to do all the things I aspired to, without the Lord's rule and reign in those facets of my life, it would all be for nothing.[71] To become a kingdom builder, we must hear from the king and then do what He says. Otherwise, we may find that we are building our own kingdom instead. And in the end, it is only God's kingdom that will stand.

I proceeded to cry out to the Lord asking for help and, as an act of my will, laid down all my hopes, all my dreams, all of myself that I could. I had come to a place where if God never did the things in my life that I wanted or thought He had called me to do, it would have to be okay—but I couldn't possibly live without Him. And as for ministry being on my right hand, I mean, ministry is a good thing, right? Not if it is a means of attaining self-worth or approval from others. Only Jesus can give us self-worth, and He has done that by giving His life for us. What could possibly give our life more significance than knowing the God of the universe laid His life down for us and invites us to come and enjoy His love and fellowship for all eternity? Only Jesus can give us approval which He has already done by giving us His righteousness. In the long run, whose else matters? Indeed, those who have placed their faith in Him have already become the righteousness of God in Christ.[72]

In heaven, we will know and be known by all. But right now, living in this flesh house, we contend with and are susceptible to all the fallacies connected to the fall of man. Thank God for Jesus. He alone can save us from idolatry, and that He will do if we allow Him to come in and help us lay the ax to the root of every wrong motive in our hearts. The Word, prayer, obedience, and time will enable us to learn and walk in the truth, freeing us from the need to strive, and as the apostle Paul wrote, "…godliness with contentment is great gain" (1 Timothy 6:6).

To my surprise, after laying down my hopes, my dreams, and myself, an incredibly wonderful thing happened. Jesus baptized me in His love. For nearly two weeks, this euphoria enveloped my mind and heart, and for the first time in my life, I understood how people willingly lay down their lives for Christ. I felt a heightened love for God that went way beyond my day-to-day love and respect for Him, and I could feel His love for others like never before; it is off the chart! During this time, I also discerned very clearly the hidden motives of why people say and do things without becoming judgmental of them; there are reasons people behave the way they do. But I could only feel God's total love and acceptance of them. And I felt free. This freedom was like nothing I had ever experienced before. I remember telling my friends I felt like the scarecrow in the *Wizard of Oz* when Dorothy loosed him from the pole he had been hanging on. It was one of the most profound experiences God has ever given me.

Jesus said in John 8:32, "And you shall know the truth and the truth shall make you free." This axiom of truth can be applied to break virtually any bondage that others, the enemy, or even we have put on ourselves, beginning with the most important truth of all: *Jesus is Lord!* If we allow Him to bring His rule and reign into our hearts, not just initially but daily, we begin to see things the way He does. And seeing things from His perspective will change us in the deepest levels of our soul and spirit. God used an incredibly compelling movie and a word of knowledge to create a sincere desire for Him to search my heart. I had to trust Him in whatever it was that He would reveal; He already knew what was in me. As a result, it opened the door for me to see for myself who was really ruling in my life (me). And as a Christian, this was absolutely unacceptable.

People usually do not realize they are bound in some way or that they have idolatry in their hearts. The Pharisees of Jesus' day did not realize it, and many Christians do not either. That does not mean they are not sincere—I was sincere. But self-idolatry was occupying the place in my heart that Jesus should have rightfully occupied if indeed I belonged to Him. And "ministry" in my mind was more like having a position rather than loving, serving, and giving freely to others. I couldn't repent of something I was unaware of; a deception had enveloped my mind. The world utilizes deception against unbelievers and Christians alike. The fall of man has produced an inward bending or perversion that causes us to look at everything through "what's-in-it-for-me?" glasses. The enemy plays on this. And he has been successful, even in the church.

As I pondered this vision, I realized I had been violating the two most important commandments. Jesus condensed the ten commandments given to Moses at Mount Sinai into two categories that, in a nutshell, comprise the entire law of God (see Exodus 20:1–17). The first four concern our relationship with God, the following six our relationship with others. In Matthew 22:37, 39, Jesus said, "You shall love the Lord your God with all your heart, all your soul and all your mind," and "you shall love your neighbor as yourself." Our love for God should enthrone Jesus Christ in our hearts as Lord. When we are in right relationship with Him, it naturally flows to others that we may love, serve, and bless them. It is a product of who He is in us and us in Him. But when we have idols, things we have given a place of exaltation compete for God's place in our heart. We are unaware of what is happening, but soon our prayer life is hindered, our desire for the things of God is weakened, and we experience a degree of doublemindedness.

I realized I couldn't love the Lord with *all* my heart; on my own, I did not have the ability. And if I couldn't love Him, how could I even venture to think I could love my fellow man? As an act of our will, we can worship God; we can bless and serve others—and those things in themselves are not insignificant. God will honor every sincere attempt to worship Him and bless those who are in our sphere. But if we feel an unsettling "feeling" that we can't quite explain, it could be there is something we are putting ahead of the Lord. Jesus knew it could only be through Him that we could fulfill God's commandments *from the heart*. As we lay our lives down for the King of Kings, He then empowers us, through the Holy Spirit, to do what God requires. He alone is the Way. He alone is the key to eternal life. There is no other.

Christians are on a journey to Christlikeness. And for that to happen, God is going to deal with us all about the contents of our hearts. A respected minister once said that if He showed us everything in us at once, it would kill us! So, God, in His mercy and timing, reveals things that we must know to grow in Him and get past the stumbling blocks restraining us from increase and forward spiritual motion.

The experience of being immersed in God's love changed my perspective of life immensely. The love of God is the most powerful force in the universe. For the first time in my life, I had no doubt I was born again. Was I saved/born again before June 2004? I believe I was because of God's Word regarding salvation in the Bible, the many times He gave me peace that passes understanding and baptizing me in the Holy Spirit in 1983. Also, because the new birth takes place in our spirit, idolatry takes place in the soul. I didn't realize I had idolized my own self. And no wonder; the culture of this world could be defined with one phrase: "It's all about me!" We deal with it in relationships, we see it rampant in the media, and our flesh is quick to jump on the "me" bandwagon—"I want my fair share!" It takes the truth of God's Word and the Spirit's revelation to bring us to the place where we make God-centered instead of self-centered decisions. The apostle Paul knew full well about the inward struggle of flesh and spirit and wrote about it in Romans, 1 Corinthians, Galatians, and Colossians.[73]

I have read about "dying to self," have heard it preached, but never did I understand what was taking place in my soul until the Lord gave me this vision. In effect, my idolatry was "eclipsing" Jesus' lordship in a particular area of my heart, and God graciously let me see I was not alone. For human beings to have idols, self must be ruling—at least in a particular area of our heart/soul. Dealing with self-idolatry is the first step to taking down all other idols, the love of which is rooted in our flesh, or old man, and fed by the fear of death which came in at the fall of man. The fear of death is what the enemy uses in all our lives to push us into making selfish decisions, with self-idolatry being an attempt to achieve significance in life apart from God's rule, even if it appears religious. Taking it down is the key to the beginning of our freedom in Christ.

Friends, have you ever stopped to consider why God chose the instrument of the cross for Jesus' death and why His blood was shed through certain means? The cross and Jesus' blood being poured out is a vivid picture of what "dying to self" is. When praying in the

Garden of Gethsemane, Jesus sweated great drops of blood, signifying the importance of God's will being accomplished in our lives (Luke 22:42). He allowed the Roman soldiers to violently press a crown of thorns onto His head, signifying that we should no longer allow our carnal thinking to rule but to set our minds on things above (Colossians 3:2). Although Jesus never sinned in any way, He took chastising stripes on His back, bearing our sickness and infirmities, signifying that we should no longer live to sin but rather live unto righteousness (1 Peter 2:24). He allowed His hands to be nailed down, signifying that our works should henceforth be done in God (Ephesians 2:10). He allowed His feet to be nailed down, signifying that our walk should now be led by the Spirit (Galatians 5:16).

God deals with each of us individually, but whatever it may concern, there are others He is dealing with about the same thing (1 Corinthians 10:13). During this intense time of allowing God to search my heart, He gave me yet another vision. I saw a church filled with people, and in front of about 85 percent of them was a little golden statue on their laps. I couldn't tell what it was, so I asked Holy Spirit if I could see it more clearly, and immediately, He gave me a close-up view. It was the Oscar statuette handed out at the Academy Awards every year! Only the best actors win Oscars, and we may fool others or even ourselves, but nobody fools God.

There are many Christians who appear to be in right relationship with the Lord, but they have been deceived somehow. If Jesus is resident in your life, but not president, take a step of faith and ask Him to search your heart. He is truthful and kind; if there is an area that needs to be submitted to Him, He will help you. First Corinthians 11:31 says, "For if we would judge ourselves, we would not be judged." Therefore, it is wise for us to humble ourselves under His mighty hand, allowing Him to continue His sanctifying work in our hearts; no one is exempt. If the picture the Lord allowed me to see is accurate and a microcosm of the body of Christ, there is much displacement of the authentic rule of God in the lives of those who say they believe.

In asking the Lord to search our hearts, we must remember that He loves us with an everlasting love and wants us to be free to enjoy all He has prepared for us in this life and the next. Our spirit will not grow properly if this truth is ignored, but when we put things in the prescribed divine order, there is no telling how fast and how far God will take us when He's in the driver's seat of our life. If we never allow Him to do this, it may not affect our eternal security, but it will affect the parameters and quality of our Christian influence. According to 1 Corinthians 3:12–15, our service to God will be tried by holy fire at the Judgment Seat of Christ. For a Christian to produce fruit that will endure this time of testing, he/she must have the same mentality as John the Baptist: "He must increase, but I must decrease" (John 3:30). The old nature in our flesh will contend for the life and years we have been given, consuming rather than producing. By investing our lives in Jesus and allowing Him to cultivate His kingdom in us, we will enjoy blessings in this life, with far greater blessings to look forward to in the next. Please understand that Jesus must not only be our Savior but also our Lord, the Ruler of our lives, for He alone can free us from ourselves.

If you have never received Jesus as Savior and Lord, you can do it right now; you can be born again and know that your name has been written in the Lamb's Book of Life.[74] If you have already asked Christ into your heart but want to recommit your life to Him, or if you are a practicing Christian but would like the Lord to help you pull down the idols that may be hindering your walk with Him, please pray one or both of the following prayers with me:

Prayer for Salvation:

Heavenly Father, I come to you in faith, recognizing I am a sinner in need of a Savior. I now turn from a life of sin and self-seeking and ask that you wash me with the precious blood of your Son, Jesus Christ of Nazareth. Come into my heart, Lord Jesus, and make it your home, for I now confess you as Savior and Lord of my life. Fill me to overflowing with your Holy Spirit that I may be empowered to live for you from this day forward. Thank you, Lord, for coming into my heart and for receiving me into your kingdom. Let my life bear much fruit and be pleasing to you, bringing you glory and honor as long as I shall live. ~ In Jesus' name, Amen.

Prayer for Dealing with Specific Sin(s):

Heavenly Father, how I thank you for your love, truth, grace, and mercy! I now confess and turn from my sin(s) of _____, trusting your Word that says if I confess my sins, you are faithful and just to forgive me of my sins and to cleanse me from all unrighteousness, according to 1 John 1:9. Please restore my fellowship with you on deeper and more intimate levels than ever before. Search my heart, Father, and see if there is any wicked way in me. Grant me repentance for anything that has kept me from your perfect will. I hereby renounce the fear of death and ask you to help me to identify every deception, including self-idolatry, that I have allowed access to my heart and soul. By the power of your Word and Holy Spirit, help me to fall out of agreement with every entrapment of idolatry. Teach me your ways and fill my heart with love for you, my brethren in Christ, and the lost.

~ In Jesus' mighty name, I pray, amen.

Fill 'er Up!

During my early years, I had no clue as to the very real, the very costly war constantly raging in the spirit realm. That is until the enemy decided to launch an attack against my soul that would forever alter the course of my life. For nearly seven years, I was like a boxer in the corner of the ring, getting the stuffing knocked out of him. I didn't know what I was fighting or how to defend myself, much less fight back. I couldn't and wouldn't tell anyone what I was dealing with because I knew they wouldn't understand—I didn't understand. Then I attended a full Gospel meeting and began to see a way out of the mental prison I had been held captive in for so long. Slowly but surely, I began to learn how to pull out and fend off the enemy's fiery darts aimed at my thought processes. It wasn't easy, but I learned for myself that God has unquestionably provided spiritual protection and has given us holy armor that withstands the enemy's assaults. He has also given us weapons, tools, and keys that free us, free others, and put the enemy on the defensive—where he needs to be! But we must use them. And we must learn to discern and follow the directives of the Commander-In-Chief, Jehovah Sabaoth, the Lord of Hosts, who is Jesus Christ, King of Kings and Lord of Lords.

To position ourselves to fight the invisible foe (the devil and his dark kingdom), we must first make sure we have submitted to and are in good standing with Almighty God, the Father of lights. Jesus, the Light of the world,[75] has provided the only way for this to be possible by believing in Him for salvation and asking Him to become not only our Savior but also our Lord and everything that entails. When we do, Colossians 1:13 says, "He has delivered us from the power of darkness and translated (transferred) us into the kingdom of the Son of His love." He also gives us the gift of His precious Holy Spirit,[76] through whom we are born again. At that moment, our spirit becomes alive. We may or may not feel anything, but instantly or shortly after, we know in our heart something is different. Many of our attitudes begin to change, and a desire for the things of God is sparked. As we learn to abide in Him, we soon discover the fruit of the spirit is being developed in our character.[77]

This emerging fruit—love, joy, peace, longsuffering, kindness, goodness, faithfulness, meekness (humility), and self-control—should become increasingly apparent as we learn to abide in Christ. But like everything the Lord brings forth in our lives, we have a choice to yield or not to yield to the truth of the Word and the leading of the Spirit. Consequently, our obedience, or lack thereof, increases or hinders the growth of spiritual fruit. We usually produce more fruit in certain areas than others, but the Lord desires for us to be well-rounded in Him. Like a fruit tree, the seeds in the fruit we bear are planted in the lives of those we daily interact with, good or bad. The more we abide in Christ, the more fruit of the Spirit we will produce and the more freedom we will attain. Blockages or hindrances to the Spirit's operation in our lives will be dealt with and removed, one by one, allowing a place for the Spirit to rule and reign where He was previously prevented from going. The fruit of the Spirit embodies and comprises the sum of Christlikeness for believers.

And God is looking for fruit. Every born-again Christian should have evidence of those nine fruits being produced in his or her life. The fruit of the Spirit also provides balance for the gifts of the Spirit as evidenced by the bells and pomegranates woven into the hem of the priest's garment in Exodus 28:33. The gifts of the Spirit are a function of the ministry of the Holy Spirit, made accessible to those who receive the baptism of the Holy Spirit.[78] When we receive the baptism of the Holy Spirit, there is an initial infilling, but the Scriptures encourage us to be refilled (Ephesians 5:18) because it tends to leak out. The presence of the Holy Spirit within our spirit never leaves, but the experiential power (not the residential power) that is manifested at His infilling, or baptism, wanes for a variety of reasons, one of which being, "...we have this treasure in earthen vessels, that the excellence of the power may be of God and not of us," (2 Corinthians 4:7). Allowing the Lord Jesus to fill and refill us with His Spirit is vitally important if we are to understand and deal victoriously with the goings-on of the spirit realm. Mary Garrison, in her book, *How to Try a SPIRIT,* said, "The gifts of the Holy Spirit are given to us that we may not depend upon our own capabilities, but that we may work in the power of the Holy Ghost, as Jesus also did. They were given that we may work in God's ability."[79] The new birth prepares us for heaven, but the Holy Spirit's baptism equips us to live victoriously here on earth.

As mentioned in chapter one, there is at least a three-fold impartation when we receive the baptism of the Holy Spirit, with each part containing another aggregate of three. First, let's examine the impartation of supernatural revelation. Matthew 3:16 has an account of what transpired immediately after Jesus' baptism in the River Jordan. It says, "the heavens were opened to Him and He saw the Spirit of God descending like a dove and alighting upon Him." Likewise, when a believer receives the baptism of the Holy Spirit, he/she becomes more aware of activities in the spirit realm, both positive and negative; like an invisible curtain has been pulled back revealing what is happening "backstage" in many events in his/her own sphere and the world in general. With time, prayer, and study of the Word, the Holy Spirit will develop the believer's discerning capacity, whereby one or all three of the revelatory gifts may begin to operate through his spirit, as the Holy Spirit wills, in his/her life: word of wisdom, word of knowledge and discerning of spirits, as listed in 1 Corinthians 12:8–10.[80]

Very simply put, the word of wisdom is a supernatural directive, giving divine insight and/or guidance to the believer regarding current or future events. An example of the word of wisdom can be seen in 1 Chronicles 14:14–15 when God gave David instructions to defeat the Philistines, including how to recognize the Lord's precise timing. The word of knowledge is a supernatural disclosure of facts, conditions, occurrences, etc., that the Holy Spirit reveals, giving the believer greater perception and understanding concerning things past, present, or future. An example of the word of knowledge would be in 2 Kings 6:8–12, where God disclosed the words of the king of Syria to the prophet Elisha who promptly warned the king of Israel. Discerning of spirits allows the believer to see into the spirit realm, to be able to supernaturally recognize what kind of spirit, angelic or demonic, is operating in a situation or what kind of spiritual "structure" is being utilized by the enemy to run his operations or exert pressure on an individual or group. A biblical example of discerning of spirits is found in 1 Kings 22:19–23, where the Lord gave the prophet Micaiah a heavenly vision of an unfolding plan that would lure King Ahab to his death, and 2 Kings 6:17 when Elisha prayed for God to open his servant's eyes to see "the mountain was full of horses and chariots of fire all around Elisha."

The second aspect of this three-fold impartation is the releasing of supernatural power. Jesus said in Acts 1:8, "You shall receive power when the Holy Spirit has come upon you; and you shall be witnesses to Me in Jerusalem, and in all Judea and Samaria, and to the end of the earth." This "power" Jesus says we will receive corresponds, but is not restricted to, the power gifts, which are also listed in 1 Corinthians 12. They are faith, gifts of healing, and the working of miracles. The power of God can manifest in any possible way. It can be a tangible occurrence within a person's spirit, soul or body, the earth, the atmosphere, or the heavens. The supernatural power of God can strengthen us spiritually, emotionally, or physically that we may step out and do what God is calling us to do, which includes power to boldly share the goodness and faithfulness of the Lord.

I remember a specific incident when the Holy Spirit operated in this fashion through Bennie and me. We had just arrived at my Aunt Etha's house for another Thanksgiving dinner when we saw my cousin Deb's husband, Paul, sitting outside. Paul was a Christian; he had accepted Jesus Christ as his Savior, but he, like so many others, seemed to be dealing with an issue where normal prayer appeared to be fruitless. Although "normal" prayer is never fruitless, it brings us to the place where God can facilitate a breakthrough if we persevere. Paul's hands were shaking, and they were bandaged tightly because he had contracted an infection that caused them to break out terribly. I asked him if we could pray for him; he said "yes." I did the praying, and Bennie did the agreeing. We cursed the infection (like Jesus cursed the fig tree; Mark 11:14) and commanded it to come out of his hands in Jesus' name, then anointed his knuckles with oil, asking the Lord to bring healing and restoration. Nothing happened immediately, but Paul did seem to feel a little better. However, the next day Aunt Etha called me and said later that evening, a black substance came oozing up and out of the back of Paul's hands. By Christmas, Paul's hands were completely restored!

The power of God was working through faith (commanding the infection to come out) and a gift of healing. This also ties into the authority Christ has given His disciples. As stated in chapter one, authority belongs to every genuine Christian believer (even those who have not received the Holy Spirit's baptism) because when we become a part of Jesus' body, we are directly connected to the head, who is Jesus Christ. The Father has committed all authority in heaven and Earth to Jesus (Matthew 28:18). Jesus, in turn, manifests that authority primarily through His body, which is you and me (if He is our Savior and Lord). Scripture records that Jesus gave His disciples authority "over all power of the enemy" (Luke 10:19).[81] The word here for authority is exousia,[82] which means authority, jurisdiction, power, right, strength.

Regarding authority, John A. MacMillan, in his book, *The Authority of the Believer*, points out that since Romans 6 states the death and resurrection of Christ include His people, "The believer is thus made a full partaker of Christ's righteousness. But Ephesians lifts the believer with the ascended Christ to the heavenlies where he is made a partaker of Christ's throne."[83] "The elevation of His people with Him to the heavenlies has no other meaning than that they are made sharers, potentially for the present, of the authority which is His."[84] The Lord gave me a vision of myself seated in the heavenlies, and I had long hair! (My hair has been short since the '90s). If we are Jesus' disciples, and He is the same yesterday, today, and forever (Hebrews 13:8), then *we* have authority! However, usually, only those who receive the Holy Spirit's baptism will function in this capacity of authority because the Spirit's infilling releases supernatural power.

Concerning faith, all believers have been given a measure (Romans 12:3); it is through faith that we receive salvation and the baptism of the Holy Spirit, but the supernatural gift of faith is a purposeful endowment given to the believer by the Spirit for a specific need that moves the hand of God. Pat Robertson says the gift of faith is for "defense and protection or for the accomplishment of some extraordinary task far beyond the ability of an individual."[85] A scriptural example of the gift of faith operating is in Joshua 10:12–14, where Joshua commanded the sun and moon to stand still until Israel had annihilated the five armies of the Amorites. The sun and moon complied.

Gifts of healing release God's supernatural power to heal and bring restoration physically, emotionally, or mentally. King Hezekiah, in 2 Kings 20:1–7, was sick and near death, but he prayed earnestly to the Lord and was healed by the Word of the Lord spoken through Isaiah the prophet and a lump of figs applied to a grievous boil. Today, as covenant believers, we are told to lay hands on the sick in faith and/or anoint them with oil, and they shall recover.[86] My friend Pat moves in the gifts of faith and healing. I was healed of a painful cyst in my hand the day after she anointed it with oil; she also laid hands on my sinuses, and they opened the next morning. No matter what kind of disease, malady, injury, etc., God is willing and able to heal us because Jesus took stripes on His back to provide legal ground for Him to do so. In fact, if you can receive it, it's already done!

The third power gift, working of miracles, takes place when God uses a person, place, or thing to suspend the natural laws of existence, revealing His ability, power, and authority over creation as we know it.[87] In 1 Kings, 17:8–16, Elijah the Tishbite was ordered to go see a widow in Zarephath through whom God would supply the prophet with food during a three-year drought he had prophesied to King Ahab. The widow followed Elijah's instructions resulting in her flour bin and jar of oil not being used up until the rain fell in Israel. New Testament miracles include Jesus turning the water into wine at Cana of Galilee (John 2:1–11) and Peter's angelic release from prison through prayer (Acts 12:7–11).

Finally, the third, and possibly most important of the three-fold impartation made possible by the baptism of the Holy Spirit: gifts of utterance. Speech is of great importance because God has chosen the vehicle of language to reveal Himself, for the most part, to human beings, although He is certainly not limited to it. When a person is baptized in the Holy Spirit, the initial evidence is tongues. On the day of Pentecost, the tongues manifest were tongues of known languages so those present in Jerusalem could hear the disciples speaking the gospel and glorifying God in their own languages (Acts 2:1–12). However, once activated, tongues can be used as a "prayer language" privately exercised by the individual Christian. Jesus gives an indirect reference to the phenomenon of tongues in John 7:38: "He who believes in Me, as the Scripture has said, out of his heart will flow rivers of living water." Then John clarifies this statement in verse 39: "But this He spoke concerning the Spirit whom those believing in Him would receive; for the Holy Spirit was not yet given, because Jesus was not yet glorified."

When we receive Jesus as Savior and Lord, He breathes life into our spirit, which is likened to receiving "living water." In the Holy Spirit baptism, the Lord also releases the fire of God, which burns off the chaff (hindrances) of our flesh nature, and the living water deposited in the born-again spirit is released to overflowing. The outward manifestation is tongues. A type of the Holy Spirit baptism is seen in 1 Kings, where Elijah, the prophet, confronted the prophets of Baal. Verses 18:37, 38a: "'Hear me, O Lord, hear me, that this people may know that You are the Lord God, and that You have turned their hearts back to You again.' Then the fire of the Lord fell and consumed the burnt sacrifice, and the wood and the stones and the dust..." Dust is a type of our flesh nature.

Jesus said in John 4:23–24: "But the hour is coming, and now is, when true worshipers will worship the Father in spirit and truth; for the Father is seeking such to worship Him. God is Spirit, and those who worship Him must worship in spirit and truth." Can this be Spirit-anointed words of understanding that flow forth from a believer's heart? Yes, but in nearly every recorded instance where the Holy Spirit fell in the book of Acts, tongues were the manifest evidence.[88] And tongues, unlike thought-laden human language, flows forth like a stream of water from our spirit, not from our intellect, which is in the soulish realm.

From the outside looking on, tongues appear to have no significance and may seem foolish to those who have not received this infilling. But speaking in tongues is something to be embraced for several reasons. The Bible reveals that tongues are a means for Holy Spirit to bring refreshing, rest, and strength[89] to a believer's spirit. The Holy Spirit intercedes through us when we pray in tongues and do not know what we should be praying for at the time (Romans 8:26). And there is the potential for supernatural revelation from our spirit flowing into our mind through praying in tongues. First Corinthians 14:14–15 says,

> For if I pray in a tongue, my spirit prays, but my understanding is unfruitful. What is the result then? I will pray with the spirit, and I will also pray with the understanding. I will sing with the spirit and I will also sing with the understanding.

This Scripture reveals our spirit man praying first, then our soul man, which is the intellect, emotions, and will. Jesus said God is seeking believers who will worship Him in spirit and in truth. What better way is there than to worship and commune spirit-to-Spirit with

God through tongues and then receive *revelation* on how we should worship and pray with our understanding for a particular situation?

First Corinthians 14:14 says our soul man doesn't understand the words pouring from our spirit. But many times, while praying in tongues, either during or soon afterward, I have received revelation, understanding, or direction in my prayers. Tongues can be an instrument, or pump, to pull revelation from our spirit into our minds, for within a Christian's spirit, the Spirit of the Lord resides, who is and possesses continual access to the throne of our all-knowing, all-powerful God. This Scripture also reveals tongues can be prayed as an act of volition, "I will pray with the spirit; I will also pray with the understanding," meaning we don't have to wait for a setting where the Spirit is moving outwardly before we can pray in the spirit. There *are* times when the Spirit of God is being poured out afresh, and we experience tongues afresh. But we have been given power to release His moving within ourselves and the atmosphere by simply choosing to speak!

When we pray in tongues, we may not know what we're saying, but God does! One of my most powerful experiences concerning tongues was on a Sunday morning at Community Church. The person next to me needed healing but was not willing to ask for prayer. In the spirit, I saw a dark figure pressing down on his shoulders, but I was unsure as to how to deal with the situation.

Not long before this, I asked the Lord if He was present in another church I was visiting because the traditions and service itself seemed devoid of the presence of God. As a result, I was given a vision that revolutionized my thinking in a certain area. And so, I once again asked Jesus, "Lord, are You here?" In an instant, my eyes were opened to see Jesus standing beside our pastor, David Berkheimer. The Lord had His arm around him, as if He were commending him in what he was about to say. Pastor was waiting for our music director to bring the worship to a pause. When everyone was silent, right before Pastor David began to speak, Jesus stepped away as if to give the Word that was about to be read great honor.

Pastor David read James 5:14–15, then asked the praying elders to come so that anyone who needed healing could receive prayer. The person next to me didn't budge. Perplexed as to how I or anyone else could help him, I asked, "Lord, who else is here?" Then I saw the most beautiful scene. A host of large angels, in what appeared to be glowing steam, was hovering over the praise and worship team. I thought—*this is something!* The Lord is here, the angels are here, and that dark, oppressive being is also here, attempting to suppress my friend's asking for help. What can I do? I thought to rebuke the evil spirit over my friend, but if he was in agreement with it (the enemy deceives in order to secure a place of agreement in our minds), my rebuke might not do any good. So, in desperation, I began praying in tongues. In an instant, an angel from the heavenly host in front flew with lightning speed over to where we were in the sanctuary, his white-hot, glowing sword drawn. As this angel maneuvered the sword with warrior precision, the dark presence took its hands off the person next to me to evade any contact with the angelic "lightsaber."

At that point, the vision ended; I could no longer see into the spirit realm, but I began to see the awesome value of tongues. When our spirit, which is inhabited by God's Spirit, prays, the Lord, through us, can release angels, obstruct evil, or whatever He deems necessary. The Spirit can intercede through us for a loved one, our next-door neighbor, or someone on the other side of the world. Distance is of no consequence in the spirit realm. The Holy Spirit presides in what is uttered, and the kingdom of God is benefiting in some way. When we can't sleep, we can pray with understanding and also in tongues. When we feel weak, we can pray with understanding and in tongues. When we don't know how to pray, or we have a burden for something or someone, we can pray with our understanding but let us absolutely, positively, pray in tongues!

It is no coincidence that Genesis 11:6–9 records the confusion of man's speech, producing many languages scattered over the earth and prevented the building of a tower that's sole purpose was to exalt man. Conversely, on the day of Pentecost, believers were filled with the Holy Spirit and began speaking in what was to them unknown tongues, but tongues known and understood by those who heard them. And these tongues exalted and extolled the wonderful works of God! Do you see the fullness and wisdom of the Lord? Tongues were designed by God to bring His people together. Therefore, the enemy has worked overtime to make them a point of division. Today, there are still accounts of people hearing others speak in tongues and having perfect understanding of the dialect that was spoken. Accordingly, 1 Corinthians 14:22a says, "...tongues are for a sign, not to those who believe, but to unbelievers." Although seemingly foolish to the world, tongues are God's secret weapon, releasing supernatural peace, strengthening our spirit man, pulling spiritual revelation into our understanding, and at times, bridging the gap of differing languages, revealing the wonder, power, and love of our heavenly Father.

My daughter, Gerrah, and I went on a mission trip the summer of 2013 with Villages of Hope, Africa, and Community Bible Church in San Antonio, Texas, which has a sister church in Gulu, Uganda. We spent nearly two weeks visiting the surrounding villages sharing the love of Jesus, witnessing, praying for the sick, leading the lost to Christ, and baptizing new believers. Our leaders asked Gulu's CBC to send interpreters so we could share with the villagers, who primarily speak the Acholi language. One of our interpreters, named Jacob, helped Gerrah and I immensely. He is a bright young man with a comical, dry wit and a sincere desire to see the fullness of God released in the Acholi people. I was amazed to learn that Jacob knew over fifty African languages, including Acholi and Swahili! There are, by some counts, over 3000 languages spoken natively in Africa.[90]

When a believer speaks in tongues, be it his/her initial infilling or prayer language (which requires no interpretation) or the corporate gift of tongues (which *does* require an interpretation), he/she may be speaking one of the 6,909 known languages[91] in the world or the tongues of angels (1 Corinthians 13:1). The Bible says that no language is without significance (1 Corinthians 14:10), even if we have not a clue as to what is being said. When spoken under the direction of the Holy Spirit, we can rest in God's faithfulness to bring rest, peace, revelation, assistance, deliverance, or whatever is needed. No matter the sound, when our spirit is praying, we are communing with the Lord on a level our intellect is not capable of achieving without divine intervention, and tongues are the vehicle selected by the Holy Spirit to divinely intervene on our behalf. Therefore, if you have received your prayer language, I encourage you to not only use it but use it often, and you will begin to perceive a definitive difference in your walk with the Lord.

The gift of tongues has a variety of applications in the believer's life, some private and some public. In most corporate full Gospel settings today, the manifestation of tongues is an indication that a prophetic word is about to come forth. This prophetic word, when it follows tongues, categorically is known as the gift of interpretation of tongues, which can be a direct translation of what was spoken, but usually, it is a revealed thought or concept to the interpreter and confirmation that the Spirit of prophecy is moving and speaking in a particular vein. My friend, Gail, shared an experience where she and a friend were praying in tongues, and Holy Spirit gave them both the same exact interpretation at the same time. Besides what the Scriptures record, I have only heard of two people translating a message in tongues in a corporate setting. I have also heard of people praying in tongues on airplanes, etc., and the person next to them understood what was spoken. If the Holy Spirit impresses you to bring a message in tongues to a group of believers, pray you may also know what the heart of God is if no one steps up and gives the interpretation. People have free wills, and if they are timid or fearful of speaking publicly, Holy Spirit will not force them, even if He desires to use them in this dimension. "Therefore, let him who speaks in a tongue pray that he may interpret" (1 Corinthians 14:13).

While writing about tongues in this book, one Sunday morning, the Lord said to me, "I want you to go to Community today and give the message in tongues." At this point, my husband had wanted to go back to his roots—the Baptist Church, but on this particular weekend, he was hunting, so I decided to attempt to follow the Lord in releasing a message in tongues if the opportunity presented itself. On the short drive to church, I was praying earnestly for the interpretation. During the praise and worship, the music and singing slowed down to a hush; I knew I had been given the mandate to step out and bring this word and thank God the anointing was there to give it. Moments later, someone on the other side of the sanctuary gave an interpretation. I was relieved, but I was also ready to give the interpretation the Lord had deposited in my heart—just in case.

Of the nine gifts of the Spirit listed in 1 Corinthians 12, seven were already in operation in the Old Testament as the Spirit moved through prophets, priests, or kings. In the New Testament, tongues and interpretation of tongues were the hallmarks of the Holy Spirit's ministry entrance in the Earth. Tongues and interpretation are unique to the birth of the church and were released specifically for this dispensation; they are more powerful than we can know unless we personally partake of this peculiar but potentially life-changing power that is released through tongues.

Tongues plus interpretation of tongues equals prophecy, which brings us to the last, but certainly not the least, of the utterance gifts—the gift of prophecy. Sylvia Thompson, who moved in the prophetic gifting with more concise clarity than anyone I have ever known, once said that prophecy can be "both foretelling and forth-telling," meaning a prophetic word can reveal future events, and it can also disclose the thoughts and intents of a heart. But all true prophecy will ultimately point to the Person of Jesus Christ because "the testimony of Jesus is the spirit of prophecy" (Revelation 19:10b).

In the Old Testament, prophecy had more to do with the foretelling of future events, which ties into an intricate pattern woven throughout the Scriptures bringing the reader through the verity of man's original state, fallen state, and God's one and only prescription for restoration: Jesus Christ. His appearance in humanity fulfilled many of the prophetic words recorded in the thirty-nine

Old Testament books and simultaneously brought clarity to many more in both Old and New Testaments that have to do with His second coming. When considered from a mathematical standpoint, the odds of Jesus fulfilling the following eight prophecies is 1 in 10,000,000,000,000,000,000,000,000,000; yet He most certainly, indisputably did![92]

- Christ would be born in Bethlehem; Micah 5:2
- There would be a forerunner of Christ; Malachi 3:1
- Christ will enter Jerusalem riding of a donkey; Zechariah 9:9
- Christ is betrayed by a friend; Psalm 41:9
- Christ is betrayed for 30 pieces of silver; Zechariah 11:12
- 30 pieces of silver used to buy a potter's field; Zechariah 11:13
- Although innocent, Christ is silent when on trial; Isaiah 53:7
- Christ is crucified; Psalm 22:16

"A prophet is defined as 'one who speaks on behalf of another,' and prophecy is the message that he conveys," write authors Tim Lahaye and Thomas Ice in their book, *Charting the End Times*.[93] The Old Testament is replete with prophetic utterances from men and sometimes women God used as His mouthpiece, including an interesting passage from the prophet Isaiah, verses 46:9–10:

> Remember the former things of old, for I am God, and there is no other; I am God, and there is none like Me, declaring the end from the beginning, and from ancient times things that are not yet done, saying "My counsel shall stand, and I will do all My pleasure."

Through the gift of prophecy and eventual fulfilling events, God declares His sovereignty and reveals His ability to bring to pass all things He has spoken. In the Old Testament, the Spirit would light upon or temporarily fill a prophet, relaying revelatory information to those to whom God wished to speak.[94] This ministry gift is seen in various places throughout the Old Testament up until the time of Christ, with a span of 400 years of silence between the prophet

Malachi and the arrival of John the Baptist, whose appearance is recorded in all four of the Gospel accounts.

With the New Testament gift of prophecy, as one of the nine manifestation gifts in 1 Corinthians 12, emphasis is not as much on foretelling, but in forth-telling, speaking "edification, exhortation and comfort to men" (1 Corinthians 14:3). Because all born-again believers in Christ have the Holy Spirit resident within their spirits, the potential to prophesy (as well as move in the other eight manifestation gifts) is also resident. However, sensitivity to the Spirit's moving in this capacity usually only takes place within those who have received the Holy Spirit's baptism. This is because He brings the fire that not only burns off hindrances in the human soul but also activates the moving of the Spirit within the believer in supernatural revelatory, power, and utterance capabilities. In other words, the new birth installs the equipment to function, but until the Holy Spirit fire is lit, there is no unction to function!

As well as forth-telling, there are some in the Body of Christ who also flow in prophetic foretelling. Although any born-again, spirit-filled Christian may prophesy, whereby the Spirit is edifying, exhorting, and comforting others, or even ourselves, not everyone is called to hold the office of a prophet, which is one of the five-fold ministry gifts listed in Ephesians 4:11. Ordinarily, the person holding the office of the prophet will be used in foretelling as well as forth-telling. The office carries a heavier responsibility and accountability to speak what the Spirit of God is saying. All ministry offices are appointed by the Holy Spirit, not us (Hebrews 5:4). According to Kenneth E. Hagin, who was a pioneer of the modern-day faith movement, a person holding the office of a prophet must have at least two of the revelatory gifts (word of wisdom, word of knowledge and/or discerning of spirits) moving in his/her life, as well as prophecy.[95]

The great news is we don't have to be prophets to move in this gift because the Scriptures encourage us all to aspire to prophesy regarding exhortation, edification, and comfort. First Corinthians 14:1 says, "Pursue love, and desire spiritual gifts, but especially that you may prophesy." This is because prophecy is the gift that reveals the heart and desire of God *and* men.[96] Prophecy is incredibly valuable to the Church. First Corinthians 14:4 says, "He who speaks in a tongue edifies himself, but he who prophesies edifies the church." The word for "edifies" here is "oikodomeo,"[97] which means "to be a house builder; confirm, embolden." Tongues (prayer language) are not about self-promotion; they are for spiritually strengthening and building up the believer; prophecy is for strengthening and building up the entire Body of Christ.

For those who desire to bring a prophetic word to the body of Christ, you can begin by praying for the Church, privately or with an intercessory prayer group. Ezekiel 22:30 says, "So I sought for a man among them who would make a wall and stand in the gap before Me on behalf of the land, that I should not destroy it, but I found no one." God is looking for people who will stand in the gap for others, and nine chapters earlier a principle is concealed in his words to the prophets of his day. Ezekiel says, "You have not gone up into the gaps (breaches) to build a wall for the house of Israel to stand in the battle on the day of the Lord," chapter 13, verse 5. Then he likens the lack of prayer to untempered mortar in the construction of a building in verse 10. Untempered mortar hasn't been brought to a proper consistency or hardness (Dictionary.com). There is a connection to intercessory prayer and the release of true prophetic words from heaven. During Kathy Lechner's ministry time at Community Church a few years ago, the Lord spoke to me, "Your prophesying will be directly proportional to your intercession." Therefore, as we purpose in our heart to intercede for others fervently, it will, in turn, prepare the way for the Lord to use us in prophetic revelation and utterances in the building of His kingdom—desire that you may prophesy!

Spiritual gifts can be conferred on believers through prophecy. First Timothy 4:14 says, "Do not neglect the gift that is in you, which was given to you by prophecy with the laying on of the hands of the eldership." Prophecy can give direction, affirmation, and stability to one's calling and spiritual duties (1 Timothy 1:18). Prophecy is also a sign of the great outpouring of the Holy Spirit. In the apostle Peter's sermon at Pentecost, he quotes the prophet Joel:

> And it shall come to pass in the last days, says God, that I will pour out of My Spirit on all flesh; your sons and your daughters shall prophesy, your young men shall see visions, your old men shall dream dreams. And on My menservants and on My maidservants, I will pour out My spirit in those days and they shall prophesy.
>
> Acts 2:17–18

Prophecy is not all-inclusive; it doesn't reveal every detail concerning our situation or future. First Corinthians 13:9 says, "For we know in part and we prophecy in part." The Holy Spirit, through prophecy, issues the exact amount of information to encourage, strengthen or comfort us. Some people are afraid to hear a prophetic Word, concerned the Holy Spirit will bring to light something they don't want exposed. That is not the purpose of layman prophecy. God always deals with us privately first. When we don't listen, however, the Holy Spirit, through the office of the prophet, can bring correction for our own good. Everything God does in our lives is motivated by love. It can be exciting and igniting to receive a prophetic Word from a reliable source. True prophecy will usually confirm what the Lord has already been speaking to our heart, and it should always point us to Jesus.

The Body of Christ is comprised of many denominational groups; those reading this may or may not be familiar with the full Gospel or even be a Christian. The author's testimony is that these gifts, including prophecy, are authentic and available to flow through the Body of Christ, as the Spirit wills. The definition of faith, as stated in Hebrews 11:1, says, "Now faith is the substance of things hoped for, the evidence of things not seen." If we choose to believe the Word of God, there is no limit to what the Lord can do in our life. God spoke through the prophet Jeremiah, "Call to me and I will answer you, and show you great and mighty (inaccessible) things which you do not know" (verse 33:3). If God had a cell phone, Jeremiah 33:3 would be His phone number: I always told my preschoolers to keep it handy. What a privilege to be able to call on Him day and night; or search the Scriptures, like the Bereans, to ascertain the truth for ourselves.[98]

Many cite 1 Corinthians 13:8b as a repudiation to modern-day prophecy, *"but whether there are prophecies, they will fail* (they sometimes do, but many times do not! God's timing and our timing may be quite different in prophetic fulfillment), *whether there are tongues, they shall cease* (we won't need tongues when Jesus comes back; we will have perfect communication with Him and each other, tongues are for now!) *whether there is knowledge, it will vanish away* (the knowledge we have now cannot even compare to the perfect understanding God will give to those who serve Him in the next life). Also, 1 Corinthians 13:10, "But when that which is perfect (complete) has come, then that which is in part will be done away." Granted, Jesus *has* come the first time, and He *is* perfect, but this passage was written after the fact, so unless you are reading this after the sky has split and Jesus has touched down on the Mount of Olives near Jerusalem, that which is perfect (Him) has not come (again), but He *is* coming (again)! Until then, we need everything He has provided to grow, to assist others, and to stand against the demonic hordes of hell.

And we need these gifts now because Satan, although defeated, is still running around, making people's lives miserable. He works through sin and deception, but God has designed the gifts of the Spirit to counteract and neutralize his efforts on every side if we listen and obey. It takes a close walk with the Lord to hear what the Spirit is saying and cooperate with Him to bring victory, but that's what the gifts of the Spirit are for—to bring into manifestation the victory that is already ours through Jesus Christ. The gifts are a significant part of God's master plan, building us up internally (individually and corporately), and in the process, we grow up into the fullness of Christ in us and us in Him. Church, we are being prepared for the responsibilities that will be committed to us as the bride of Christ, when we shall rule and reign with Him in glory! I do not know what all that will entail, but Hebrews 6:6 indicates that the functioning of supernatural power in the age to come will be the norm. Now, we encounter opposition and hindrances to the operation of God's power in our lives, but we are still an extension of God Himself on the Earth because the Spirit dwells in us. One day soon, His power in us will have no limits. Praise the Lord!

Remember the service stations of yesteryear? Back in the day, people didn't fill their own gasoline tanks; there was no self-serve. When my mom or dad would pull up to a service station, an attendant would quickly come running to the driver's window asking, "What'll it be?" "Fill 'er up!" was the response every time. When we're given the opportunity to receive the infilling of the Holy Spirit, or we need a holy visitation from the Lord, "Fill 'er up!" should be our response and plea every time because, without Him, we lack the power necessary to fulfill our mission in Christ. We must be born again, unequivocally making Jesus Lord of our lives, and it's to our great advantage to also receive the baptism of the Holy Spirit. Therefore, let us be filled and refilled as needed so that "times of refreshing may come from the presence of the Lord" (Acts 3:19). What magnificent works of the Spirit of God within the believer! And just when we thought it couldn't get any better, He dresses us for success with the whole armor of God—and, um, His wardrobe doesn't malfunction.

Prayer For the Fullness of the Holy Spirit and
Activation of the Gifts of the Spirit:

Heavenly Father, thank you for making my heart your home and writing my name in the Lamb's Book of Life that I may come and live with you for all eternity. I now ask you to baptize me with your Holy Spirit and fire, filling me to overflowing with the evidence of other tongues. By faith, I receive the endowment of power that comes from this impartation and ask you to move in my life in supernatural ways that the gifts of the Spirit may be made manifest in me as the Spirit wills. Help me stay humble under your mighty hand as you bring me into a greater understanding of your will and your ways. Define your calling on my life that I may serve you with my whole heart.

~ In Jesus' name, amen!

LOCK & LOAD

Some of the best times Bennie, Julianne, Gerrah, and I had were the skiing vacations we took with family and friends. Everyone could easily ski the blues except Gerrah and me, but we sure tried! When our skis were snapped into place, and the gang was ready to head for the ski lift, we would hear our fearless leader, Hammon, speak that unmistakable phrase, "Lock and load!" We were rockin' and ready to tackle the high altitude, snow-covered terrain with ski poles and a prayer. It would have been pure folly to ascend that mountain without some faith and our ski equipment in order. And it is pure folly to think that as a Christian, we won't be buffeted by the forces of darkness or ever "wrestle with the devil." When attacks come, and they will, the serious-minded Christian needs dependable and effective protection, and there is undeniably no substitute for the full armor of God.

Through the new birth, we are given the ability to submit to God; renewing our minds with the Word helps us recognize where He desires to work. Although the extent and impregnability of the Christian's armor are developed to greater degrees as we obey and walk with the Lord through spiritual discipline, we can still activate this invisible protection through a verbal profession of faith. God has given us this armor, and the apostle Paul skillfully depicts how each piece protects the Christian in a specific way. Ephesians 6:10–11 says, "Finally, my brethren, be strong in the Lord and in the power of His might. Put on the whole armor of God that you may be able to stand against the wiles (schemings) of the devil." Something shifts in us and/or the atmosphere when we verbally appropriate[99] the full armor of God. It should be part of our daily dress for success, but *anytime* we feel uneasy, anxious, or apprehensive, we can put it on by faith.

Bennie and I were traveling to east-central Texas one day, and the closer we drew to our destination, the more uneasy I felt. These feelings were rooted in past experiences, but now I could do something about it. The Holy Spirit quickened me to put on the armor and declare that "no weapon formed against me will prosper and every tongue that rises against me in judgment I shall show to be in the wrong because God has given me his righteousness" (Isaiah 54:17, AMP), along with declaring other spiritual truths into the upcoming situation. I did this silently as we rode forward—and it worked.

Jesus referred to people, animals, and objects that humans are familiar with to explain spiritual truths: landowners, farmers, judges, widows, sheep, wolves, lamps, clothing, wineskins, and trees, etc. Paul utilized this type of analogy also. By comparing the Christian to athletes, the human body, and Roman soldiers, he enabled those who read his letters to comprehend the realities of the spirit realm. To equip God's people concerning the forces of darkness, the Roman soldier's armor efficiently defines God's provision for protecting our vulnerabilities. Ephesians 6:10–18 describes six indispensable pieces of armor the Christian needs to withstand the evil generated by the enemy of our soul. These pieces are more than acknowledgments of characteristics of the Word; they are disciplines for the maturing Christian. But the Word also provides a spiritual "undergarment," offering protection against one of the enemy's most insidious deceptions: pride.

First Peter 5:5b says, "Yes, all of you be submissive to one another and be clothed with humility for God resists the proud but gives grace to the humble." The word for "clothed" is "eckomboomai,"[100] which means "to engirdle oneself." We have all been inflated with pride at one time or another. Dictionary.com defines pride as "a high or inordinate opinion of one's own dignity, importance, merit, or superiority, whether as cherished in the mind or as displayed in bearing, conduct, etc." In the world, people have come to accept, even promote, the idea that it is okay to step on or manipulate whoever they must to advance their personal goals. Even in church, strife, which is rooted in pride, can come between Christians. Proverbs 16:18 says, "Pride goes before destruction, and a haughty spirit before a fall." Be on guard against pride. It sunk the devil and is one of his most subtle tactics in spiritual warfare. Usually, the person infected with it is completely unaware.

Like the rest of the armor, humility can be appropriated, but we must also walk it out. Waiting upon the Lord, choosing forgiveness, lifting others in prayer, showing kindness, and being "doers of the word"[101] releases God to bestow true honor on our lives. First Peter 5:6 says, "Therefore humble yourselves under the mighty hand of God, that He may exalt you in due time." Christians have Jesus as our example and leader and the Holy Spirit as our counselor and teacher. Humility is not a weakness, as the world would have us think. It positions us for blessing and promotion while simultaneously deflating pride. While listening to *The Message* on SiriusXM, I heard a member of Big Daddy Weave say, "True humility is agreeing with God concerning what He says about us,"[102] and he is right. True humility is not self-deprecating rhetoric but knowing who we are in Christ and lovingly serving others. Proverbs 15:33 says, "The fear of the Lord is the instruction of wisdom, and before honor is humility." A safeguard against pride, humility must not be overlooked and cannot be overstated, so don't go commando! Put on humility before you put on the armor.

The Belt of Truth—Our Foundational Defense Against Deception

Ephesians 6:14a, "Stand therefore, having girded your waist with truth..." The belt of truth is listed first because the only infallible source of truth known to man is God's Word, the Bible. The Spirit of God exhorts us to allow truth to sink deep into the core of our being. Psalm 51:6 says, "Behold, You desire truth in the inward parts, and in the hidden part You will make me to know wisdom." Pontius Pilate asked Jesus, "What is truth?" (John 18:38). World

Book Dictionary defines truth as "that which is in accordance with the fact or facts; a fixed or established principle, law, proven doctrine, etc., that which is true, real or actual in a general or abstract sense; the quality or nature of being true, exact, honest, sincere, loyal." Maybe Mr. Pilate asked this question because truth in his day, as well as ours, seemed elusive—but it's not. Jesus claimed to be *the* truth (John 14:6); truth is the Word of God; Jesus *is* the Word of God made flesh! Truth is the foundation upon which everything that will stand is built. Therefore, truth is first and foremost the foundational groundwork in the network of protection God has provided against our spiritual foe.

Jesus said, "If you abide in My word, you are My disciples indeed. And you shall know the truth and the truth shall make you free" (John 8:31–32). We cannot abide in His word until we put it into our hearts. Some say they have read the Bible, but their actions and words contradict their claim. It's not a one-time read. The Bible is a spiritual book with unsearchable depths of nourishment, wisdom, and revelation, but only through the Holy Spirit are these treasures brought forth. And it's not enough to know *about* truth; we must *practice* it.

My cousin Terry has always been a Word man. He was reading his Bible when Bible reading wasn't cool. But his devotion influenced me; I knew I needed to read my Bible but was inconsistent. Those New Year's resolutions I made usually lasted maybe two weeks. Then I heard someone say, "Ask God to give you a hunger for His Word." When I did, the Bible came alive to me. It was no longer like reading the yellow pages. Jesus said in John 6:63, "It is the Spirit who gives life; the flesh profits nothing. The words that I speak to you are spirit and they are life." When we prayerfully approach God's word asking for a hunger, acknowledging our need, the Spirit of truth[103] will, in time, guide us into all truth, revealing inexhaustible resources and a Rock-solid foundation in Christ.

By observing the functionality of a belt, we see it can hold different tools, keys, and weapons needed for any situation. The belt of truth has the same practicality in facing the scope of uncertainties in life, making a working knowledge of the Word expressly vital. In another sense, a belt holds up the portion of outerwear covering our reproductive organs. Without the belt of truth, we will reproduce the world and its opposition to spiritual veracity. My friend Sarah shared that we will unknowingly receive and multiply the burdens of generational curses instead of allowing the Word to break them in our lives, liberating us and giving our children an honest chance to be free in the Lord.

To seek truth, we must ask Holy Spirit to reveal areas where we or our ancestors have been deceived and consequently promoted deception and sin. He can reveal deception and lead us out of it. By repenting of sin, repenting for listening to the enemy, repenting for our ancestors, and renouncing all association with the sin and/or deception, we then ask Jesus to cleanse and help us abide in His truth in this area of our lives. We remain vigilant by asking Holy Spirit to alert us when the enemy is up to his old tricks. Abiding in truth with God and with each other allows His Word to work decisively in our lives, but remember, we are all at different stages in our walk with Christ.[104] When others are struggling, we must pray for them until they are ready to deal with issues in their life.[105] In God's timing, speaking the truth in love will enable us to grow up in all things in Christ (Ephesians 4:15). Truth's power delivers from doublemindedness,[106] and Jesus said we are sanctified, or set apart, by God's truth.[107]

The enemy's greatest weapon is deception. He used it against Adam and Eve and still uses it today. Jesus, when facing the cross, said, "I will no longer talk much with you for the ruler of this world is coming, and he has nothing in Me" (John 14:30). Satan couldn't feed Jesus a lie and thus, couldn't subjugate His mission. Jesus claimed to be the personification of Truth. Jesus also said Satan has *no* truth in himself (John 8:44); he is a liar and the father of it. The belt of truth is symbolic of eternal truth available only in Christ, the Word of God. Jesus bore witness to the truth, and everyone who is of the truth will hear His voice.[108] His truth is freedom. His truth is life. His truth *is* truth.

The Breastplate of Righteousness—
Positional *and* Obedience Righteousness

"Having put on the breastplate of righteousness" (Ephesians 6:14b). A breastplate is designed to cover the heart and lungs, two vital organs without which we could not survive. Spiritually speaking, the heart of man is of great concern to God and a prime target of the enemy. Proverbs 4:23 says, "Keep your heart with all diligence, for out of it spring the issues of life." Whatever incubates in our heart has the potential to come out of our mouth.[109] In the natural, our lungs give airflow for words to come forth from our mouth; but words have spiritual power—both positive and negative, and the course of our life will follow our words.[110] Therefore, the breastplate that protects our spiritual heart, greatly affecting the words we speak, is called the breastplate of righteousness for at least two reasons.

Pastor David once said, "Righteousness has two wings—and neither one can fly alone. It takes *both positional righteousness* and *obedience righteousness* to fulfill God's plan for your life."[111] Understanding, walking in, and appropriating these two sides of righteousness will provide ample protection for our hearts. Positional righteousness is the righteousness of faith; God has given us His righteousness through Jesus Christ. In Matthew 6:33, Jesus said if we "seek first the kingdom of God and His righteousness," then all things we have need of will be added to us. People tend to skip the second part of that directive—to seek God's righteousness. We cannot earn righteousness; it is freely given to those who trust in Christ.[112] This is problematic for people who like being their own boss and paying their own way—that pride thing again. In Romans 10:2–3, Paul described this same problem in his day: "For I bear them (the Jews) witness that they have a zeal for God, but not according to knowledge. For they, being ignorant of God's righteousness, and seeking to establish their own righteousness, have not submitted to the righteousness of God." Through humility, we can accept the truth and receive.

We tend to view success or failure according to what we have learned, earned, or accomplished, which isn't the right measure, my friend Terri has pointed out. Sometimes we're unsuccessful, or we don't measure up. We look back and see defeat or disappointment, and we become discouraged while the enemy is making accusation and inciting regrets. But God wants us to know His mercies are new every morning (Lamentations 3:23), and since He has given us His righteousness through Christ, we have assurance our failures and disappointments are under the blood of Jesus. We can come boldly to His throne of grace in time of need (Hebrews 4:16); we don't have to earn His favor. Through Christ, we already have it! His righteousness is truly a breastplate of faith.[113]

Obedience righteousness is the Christian's honest attempts to live within the framework of what God reveals as right and wrong. This has nothing to do with our salvation but everything to do with our sanctification. Our obedience to the Lord and His Word is a living epistle to the world as to whom we rightfully belong. When we make a sincere effort to follow the leading of the Spirit through the truth of the Word, the breastplate of righteousness will protect our heart from demonic attack and bring us into alignment for God's blessing.[114]

Obedience righteousness also addresses the problem of presuming on God's grace. Because righteousness is a gift, some think they can do anything they want. But that is ignorant of the spiritual laws eternally put in place by our Lord. Yes, we have been given the righteousness of Christ, but the principle of sowing and reaping is still operational.[115] King David recognized this and prayed, "Keep back Your servant also from presumptuous sins, let them not have dominion over me, then I shall be blameless, and I shall be innocent of great transgression" (Psalm 19:13). We move forward, recognizing our imperfections yet endeavoring to live a life pleasing to God, knowing that His daily grace is sufficient.

How blessed we are and how thankful we should be that God's unmerited favor is continually available. Let our attitude be like Paul's, "...forgetting those things which are behind and reaching forward to those things which are ahead, I press toward the goal for the prize of the upward call of God in Christ Jesus" (Philippians 3:13–14). A close walk with God through prayer, Bible study, and connection to a biblical church provide a family of believers who forgive and undergird us should we fall. And when we do, let's be quick to repent and close the door to the enemy.[116] The longer the door stays open through grumbling, unforgiveness, anger, self-pity, etc., the worse we are going to feel and the more opportunity and legal ground we give the enemy to attack in some way.[117] Obedience to God and His Word and correct understanding of righteousness will keep the breastplate of righteousness properly positioned over our hearts.

Gospel Shoes of Peace—God's Way and God's Ways

"And having shod your feet with the preparation of the gospel of peace" (Ephesians 6:15). I love comfortable shoes, but I wear them whether they are comfortable or not because I don't like going bare-footed. Shoes provide protection and stability. Spiritually speaking, we would be wise to give ample attention to four truths revealed in this Scripture: our walk, preparation, the gospel, and peace.

When we are sincere in our walk with Christ, we find He does indeed provide protection and stability. Galatians 5:16 tells us to "walk in the spirit, and you shall not fulfill the lust of the flesh." Because our spirit is housed in an earthen vessel that has yet to be redeemed, there is constant potential to yield to the flesh, be lured by the world, or listen to demonic lies. To diligently follow Jesus, we make preparation through prayer and reading the Word that we may hear clearly from the Holy Spirit. As we walk with Him daily, we begin recognizing things detrimental to our spirit man's growth and viability.[118] Step by step, we slowly but surely reposition ourselves to be in sync with the plans and purposes of God. Sometimes we stumble or make a wrong turn, but repentance and God's grace get us back on track.

As disciples of Jesus, we are commanded to "Go therefore and make disciples of all the nations, baptizing them in the name of the Father and of the Son and of the Holy Spirit" (Matthew 28:19). This is "the Great Commission," and it is not limited to the ministry of the evangelist. We must be ready to testify and share what God has done in our lives, pointing others to Him. Having a basic understanding of the "Roman Road" supplies a Biblical anchor and a scriptural map from whence we can share the gospel (good news) to a lost and hurting world:

Romans 3:23: "...all have sinned and fall short of the glory of God." Romans 6:23: "...the wages of sin is death, but the gift of God is eternal life in Christ Jesus, our Lord."

Romans 10:9–10:

> If you confess with your mouth the Lord Jesus and believe in your heart that God has raised Him from the dead, you will be saved. For with the heart one believes to righteousness, and with the mouth confession is made to salvation.

Romans 5:1: "Therefore, having been justified by faith, we have peace with God through our Lord Jesus."

> For I am persuaded that neither death nor life, nor angels nor principalities nor powers, nor things present nor things to come nor height nor depth, nor any other created thing, shall be able to separate us from the love of God which is in Christ Jesus our Lord.
>
> Romans 8:38–39

Because we are secure, we have an obligation, a mandate, to tell others. Although Jesus would have given His life just for you or me, He sees thousands of people dying every day;[119] many of them lost for eternity. And it's not His will that any should perish.[120] If we ask and look for opportunities to share Jesus with others, He will provide them. The Lord specifically spoke to me, "Don't stop giving out tracts; you're planting seeds." If we plant a seed or water one that has been planted or perhaps lead a dear soul to Christ, it is God who is at work through our obedience.[121] Some are called to an evangelistic ministry, but all are called to be light and salt. The light of His truth shining forth in our words and actions while retaining the salt of the fear of the Lord[122] creates a thirst in others for living water. Paul tells us in 2 Timothy 4:2, "Preach the word! Be ready in season and out of season. Convince, rebuke, exhort with all longsuffering and teaching."

Finally, we must realize that God's ways are confirmed in peace. When we share, and it appears it wasn't received, commit the situation to the Lord. My aunt Babe preached for years to my cousin, Dee, with no apparent response. But when Dee experienced a health crisis, she turned to Jesus with her whole heart. Another time, Jack, my husband's friend, visited us after an Al-Anon meeting, excited about the "higher power" the twelve-step program espouses. I respectfully shared that the Bible says the only higher power we have access to is Jesus.[123] He didn't think so and left somewhat miffed. Years later, we saw him at Orange's Gumbo Cookoff, and he said, "You were right. Now I know Jesus *is* the higher power." Sometimes speaking up is uncomfortable, but if we lean into Holy Spirit, asking Him for help, He will. It frees us to share the Gospel in peace knowing He is doing the work; we are only the messenger.

The Shield of Faith— an Antidote for Unbelief and Rest in God's Promises

"...Above all, taking the shield of faith with which you will be able to quench all the fiery darts of the wicked one" (Ephesians 6:16). A shield is a barrier, and the barrier between you and enemy fire is your faith in God. It is through faith in what God has done for us through Jesus Christ that we can extinguish everything the enemy can dish out. Therefore, Paul says, "above all," because even if a soldier has no other piece of armor, he/she can still use his/her shield to fend off an enemy attack.

The word "faith" is only mentioned twice in the Old Testament[124] and 244 times in the New! Although faith is certainly an important theme throughout Old Testament Scripture, it is clarified in the New Testament. Jesus responded to or spoke about faith at least twenty-nine times in the Synoptic Gospels (Matthew, Mark, and Luke), and faith becomes a major theme in the New Testament Epistles. In Ephesians 6:16 and in most New Testament writings, "faith" is translated from the word "pistis,"[125] meaning "persuasion, credence, conviction." Our strong belief in God's holy character, unlimited ability, and sacrificial love becomes a shield against Satan and his devices.

Jesus made it clear the enemy is after the Word in our hearts.[126] This is because "...faith comes by hearing, and hearing by the word of God" (Romans 10:17). Our faith is directly connected to our knowledge of God's Word. We must be diligent in putting it into our thoughts, words, and actions because if the enemy can steal the Word from us, he can hinder our ability to defend ourselves. But Satan cannot override God's sovereignty. Therefore, we must also have faith in God's faithfulness; His faithfulness to those in covenant with Him will never fail.

Because Abraham believed God, God accounted it to him for righteousness.[127] Hebrews 11:1 gives the biblical definition of faith. Without faith, it is impossible to please God (Hebrews 11:6). Faith is our shield and our taproot connection to the invisible God. Spiritual death caused by original sin elevated the soul of man to the position God intended for man's spirit. This regrettably gave mankind's soul, governed by physical senses, primary influence in perceiving, understanding, and decision making instead of spirit discerning, spirit-ruled, and spirit-led. Once our spirit man has been reinstated through the new birth in Christ, we have a choice to make: either continue allowing our soul to govern our decisions or learn to be led by the Spirit of God and "walk by faith, not by sight," (2 Corinthians 5:7). When serving God and not ourselves, we choose the faith walk because "...as many as are led by the Spirit of God, these are the sons of God" (Romans 8:14). This should be exemplified in our words *and* our actions because "faith by itself, if it does not have works, is dead" (James 2:17). The more determined we are to walk as children of God, the more our armor will be fortified in Him, including the shield of faith.

"Faith" is mentioned frequently in the New Testament, but "shield" is only mentioned in Ephesians 6:16 and translated, "thureos,"[128] meaning a large door-shaped shield. This speaks of ample sufficiency and thorough coverage the shield of faith provides against the spiritual doors of the enemy. A spiritual door is an opening or point of entry whereby the enemy of our soul seeks admittance. It is the shield of faith that shuts him out, enabling the believer to refuse Satan's lies.

The shield of faith blocks the enemy's attempts to thwart our mission in the kingdom, allowing us to move forward in Christ. Day by day, we can strengthen our faith, and consequently our shield, simply by prayerfully reading, applying, and doing what God's Word says. If we have faith in God, we have a shield against evil. Therefore, never stop believing that God is and that He loves you. Never stop believing that if you fall, He will pick you up. Never stop believing that He who is in you is greater than he who is in the world. Hold tight to your shield of faith—above all.

The Helmet of Salvation—
Security in Christ, Necessity of Renewing Our Mind

"And take the helmet of salvation" (Ephesians 6:17a). Few of us must continuously wear a helmet (for which I am grateful—I don't want hat hair!). But for those who play contact sports, work on construction sites, ride motorcycles or engage in military conflict, going without protective headgear could be downright lethal. The helmet of salvation is equally indispensable because the helmet, like the breastplate, offers vital organ protection. The word says "take" in Ephesians 6:13, 16, and 17 because salvation and everything pertaining to it is freely offered by God through Christ, but we must RSVP to the divine offer. No one can do this for us in proxy. Although Christians can appropriate the helmet's benefits for other Christians, the initial response to receiving salvation must be made by the individual. And like all previous pieces of armor, the activation and protection of the helmet of salvation are dependent upon our obedience to the Word and cooperation with the Holy Spirit.

Salvation is described as a helmet in three different places in Scripture,[129] so there is unquestionable significance to this allusion. Nothing in God's Word is accidental or coincidental. According to E.W. Bullinger, "All things that are especially complete are stamped with this number three."[130] Knowing what we have in Christ, what He saved us from, saved us for, and resting in hope of a secure future in Him has the power to protect our minds from the daily onslaught of pressure to think, choose and act like the world rather than the Lord. As we claim the helmet of salvation, we also claim the truth that says, "...we have the mind of Christ," 1 Corinthians 2:16, which is enhanced by renewing our minds with God's Word and involves a process.

In the natural, a helmet protects the head, which encases the brain, the organ utilized by the mind. It is where conscious and unconscious decisions are made and orders given; our very own "mission control." Without the Word of God being given a prominent place in our thoughts and actions, our mind's decisions will become self-centered and world-oriented, as they perpetually were before we were saved. Remember, it is our spirit that has been born again, not our soul. Consequently, we must shore up and reinforce those parts that can be readily influenced by our flesh, the world, and the devil.

The rectification of this situation is found in Romans 12:2, "...do not be conformed to this world, but be transformed by the renewing of your mind, that you may prove what is the good and acceptable and perfect will of God." The Word of God is the mind of Christ and the godly design of the spirit of our mind (Ephesians 4:23). We search out the good, acceptable, and perfect will of God because there are levels of cooperation with the Holy Spirit; renewing our mind is the blueprint to becoming more like Jesus. Although He alone was and is perfect, He will bring us to new levels in Himself if we invest the time and prayer necessary to bring us deeper and higher. Deeper in understanding what He is doing in us and higher in understanding what He wants to do through us.

We renew our minds by accepting, meditating, and speaking forth those things the Word of God says are true. This lays the forms or framework for God's Spirit to make necessary changes in us that will produce Christlikeness. This change becomes manifest when we are faced with a decision and choose God's way over our own. We have prepared the way to obey when we read, believe, and speak God's Word. Doing what the Word says produces change within us, a divine shift in soul and spirit, bringing us closer to a more accurate reflection of Christ. In stealing the Word, Satan's goal is to ultimately control our will. By setting our minds on things above,[131] staying spiritually minded and anchored in God's Word, we allow the Helmet of Salvation to shelter the ongoing work of sanctification and keep our focus on the blessed hope of eternity with Christ.

The Sword of the Spirit—
The Power of God's Word Spoken From a Faith-Filled Heart

"And the sword of the Spirit, which is the word of God" (Ephesians 6:17b). Every piece of armor mentioned in Ephesians 6 is a dimension of a specific function of God's Word, which is truth, righteousness, and peace, producing faith and salvation in believing hearts. These defensive elements protect against contaminants and the demonic inhabitants of a fallen world. But the sword of the Spirit encompasses more; it is a weapon of defense, but primarily a weapon of offensive, driving back enemy forces and all that hinders, binds, and imprisons.

The Word of God framed the worlds[132] and holds everything together. It is alive and active. It is sharper than any two-edged sword made by human, angelic, or demonic hands. It cuts asunder to the division of what is soulish and spiritual, what is connected and contained, distinguishing and separating thought and intent in the recesses of the human heart (Hebrews 4:12). Miracles take place when we speak His Word in faith. We move mountains and spiritual forces that are bigger than we are because God is watching over His Word to perform it (Jeremiah 1:12). How valuable is the Word! How necessary for men and women to hear, receive and obey. Without God's Word, we cannot be enlightened, saved, spirit-filled, or grow into the purpose for which we were created (Hebrews 6:4–5). Without the Word of God, we have no offensive weapon against our flesh nature, the world's philosophies, and the lies, stratagems, and structures that have been devised in darkness by Satan and his associates in sin.

To effectively use the sword of the Spirit, we must regularly read and spiritually ingest God's Word, memorizing all we can. The Holy Spirit will retrieve scriptural truth that is stored in our memory, strengthening and stabilizing our soul. Because sooner or later, someone or something is going to challenge our beliefs. Therefore, we should dig deep and know what, why, and where our beliefs are staked. By practicing Scripture memorization in all the basic tenets of Christianity, and Scriptures that keep the enemy at bay in our situation, we can remind the Lord what He has spoken (Isaiah 43:26), claiming His promises by faith and inform the enemy that he is defeated. By speaking God's Word over ourselves regularly, when we are tempted, pressured, or under attack, our response will be quick and efficient.

When my girls were growing up, we learned a scripture every week. They would quote it before they received their allowance. They were only learning by rote, but I knew God's Word is powerful and will not return void (Isaiah 55:11). Jesus knew the Scriptures quite well before He began His earthly ministry. Immediately after His baptism, He was led into the wilderness to be tempted in every area the enemy uses to entice man to sin:[133] the lust of the flesh, the lust of the eyes, and the pride of life.[134] Jesus responded to every temptation by quoting the Word. He knew the power of God's Word, but while He endured the restraints of human flesh, He spoke the Word from a human perspective, not the omniscient perspective of the Almighty, from whence He had come. And it still worked! Jesus was divine *and* human, but He operated on the Earth as a human being (Philippians 2:7). God did, however, give Him the Spirit without measure (John 3:34). Jesus was and is the prototype of redeemed mankind, the image of the invisible God, the firstborn of all creation (Colossians 1:15).

He still speaks to us and rebukes the enemy through us. Every time we speak the Word of God in faith toward the enemy, we are cutting into him and his devices with the sword of the Spirit. The right word from God's arsenal will have a direct impact on him and the bondage he is attempting to lure us into or to keep us bound. The evening before I was to host a first-ever prayer meeting at my house, the Lord spoke to me as I was laying down for the night and said, "Rise up and break the devil's power over this house." Not realizing that it was Him, I pondered why that thought would flow through my mind. Then, a second time He spoke, this time stronger and louder from my spirit, "Rise up and break the devil's power over this house!" I went to every room in my house and said what the Lord said, "In Jesus' name, I break the devil's power over this house." I then went to my living room and began praying in tongues. In the spirit, I could see my house from an aerial view, with roots coming up from the ground and intertwining over the top. It was completely bound and entangled. Then a huge arm came down from heaven holding a sword. The sword slipped under the roots and cut them asunder like a hot knife through butter.

By speaking this to me at that particular time, I believe the Lord had a specific purpose that had to do with the house I currently lived in, for demonic beings can hang out in locations where they have not been opposed and cast out through the authority of Christ, but He was also revealing to me that I could use His Word to free myself from every lie and vestige the enemy had used to keep me bound. In one sense, the house was the house, but in another sense, the house represented me. After all, our bodies are only the "house" our soul and spirit live in. According to Scripture, roots are generally symbolic of sinful hidden attitudes[135] which need to be severed. We can do this through the leading of the Holy Spirit and the Word of God, and we have been given the authority to do so. Through this incident, my resolve was strengthened to become strong in logos[136] (the total inspired Word of God) and strong in rhema (hearing a specific Word from the Holy Spirit), as my friend, Pastor Benny Thomas, has said.

Ephesians 6:10–17 describes the supernatural armor God has given us for protection against evil. In the next verse, we see the reason the Lord has furnished these six pieces of devil-busting, world defeating, flesh crucifying protective gear: Ephesians 6:18, "praying always with all prayer and supplication in the Spirit, being watchful to this end with all perseverance and supplication for all the saints." The words "praying," "prayer," and "supplication" come from two different Greek words basically meaning the same thing: speaking or communicating to God in the variety of expression that flows from a posture of worship. Prayer items to God consist of conversing with Him, giving thanks, praising, worshiping, and voicing our petitions.

Paul is saying, "put that armor on, then pray, pray and keep praying!" And while we must pray for ourselves, we must not stop there. There are many souls and institutions in our sphere needing prayer as well as our immediate and extended family. Even more specifically, Ephesians 6:18 says, "for all the saints," meaning our local church family, missionaries, and all those who are functioning within the body of Christ doing kingdom work inside and outside the church walls. The lost need prayer, our cities, and the nations, but those who are living for Jesus are the ones we are called to spe-cifically intercede for. And our prayers are not insignificant. Our prayers are needed, desired, and powerful. The effective, fervent prayer of a righteous man avails much (James 5:16b). A true mark of Christian maturity is a change of focus from selfish concerns to genuine concern for others, ministering to them, and a sincere desire to fulfill God's will more than our own.

Ephesians 6:18 also contains the phrase "in the Spirit." As pointed out in Chapter four, this is usually thought to mean praying in tongues. Tongues are part of our spiritual sword and can be used by the Holy Spirit within us to accomplish many things, some of which we may never know until we arrive at the pearly gates. But there it is, in black and white, from the apostle who was used by God to write 31.57 percent or thirteen of the twenty-seven books of the New Testament (not including Hebrews).[137] Many times the "sword of the Spirit" is not only used as a prayer item, whereby we pray the Scriptures concerning our needs or the needs of others (Isaiah 43:26) but as a power item toward the enemy. When the Word is used in this fashion, it would not be considered prayer (because we don't pray to the devil), but instead a decree or prophetic declaration into the spirit realm (Job 22:28) toward things opposed to the rule of Christ and/or to establish or confirm a kingdom proclamation.

Sometimes people ask the enemy to go or pray for God to make him leave them alone. The only way he is going to do that is if we kick the bucket and head on up to heaven *or* take authority over him in Jesus' name. If there is anything we can give the devil credit for, it is his persistence; always looking for an opportunity to harass the Lord's Beloved or cause destruction, dejection, depression, and despair. If the enemy had a theme song, it would probably be, *I've Gotta Be Me!* (no offense to the people who wrote or sang that song) because his nature is the epitome of evil, and the fruit of his nature is manifest in all his doings. He may deceivingly appear at times to be an "angel of light," but his works bear witness that he is full of darkness, his job being to oppose anyone and anything that would give rightful glory to Almighty God. But—hallelujah!—our Lord and Savior Jesus Christ, who lives in us, has thoroughly defeated him!

Proverbs 18:21 says the words we speak have the power of life or death in them; how much more power when our words agree with God's eternal Word? We have the authority to directly oppose the works of darkness using the sword of the Spirit at the Lord's direction. And when we are in line with the Word and will of God, the declarations we make in faith have the capacity to change the course of our lives or the ones we are interceding for, bringing us or them into greater alignment with the purposes of God. Jesus said, "For assuredly, I say to you, whoever says to this mountain, 'Be removed and be cast into the sea' and does not doubt in his heart, but believes that those things he says will come to pass, he will have whatever he says" (Mark 11:23). The entirety of God's armor provides the Christian with protection and more; the armor is a vehicle by which we come into greater alignment with the Word on different levels, increasing our spiritual effectiveness. Prepared, clothed, and armed with the Lord's defensive and offensive implements, we have a sure footing in executing the Word from God that will hinder, dismantle, and ultimately break Satan's efforts to advance the gates of hell.

First Thessalonians 4:4 says, "that each of you should know how to possess his own vessel in sanctification and honor." The armor of God offers insight into how this is done. Each discipline will take shape in our lives through studying and obeying the Word. There are volumes written about this subject by people who have much greater understanding, but the Holy Spirit has graciously provided some short vignettes. It is good to integrate various elements essential to Christian growth because becoming more Christ-like with each passing day is imperative for protection and deliverance from the effects of selfishness residing in our flesh, the allure of the world, and the deceptions of Satan.

Our adversary is seeking whom he may devour.[138] Therefore, we must "lock and load" by holding fast to the truths of God's Word and allow the Holy Spirit to fill us with understanding concerning the spiritual protection, weapons, and ammunition we have in Christ. In so doing, may we overcome in every area of our lives and simultaneously be salt, light, and strength to those we have been given the opportunity to serve for His glory.

Heavenly Father, thank you for everything you have provided to bring protection, preservation, and power into my life, including the full armor of God. By faith, I now put on the belt of truth, which provides a foundational safeguard against deception; and the breast-plate of righteousness, receiving your righteousness and choosing obedience righteousness. I cover my feet with the preparation of the gospel of peace by choosing your ways and your way. Above all, I take the shield of faith, with which I quench the fiery darts of the wicked one because I choose faith, and I rest in your promises. I take the helmet of salvation, knowing I am secure in Christ and renewing my mind with your Word. I take the sword of the Spirit, which is the Word of God, and make myself ready to speak it forth in the power and anointing of the Holy Spirit. Reveal those you would have me pray for today and anoint me to intercede on their behalf. ~ In Jesus' name, amen!

The Enemy Exposed

"For this purpose the Son of God was manifested, that He might destroy the works of the devil" (1 John 3:8b). Jesus alone defeated Satan, and for Christians, our faith in and obedience to the Lord has provided our victory as well. The Son of God is reaching out to humanity, offering new life in Himself and Holy Spirit power to all who repent, believe, and receive. As we walk with and learn to abide in Him, He develops the fruit of the Spirit in us and bestows supernatural giftings to strengthen, heal, deliver, and equip us for service. He provides armor of light to help us maneuver through the darkness of this world, and He has given us weapons of war with which we can displace forces greater than ourselves.

And we are never alone. Jesus said He wouldn't leave us orphans (John 14:18); He sent the Holy Spirit to be our comforter, counselor, teacher, and guide[139] in all things, including spiritual warfare. The full armor of God protects His children from deception and condemnation; it prepares us, strengthens our faith, protects our minds, and empowers us to advance the kingdom of God; "For we wrestle not against flesh and blood, but against principalities, against powers, against the rulers of the darkness of this world, against spiritual wickedness (some translations say wicked spirits) in high places," (Ephesians 6:12, KJV). Our unseen foe is extremely systematic and militant in pursuit of control of the world, utilizing a demonic mega structure that answers to Satan himself.

There are three forms of assault the enemy uses to ensnare the souls of men: our own flesh nature, the world's temptations, and the forces of darkness who have pledged allegiance to him (i.e., our flesh, the world, and the devil). Ephesians 6:12 reveals three characteristics of spiritual warfare with evil spirits: (1) wrestling denotes a grappling or hand-to-hand struggle with demons that is close by or within our sphere or minds; (2) people are *not* our enemy; and (3) our spiritual opponent has at least four levels of operation, maybe more.

Because Satan isn't omnipresent like God, he cannot be everywhere at the same time, so he developed a highly organized, strategic network of demonic subordinates. The word "high" in Ephesians 6:12 is translated from the Greek word "epouranios,"[140] meaning "above the sky." These evil assistants traverse and occupy the realms of darkness below, on, and above the Earth's surface. The sky and atmosphere we see are called the first heaven; the space above our atmosphere is known as the second heaven. From there, the demonic net monitors the Earth's surface to keep as many geographical areas in spiritual darkness as possible while simultaneously attempting to extinguish outbreaks of the light and presence of God. The third heaven is the place of God's throne (2 Corinthians 12:2), where Satan and his fallen angels can no longer enter legally, although they did have access until Jesus' blood was shed at Calvary and sprinkled upon heaven's mercy seat.[141]

Satan (which means adversary) was not always a devil. Isaiah 14:12–17 and Ezekiel 28:12–19 give a general description of his fall from the position he was created for. This fall probably happened between Genesis 1:1 and 1:3, which could contain eons of time. We know this because he was in the garden of Eden exhibiting his current diabolical nature (deceiver, tempter) in an endeavor to execute his maleficent agenda: pollute God's glorious creation with the stain of sin and usurp authority God had given to man. This is a far cry from what God originally created him to be—a covering cherub (angel of high order) named Lucifer, known for his brilliance, beauty, wisdom, and musical abilities. Although Satan and the fallen angels were once in perfect fellowship with God, he knowingly defiled himself with prideful activities and then persuaded other angels to follow him in rebellion against the righteous rule of God. Revelation 12:7–8 says, "And war broke out in heaven: Michael and his angels fought against the dragon (who is Satan); and the dragon and his angels fought, but they did not prevail, nor was a place found for them in heaven any longer." Revelation 12:4 reveals it was one-third of the angelic host created by God who lost their original estate in heaven because of their participation in that rebellion.

The following paragraphs provide some insight into the demonic ranks and their functions. A website called *Kings, Prophets, and Intercessors* writes that principalities have authority over nations/cities, powers have authority over cities/institutions, rulers of darkness over families/individuals with spirits of wickedness being the lowest level of demonic (spirits of lust, pride, confusion, etc.). However, this may or may not be a correct representation of fallen angels and/or demonic regimentation. We simply do not have vast amounts of Scripture defining these beings, their nature, and operations, but we can stand and be victorious with what Scriptures do reveal. We should not fear them because the greater one lives in us, but we would be wise to never presume and always keep our spiritual walk close to Jesus. Ephesians 3:10 says the wisdom of God is variegated or many-sided, so let us humbly and prayerfully approach this subject that we may navigate it successfully, acquiring a greater understanding of just what we are wrestling against.

Principalities, the first group referenced in Ephesians 6:12, comes from the word "arche,"[142] meaning "commencement or chief." The word "principality" has to do with governmental authority; a territory ruled by a prince, their position, authority, or jurisdiction (Webster's Online Dictionary). My friend, Pastor Chris Houghton, pointed out that the modern English word "architect" is derived from this Greek word, "arche." An architect is a person who designs and guides a plan or undertaking.[143] Rick Renner, a highly respected Bible teacher and leader in the international Christian community, states that principalities are "those that have held the highest seats of power since the most ancient times."[144]

The book of Daniel mentions two territorial princes, the prince of Persia and the prince of Greece (Daniel 10:13, 20). Gabriel,

God's messenger angel, could not overcome the prince of Persia's atmospheric territorial obstruction without help from the archangel, Michael, who is also known as a chief prince of heaven. Daniel's twenty-one-day fast directly coincides with the spiritual warfare taking place in the heavenlies, ultimately ushering in the "big guns" (Michael) to get a breakthrough. The prince of Persia was a principality that exercised governmental control over the entire region of Persia. Likewise, today there are ruling principalities over regions that exercise executive governing capabilities over areas within their domain. Principalities are most likely fallen angels who hold high-level spiritual positions, supervising their definitive kingdoms, categorically or geographically.

Powers,[145] the next level of demonic beings listed in Ephesians 6:12, is translated "exousia,"[146] meaning "privilege, force or mastery." According to Renner, powers "have received license to do whatever they want to do wherever they want to do it. These are roaming spirits that have been delegated spiritual power by principalities."[147] Their work may be to draw multitudes into idolatrous bondage. Powers may also be fallen angels whose main function is to inject or exude tangible power from the spirit realm into the natural world (Acts 19:35).

There is a direct correlation between the ruling prince over a region and the powers which assist in acquiring legal permission to occupy a specific territory. In Daniel 10:20, Gabriel, the messenger angel, said, "Do you know why I have come to you? And now I must return to fight with the prince of Persia, and when I have gone forth, indeed the prince of Greece will come." History records the Persian empire continued until Alexander the Great, who ruled the Greek kingdom of Macedon, conquered Persia and much of the known world. Alexander was a pawn of the prince of Greece and therefore authorized to conquer through the spiritual powers in allegiance with the Grecian prince. Powers use human beings of prominence and preeminence to fortify or dethrone a ruling prince. They may also work with rulers of darkness to establish certain sins as prevalent in a specific area. When traveling through different cities or parts of the country, notice the observable manifest bondage, which is an indication of the type of spirits who have gained legal (although unscrupulous) influence over an area through idolatry and sin of human residents in that region. In every New Testament reference, where principalities are mentioned as demonic entities, powers are mentioned with them.[148] Like Pastor Chris said, "They work together."

Rulers are listed third in Ephesians 6:12 in the ranks of fallen angels or demons. The Greek word for "ruler" is "kosmokrator,"[149] meaning "a world-ruler; an epithet of Satan." The Amplified Bible calls this group "the master spirits who are the world rulers of this present darkness." Dictionary.com defines "master" as a person with the ability or power to use, control, or dispose of something, an owner of a slave. Kenneth Hagin, in his book, *The Origin and Operation of Demons,* says, "the highest type of demon we have to deal with on earth is 'rulers of the darkness of this world.'"[150] In other words, principalities and powers mostly operate in the second heaven, while rulers and wicked spirits mostly operate here on the Earth. Ruling spirits could possibly be the master spirit in a demonic grouping or stronghold, the "strongman" that Jesus spoke of in three of the gospel accounts.[151] "When a strong man, fully armed, guards his own palace, his goods are in peace. But when a stronger than he comes upon him and overcomes him, he takes from him all his armor in which he trusted and divides his spoils (plunder)" (Luke 11:21–22).

John A. MacMillan, in his book, *The Authority of the Believer,* wrote,

> Rulers of the darkness of this world (are) a class of beings whose ministry is the keeping in darkness of the masses of mankind. From them doubtless proceed those cunningly devised heresies, such as evolution, which backed by no genuine evidence, is yet accepted by the intelligentsia of our day, is defended with a pathetic loyalty, and is forced upon the young in our schools as a reality.[152]

And Kenneth Hagin wrote, "...rulers of darkness are the most intelligent type of spirits. They rule over other spirits and tell them what to do. Besides dominating the unsaved, they dominate Christians who will walk in darkness."[153] The two words that make "kosmokrator" are "kosmos," meaning "an apt and harmonious arrangement, or constitution, order, government,"[154] and "kratos," meaning "force, strength."[155] The term "kosmokrator" is indicative of the ruler's ability to organize and utilize the strength of evil spirits to systematically attack, block and hinder the saints of God.

The word for "spiritual" in Ephesians 6:12 is "pneumatikos,"[156] meaning "non-carnal, ethereal, spirit," and "wickedness" is "poneria,"[157] meaning "depravity, malice, plots, sins." Spiritual wickedness, or wicked spirits, could be fallen angels, demons, or both comprising the various levels of devils in the echelons of darkness. Without Jesus' victory over Satan and his entire organization, we would be helpless against them. But He did defeat them, and we are not helpless. Nevertheless, we are still challenged and buffeted by wicked spirits, whether we realize it or not. Without the new birth or the baptism of the Holy Spirit, we have no way of knowing their presence or activities unless they manifest in some way. When they do, it is usually to scare people (which creates an opening for a spirit of fear) and/or mislead them into worshiping something other than God. Wicked spirits' strategy is to work on the individual with the goal of obtaining a place of manipulation or control through generational curses, carnal and/or ungodly beliefs, and wounds to the soul and/or spirit.

The Bible mentions several by name:

- Familiar spirit, Leviticus 19:31
- Jealous spirit, Numbers 5:14
- Spirit of disaffection (ill will), Judges 9:23
- Unclean spirits, Matthew 10:1
- Dumb and deaf spirit, Mark 9:17
- Spirit of infirmity, Luke 13:11

– Lying spirit, 2 Chronicles 18:22

– Haughty spirit (pride), Proverbs 16:18

– Perverse spirit, Isaiah 19:14

– Spirit of slumber, Isaiah 29:10

– Spirit of heaviness (depression), Isaiah 61:3

– Spirit of whoredoms, Hosea 5:4

– Spirit of divination, Acts 16:16

– Spirit of bondage, Romans 8:15

– Seducing spirits, 1 Timothy 4:1

– Spirit of fear, 2 Timothy 1:7

– Spirit of anti-Christ, 1 John 4:3

– Spirit of error, 1 John 4:6

Many are not recorded specifically in Scripture. Frank and Ida Mae Hammond, in their book *Pigs in the Parlor*, list 53 demon or evil spirit groupings that are usually found together.[158] Are demons fallen angels, or are they a different type of spiritual being? Some people believe that wicked spirits (lowest in demonic order, the ones who pester humans) are the disembodied spirits of beings that existed on earth in a pre-Adamic creation.[159] Others believe they are the disembodied spirits of the Nephilim, which were giants and superhuman beings produced by intermarriage between some of the fallen angels and human women in Genesis 6:2–4.

However, certain characteristics in Scripture are associated with specific evil spirits. Fallen angels can possess unsaved people because Satan entered Judas.[160] Battalions of evil spirits occupy heavenly realms.[161] Jesus and the disciples cast out different types of spirits who had taken residence in people's bodies; demons apparently needing a physical body to manifest their character. Because principalities and powers mostly function in the second heaven, with no mention of them needing some type of physical body for expression, the existence of disembodied spirits would explain why some demons seek to gain entrance into or attachment to a physical body here on Earth; and once they have moved into a person or their sphere, they think of the host body as their house.

Jesus revealed why these wicked spirits or demons search for habitation inside the bodies of living organisms, be they human or animal.[162] The human body is composed of 50-75 percent water.[163] Matthew 12:43–44 says, "When an unclean spirit goes out of a man, he goes through dry places, seeking rest, and finds none. Then he says, 'I will return to my house from which I came.' And when he comes, he finds it empty, swept, and put in order." Living organisms provide rest to these beings. It seems they prefer humans, probably because human bodies and souls provide a greater range of expression, enabling them to gain influence over others, but they will inhabit animals if given permission (Mark 5:12–13).

Demons must have spiritual doors to gain entrance to the soul or body of any living being. A door is an opening or landing strip where the enemy has obtained permission to land, hence the word "legally;" they cannot come in just because they want to. It is a place where the host or someone in authority over them has agreed with darkness in thought, word, or deed. The principle of agreement is found in Amos 3:3, *"Can two walk together unless they are agreed?"* The enemy acquires permission through generational or word curses, lies presented to and accepted by the mind, and wounds to the soul and/or spirit resulting from our sin or sin others have done against us. Sin and/or deception has the propensity to open the door to demons, and we have all been influenced by them before our salvation, but also afterward when we have allowed the lust of our flesh, the dictates of the world, or the lies of the enemy to affect our thoughts and decisions rather than submitting to the Lord in that area of our life. A Christian who is oppressed by demons is not possessed but is being influenced by the enemy's application of pressure somewhere in his/her soul.

These spirits work to gain access and eventually build a house of thoughts, a dwelling, or a stronghold that provides fortified protection for their presence. The thoughts they present to the mind are comprised of arguments, imaginations, and an endless plethora of rhetoric that exalts itself against the knowledge of God. These strongholds, although originating in the mind, can affect other parts of the soul as well, stirring feelings (positive or negative) in our emotions and asserting pressure to our will, all for the purpose of concealing and continuing their mandate to take more ground within the individual or the individual's sphere.

Demons have a close relationship with the works of the flesh because of the curse God pronounced upon the serpent (Satan in disguise) after man's fall. Genesis 3:14b says, "...and you shall eat dust all the days of your life." Man was formed from the dust of the ground (Genesis 2:7); the enemy and his demonic crew feed upon man's flesh nature. When we live by the dictates of our flesh, we give the demonic opportunity to attach to ourselves or invade our soul or body in some way. The works of the flesh provide ground for the demonic to put down roots that feed evil spirits with short-lived pleasure the indulgence provides them and our carnal man. These flesh works are listed in Galatians 5:19–21 and provide a smorgasbord for demons: adultery, fornication (sexual immorality), uncleanness, licentiousness, idolatry, sorcery, hatred, contentions, jealousies, outbursts of wrath, selfish ambitions, dissensions, heresies, envy, murders, drunkenness, and revelries. Any time someone participates in these and similar flesh works, demons are involved on some level. The Word goes on to say, "...those who practice such things will not inherit the kingdom of God."[164]

No *mature* Christian is going to practice, as an act of his/her volition, something the Bible defines as sin unless they have allowed themselves to be bound with enemy lies. But even the most vigilant Christian can become entangled in a work of the flesh, producing sin's bondage. We all have experienced bondage to some degree before salvation and sometimes after. We may have repented many times, and God does forgive us every time we repent,[165] but understanding bondage has its roots in our flesh nature and is reinforced by the lies of the enemy helps us see areas we must begin cooperating with the Holy Spirit to regain our freedom.

Sometimes people are bound in areas the Bible does not specifically define as sin, but an area of concern; we may feel out of control or that something "just isn't right." Pastor David taught this could be due to a weak or defiled conscience,[166] which condemns things the Bible says is pure.[167] He wrote, "In these cases, we must learn the Word of God in its completeness and become understanding of the Father's love. The Word supersedes our conscience (1 John 3:20)." We can adjust our conscience by believing and practicing God's Word. However, when help is needed, find a trusted Christian friend to whom you can confess your faults and receive sound counsel. James 5:16 (KJV) says, "Confess your faults to one another, and pray for one another, that ye may be healed." The word for "faults" is "paraptoma,"[168] which means "unintentional error," but can also mean "willful transgression." There is freedom in bringing things to light by sharing and examining them through the filter of truth.

Satan uses our flesh and the world system as allies in bringing souls into bondage. When Eve was tempted by the serpent, Genesis 3:6 says, "...the woman saw that the tree was good for food, that it was pleasant to the eyes, and a tree desirable to make one wise." Works of the flesh are a product of succumbing to one or a combination of any three temptations in the previous Scripture. This is further defined in 1 John 2:16, "For all that is in the world—the lust of the flesh, the lust of the eyes, and the pride of life—is not of the Father but is of the world." Jesus was tempted in all three areas during His forty-day wilderness fast.[169] We too are tempted in every area. Concerning the lust of the flesh, He was tempted to misuse His power and authority to meet His personal need. God knows we need food, clothing, and shelter, and He has promised to provide them when we seek Him first in our lives. However, works of the flesh don't always involve food but rather something that feeds our senses and selfishness disproportionately. Gotquestions.org says, "Lust has as its focus pleasing oneself, and it often leads to unwholesome actions to fulfill one's desires with no regard to the consequences."

When we are born again, in our spirit, we no longer desire to partake of things that are an affront to God.[170] But because our spirit lives in a flesh house (our body), we still face temptation and sometimes gravitate toward it. The apostle Paul recognized this enigma and wrote about it in Romans 7:7–25. The "sin principle," or the tendency to give in to sin, is ever-present in our flesh nature and will be until we get our new resurrection bodies upon the Lord's return. It's been said that "you can't cast out the flesh, and you can't discipline it either." Yet if we are to live victorious Christian lives, this is an area we must deal with on a regular basis. For if we choose to ignore the Scripture's exhortation to, "Walk in the Spirit, and you shall not fulfill the lust of the flesh" (Galatians 5:16), we have no defense against the base desires resident within every human being. Eventually, we will reap what we have sown (Galatians 6:7–8), which can mean sickness and disease in our body, along with bondage and error in our mind, emotions, and will. As an added "bonus," we unintentionally pass these tendencies and bondages to our children because we have not allowed the Word to do its ongoing work in our mind, will, and emotions as it did within our spirit when we were born again and Spirit-filled.

Bondages are not always apparent, although many are evident and accepted by society due to the enemy's lobbying through individuals devoid of God's spiritual laws, laws such as the Law of Dominion.[171] Romans 6:16 says, "Do you not know that to whom you present yourselves slaves to obey, you are that one's slaves whom you obey, whether of sin leading to death, or of obedience leading to righteousness?" and 2 Peter 2:19b, "…for by whom a person is overcome, by him also he is brought into bondage." The Law of Dominion is framed in Goliath's words as he challenged Israel to send a man to fight him instead of all the Philistines and Israelites duking it out, "If he is able to fight with me and kill me, then we will be your servants. But if I prevail against him and kill him, then you shall be our servants and serve us" (1 Samuel 17:9). The Law of Dominion provides a door for the enemy when humans yield to him rather than honoring and upholding the Word of God.

The Lord allowed me, on a certain occasion, to see into the spirit realm concerning evil spirits and their connection to man's physical being. A friend of my husband's and his wife came to visit.

As we were standing on our back patio talking, I saw (in the spirit, but also with my eyes; an open vision) three black insect-looking things fly towards this man, two from the upper right, one from the upper left. They disappeared behind his back as if they were coming in for a landing like bees on the same flower and were the size of squirrels. This man was a chain smoker at the time, and I wondered if their presence had anything to do with his smoking. Suddenly, he looked around and said, "I gotta have a cigarette!" and proceeded to light up. It seemed their presence triggered this craving. I could not see what was happening inside of him, but I surmised the demonic creatures were partaking of the smoke inhalation in his lungs. He eventually was able to stop smoking, but sadly, many are not—just one of many vices the enemy uses to keep humans bound.

Our spirit and soul live in a flesh body, and that is *not* evil. Our bodies are fearfully and wonderfully made by God (Psalm 139:14). We are also made in His image (Genesis 1:26). But we experience ongoing internal conflict due to the flesh nature residing within us inherited from original sin.[172] The flesh nature, or the carnal mind, is a fallen spiritual state within our soul and body that vies for rulership in our heart. Romans 8:6 says, "For to be carnally minded is death, but to be spiritually minded is life and peace." Thank God for Jesus Christ, who made it possible for us to be spiritually minded and Spirit-led despite the presence of the flesh nature within us.

God's Word and Holy Spirit help us distinguish between thoughts, words, and actions rooted in selfishness as opposed to those rooted in Christ. By renewing our mind with the Word (reading and ingesting our Bible) and walking in the Spirit (living a life of truth and love for God and others), we can "put to death the deeds of the flesh" (Romans 8:13). James 1:21 says, "Therefore lay aside all filthiness and overflow (abundance) of wickedness and receive with meekness the implanted word, which is able to save your souls." It is dying to self and living to God, deliberately retraining our thought processes by reading and meditating on the Word, affecting our speech and actions. This is further galvanized within our soul through spending time in the Lord's presence in prayer and worship. Instead of focusing on our problem, attempting to fix it in our own strength, we begin by focusing on the Lord, allowing Him to lead us to the place of freedom. We become spiritually proactive.

I once heard my cousin Terry say, if we can whip the flesh, the world and the devil would be a cinch. I must agree that sometimes, if not most of the time, we are our own worst enemy. The apostle Paul said, "All things are lawful for me, but all things are not helpful (profitable). All things are lawful for me, but I will not be brought under the power of any (anything)" (1 Corinthians 6:12). It's not that God doesn't want us to enjoy life; He does (1 Timothy 6:17), but we must beware of the dangers of crossing invisible lines and indulging in excesses. When we fall, let's get back up again, and thank God for the victory we have in Jesus (He has overcome, and we are in Him) *and* our coming manifest victory. Condemnation will attempt to push us farther down, but Jesus is not condemning us (Romans 8:1).[173] He knows we are fighting a war within our own being, the spirit versus the flesh, with our soul caught in the middle. Even born-again believers must renew their mind, or the soul will incline toward the flesh over time. The enemy knows this; that is why he fights Bible reading so intently. With enough time and spiritual neglect, he hopes to gain legal ground in our life to bind, afflict, manipulate, and control us in some way. Because of this, we must ask Holy Spirit to bring us to a holy discipline in renewing our minds with the Word, that wrong attitudes, ideas, or thinking patterns may be dealt with. In so doing, we discontinue giving the enemy fuel.

Diane Sloane, in her book, *Honey, I Shrunk the devil!*, says the Lord told her to "Feed your passion and starve your fears."[174] This principle works in any area of life, including dealing with the flesh nature. When we give the things of God greater attention and weight and our personal agenda less attention and importance, we will see spiritual progress. Through the leading and indwelling power of the Holy Spirit, and the renewing of our minds with the Word, we can diminish the negative in our lives by replacing it with positive choices that are rooted in Christ-exalting motives. *The Christian's victory over his/her flesh is through the power of the Holy Spirit.*

This first of the world's three forms of temptation is the lust of the flesh. The second is the lust of the eye. In Luke 12:15, Jesus said, "Take heed and beware of covetousness, for one's life does not consist in the abundance of the things he possesses." Ecclesiastes 5:11 says, "When goods increase, they increase who eat them. So what profit have the owners except to see them with their eyes?" These Scriptures help us understand the deception of the lust of the eye: we think the thing we see and desire will bring satisfaction, when in reality, only God, whom we cannot see, can do that. When Jesus was tempted in this way, He was offered the world's kingdoms if He would bow down to Satan (Luke 4:5–8). Seeking a kingdom of our own constitutes worship of something other than God. And guess who is behind that something?—Satan (Where's the church lady when you need her?). Jesus set the devil straight on who was supposed to be bowing to whom.

We all desire things we see that appeal to us personally, but when we attain that thing we have desired, we soon tire of it and want something else. People spend their entire lives building their own kingdom, just to die and leave it behind. Listen, God doesn't mind if we have things because 3 John 2 says, "Beloved, I pray that you may prosper in all things and be in health, just as your soul prospers." But he *does* mind if things have us. We cannot serve God and money.[175] Ever since our eyes were "opened" in the Garden of Eden, the enemy has been using the human eye gate as his primary point of influence. Even Christians can spend their precious time on Earth chasing the "American Dream" or their own kingdom instead of the kingdom of God. This is folly since we cannot own anything in this life. Nevertheless, the lust of the eye continually appeals to our flesh nature. We must recognize it for what it is, and through Christ, do something about it. That something is to seek *first* the kingdom of God, the rule and reign of Jesus Christ in our lives.

Psalm 119:37 gives direction in prayer when things we see cause technical difficulties in our prefrontal cortex, "Turn my eyes from looking at worthless things, and revive me in Your way." And Psalm 101:3, "I will set nothing wicked (worthless) before my eyes... it shall not cling to me." For this area and any area of the flesh, we must find Scriptures, pray, and seek the Lord until His power fortifies our spirit man, subduing the weakness in our flesh and mind. Jesus will help us; He wants us to succeed!

The third form of temptation from the world is the pride of life. Some pitfalls of pride were covered in chapter four, emphasizing the importance of asking God to clothe us with humility. The pride of life is the temptation to acquire wisdom and knowledge apart from God for the purpose of satisfying the excessive desires of our flesh and eyes and exalting ourselves. It is an indicator as to where our true allegiance lies. When Eve was tempted in the garden, she believed the serpent's lie that the forbidden fruit was something necessary to give her wisdom. But Proverbs 9:10 would later reveal, "The fear of the Lord is the beginning of wisdom, and knowledge of the Holy One is understanding."

When Jesus was tempted with the pride of life, Luke 4:9–11 says the devil set Him on the pinnacle of the temple in Jerusalem and said, "If You are the Son of God, throw Yourself down from here. For it is written, 'He shall give His angels charge over You, to keep You,' and, 'In their hands they shall bear You up, lest You dash Your foot against a stone.'" Why did Satan tempt the Lord to do something totally stupid? Because if pride had been there, He might have obliged him. After all, Jesus would later demonstrate His power over all the elements of the earth, including gravity. But unlike Lucifer's major malfunction, Jesus was, and is, the most humble—yet powerful—being in existence next to Father God. Every time He exercised supernatural power, He was operating in obedience to what the Father had shown Him to do[176] for the purpose of preparing the forms through which the foundation of the kingdom of God would be laid in human hearts.

The pride of life is a deception of the world that will cause people to take risks that common sense tells them not to do. It will cause family members or old friends to stay offended for years because they think the other person "owes them an apology." The pride of life can keep someone from receiving a precious gift from God because they are "set in their ways." It will motivate us to judge others and justify ourselves. The pride of life can cause us to disassociate ourselves with people because we deem ourselves better than them in some way or because they look, think, act, or smell different from us. It is false security on a faulty foundation, the proverbial house built upon the sand (Matthew 7:26–27). The pride of life is the culmination of all our efforts to build our lives according to the world's blueprint to succeed in life and then boast about it, no matter where we end up. The pride of life is all about self, a satanic strategy to keep us on the world's rollercoaster to ruination. Even Christians can find themselves caught in the world's deceitfulness, but there is a way out. *Our victory over the world is to love the Lord our God with all our heart, soul, mind, and strength.*

When the lust of the flesh, the lust of the eyes and/or the pride of life somehow creeps in, we should repent quickly, knowing there is forgiveness and promise of restoration through Christ. In steadfast continuance, we will grow in Him and begin to recognize the havoc our flesh nature has caused, the misleading captivation of the allure of the world, and the devil's traps and tactics used on us and our ancestors for generations. Jesus said in the world, we will have tribulation, but we should be of good cheer because He has overcome the world (John 16:33). If we trust Him and do our best to follow Him, we can too. But we can't stay infants in Christ if we want to walk in the victory Jesus has provided, including identifying and dismantling strongholds built in our souls through participation in the lust of the flesh, the lust of the eye, and the pride of life.

Second Corinthians 10:4–5 says,

> For the weapons of our warfare are not carnal (of the flesh) but mighty in God for pulling down strongholds, casting down arguments and every high thing that exalts itself against the knowledge of God, bringing every thought into captivity to the obedience of Christ.

Spiritual warfare weapons are not weaponry of natural composition. They are multifaceted truths hidden in God, enabling us to pull down strongholds. We must identify anything presented to or currently residing in our minds that is contradictory to the Word of God. A stronghold in the natural is a fortress, a fortified, reinforced, protected position. Similarly, in the spirit, the enemy builds them in our minds through wrong teaching, distorted perceptions, and worldly beliefs rooted in our flesh or carnal mind, ranging from being delicately different to diametrically opposing truth as revealed in the Bible. One of the best definitions of a stronghold is given by Frances Frangipane in his book, *The Three Battlegrounds*. He says, "A demonic stronghold is any type of thinking that exalts itself against the knowledge of God, thereby giving the devil a secure place of influence."[177]

That it is not possible for born-again Christians to be buffeted or inhabited—in their souls or spheres, *not* their spirit—by evil spirits is a well-crafted lie from the pit to keep the people of God from uncovering the root of most of their afflictions. Lies and deception are the breeding ground for all Satan's objectives. When we become a Christian is when the enemy is going to take special measures to up the ante of attack in our lives. Salvation is the most pivotal, important event in life, but to defend ourselves against our spiritual nemesis, we must receive all the Lord has provided for victory.

Strongholds exist in Christians and most certainly in non-Christians. They are formed when thoughts, feelings, and perceptions of occurrences converge within our soul and are built from the vantage point of our conscious and unconscious mind. They begin to affect other parts of the soul and even the body, consisting of ideas, attitudes, belief systems, mindsets, judgments, etc. and are grounded through agreement with fleshly, soulish, or even demonic thought. From a stronghold, the enemy conducts his operations and is not easily detected because he is hidden in a "house" of thoughts comprised of more than a single idea or belief. To stand secure, a house must have a foundation, support walls, and a covering. But even a lean-to can provide a place of shelter. A stronghold may be as impenetrable as a fortress or as flimsy as a straw house, but it is built with the purpose of securing the enemy's position in keeping the human mind and heart in darkness, away from the Light and Truth that sets men free. As people get older, they are less likely to receive salvation.[178] Or, they may get saved but never really grow into spiritual maturity or encounter obstacles that seem insurmountable even though the Word of God contains precious promises available to every believer through faith.

Strongholds are the means the enemy uses to divert humans away from the kingdom of God entirely or keep a Christian from becoming all he or she was created to be in God. Thank the Lord; many strongholds are effortlessly broken apart as we move forward in our walk with Jesus, as the truth of His Word washes our souls and renews our minds.[179] Others will take a more intensified effort on our part to seek God for revelation and humbly obey the Spirit's instructions. But even in situations where breakthrough seems impossible, through the light of God's Word and leading of the Holy Spirit, it is possible for a believer to discern and consequently dismantle even the enemy's most calculated stronghold. "All things are possible to him who believes" (Mark 9:23).

The flesh, the world, and the devil have been dealt a lethal blow; *the Christian's victory over Satan is solely through faith and commitment to God's Son, the Lord Jesus Christ.* Jesus defeated Satan; He disarmed principalities and powers and made a public spectacle of them (Colossians 2:15). He overcame the world and His flesh nature, now offering to us victory by which we may live, walk, and experience triumph—all to the glory of God! The apostle Peter wrote, "...His divine power has given to us all things that pertain to life and godliness through the knowledge of Him who called us by glory and virtue" (2 Peter 1:3). As we learn and apply the Word of God, we become spiritually stronger, wiser, and freer; positioning us to hear from the only One who can get us out of here alive and through us reach those in need, those who don't know God and those within our sphere.

Because Jesus is seated at the right hand of God, we are too, because we are His body! Ephesians 2:4–6 says,

> But God, who is rich in mercy, because of His great love with which He loved us, even when we were dead in trespasses, made us alive together with Christ (by grace you have been saved), and raised us up together, and made us sit together in the heavenly places in Christ Jesus.

We are present on Terra Firma, in our Earth suit, complete with soul and spirit, while our spirit man is simultaneously hidden in Christ and seated in heaven, all because of our spiritual position in the Lord. When buffeted by attacks from the dark side, we don't have to cower in a corner if we know who we are in Christ and who He is in us. God's Word and Holy Spirit have exposed and uncovered the enemy for who and what he really is. We are *not* to fear him because Jesus already defeated him, but we should use wisdom in our dealings with him.

We are a three-part being: spirit, soul, and body (1 Thessalonians 5:23). The enemy's strategy is to use the weakness in our flesh and our weakness toward the world's temptations to bring us into deception and bondage, then build false security through pride that renders us unteachable regarding life-saving truth. His objective is to gain entrance into the heart and mind of every human being by tapping into our old nature and taking advantage of our ignorance of spiritual processes. He then works like a spider weaving a web through the thoughts and emotions of unsuspecting souls; reinforcing mindsets and attitudes formed through "coincidence" and circum-stance, steadily moving toward his goal of capturing man's free will.

Because of our sin and fallen nature, we continually possess the propensity to be vulnerable to the enemy's wiles. And the biggest lie we buy into is that the world and everything in it revolve around us. We are the center of our universe, and we build our own little kingdoms around this fallacy. This is idolatry and fertile ground for enemy control. But by now, you already know the way out; the enemy has been exposed! God, through the finished work of His Son, and the power of His Holy Spirit can and will deliver us from the devil's lies, the world's deceptions, and the biggest challenge we will ever face in this life—ourselves.

Power Tools

Instruments that work and have an additional power source, usually electricity, other than human effort are called power tools. God's power tools are energized by the Holy Spirit, the third Person in the Trinity. The Trinity, or Godhead, is comprised of the Father, who is Creator, the Son, who is His Word and His authority, and the Holy Spirit, who is His power. The following five "power tools" are available to every Christian, but only as we recognize and utilize them will we experience their effectiveness. Second Corinthians 10:4–5 says our weapons aren't physical armaments like the ones used in mortal combat, but spiritual truths, revelations, and directives. They are enforced by Jesus' blood, God's Spirit, His angelic host and are indispensable to the serious Christian. Zechariah 4:6 helps us grasp that victory is, "Not by might nor by power, but by My Spirit, says the Lord of hosts."

The Power of Prayer

Prayer is defined as "a devout petition to God..."[180] or just talking to Him. This verbal interaction takes different forms: personal, intercessory, and corporate prayer, the prayer of consecration, praying in tongues, the prayer of faith, and the prayer of agreement; voicing our petitions, concerns, desires, and thanksgiving. Early in life, my prayers mostly consisted of rehearsing my wish list. But when spiritual warfare began, I needed more than material things and personal kudos; I needed revelation to deal with and overcome the dilemma I found myself in. The Wednesday morning meetings helped me comprehend God's provision included more than blessings and a "get out of hell" card; seeing God for who He is, not just what He gives. Standing beside spirit-filled, powerhouse women of God boldly interceding for others lit a fire in me that I pray never goes out.

Our personal prayer life is the most vital ingredient in our walk with God besides reading and/or listening to the Word. Through God's Word, the Holy Spirit releases revelation into our human spirit. By praying and meditating on the Word, we realign with God's plan and purposes. Christians can and should pray from our spiritual position in Christ, where we are seated with Him at the right hand of the Father. [181] God originally gave dominion over the Earth to mankind, but Adam gave it to the enemy when he listened to Eve and acted upon Satan's lie. Because God gave dominion to man, only a man could regain this position of authority. Jesus, although divine, operated strictly as a man born of and filled with the Holy Spirit during His ministry on earth, defeating Satan and regaining dominion. He now manifests His authority and power through those who follow and are in covenant with Him,[182] meaning Satan and his minions are all positionally under our feet.

Jesus is our Teacher, Leader, and example in prayer. He only did or judged what the Father showed Him,[183] consistently recognizing the Father's will through His knowledge of Scripture and time spent in prayer. Jesus prayed during and before major decisions, events, and works—at His baptism (Luke 3:21), before choosing His disciples (Luke 6:12), at the transfiguration (Luke 9:28), before feeding the 5,000 (John 6:11), and before walking on water (Matthew 14:23).[184] If prayer was indispensable to Jesus, who had the Spirit without measure, how much more do we need daily prayer? He even provided an outline to follow in the Lord's prayer,[185] not to be legalistic but to recognize important aspects of prayer.

Jesus said, "My house shall be called a house of prayer,"[186] and we are His house. Reading the Scriptures first can jump-start our prayers but is not essential, and the more time we spend in prayer, the stronger our spirit becomes. Some spend an hour a day in prayer because of what Jesus said in the Garden of Gethsemane, "What! Could you not watch with Me one hour?"[187] Some give a tithe of their day in prayer: two hours, forty minutes. By seeking Him early, we honor Him with the first fruits of our time; Psalm 5:3 says, "My voice You shall hear in the morning, O Lord; in the morning I will direct it to You, and I will look up." A great way to start our day, but no matter when we pray or how long we pray, we should, "Be anxious for nothing, but in everything by prayer and supplication, with thanksgiving, let your requests be made known to God," (Philippians 4:6).

Personal prayer is foundational to every type of prayer. Intercessory prayer is praying for others. Corporate prayer is intercessory prayer by a small or large group. Not everyone is comfortable praying out loud, but we can pray silently in agreement with those leading. All are encouraged to pray when led by the Holy Spirit, and prayers are in line with the Word. Praying the Word is effective because God's Word is settled in heaven.[188] The prayer of consecration is praying for those God has called to a task or ministry such as Paul and Barnabas in Acts 13:2–3. And when we pray in tongues, the Holy Spirit prays through us and will undoubtedly pray the will of God.

First Thessalonians 5:17 says we are to "pray without ceasing." God is on call twenty-four/seven. One time in discouragement, I asked God if my prayers were for nothing concerning an ongoing situation. About fifteen minutes later, He said, "Do you really believe I let you walk through this for nothing?" When He spoke, my heart melted, and I knew He had a redeeming purpose in the things I endured. Eventually, my prayer was answered, but not how I expected. The Lord spoke John 15:7 during an enemy attack, "If you abide in Me and my words abide in you, you will ask what you desire, and it shall be done for you." This promise is a target for our thoughts, words, and actions because when we are aligned with God's Word *and* our heart is right, we are positioned to receive answered prayer.[189]

God desires to bless His children, but sometimes issues block our receiving from Him. Scriptural hindrances to prayer are holding onto known sin,[190] unforgiveness,[191] failure to pray or praying with selfish or wrong motives,[192] not praying in faith,[193] idolatry,[194]enemy interference.[195]And in marriage, husbands or wives dishonoring their spouses.[196] By dealing with sin and praying the Word, we can have blessed assurance the Lord has heard our prayers. First John 5:14–15 says, "Now this is the confidence that we have in Him, that if we ask anything according to His will, He hears us. And if we know that He hears us, whatever we ask, we know that we have the petitions that we have asked of Him."

If we believed we received when we prayed, we thank God for the answer! This is the prayer of faith in James 5:15 and Mark 11:24, "…whatever things you ask when you pray, believe that you receive them, and you will have them." However, in Mark 11:25–26, Jesus said we must forgive others of their trespasses when praying, or we won't be forgiven. My friend, Mary, suffered abuse by a family member. Forgiveness was difficult, but after experiencing a dream where her abuser held her captive in hell, she, as an act of her will, forgave him. Lay every prayer hindrance down; if forgiveness is needed, forgive, release, and bless others. If repentance is needed, repent. Nothing is worth deterring our prayers because "The effective, fervent prayer of a righteous man avails much" (James 5:16b).

Finally, the prayer of agreement is probably the most effective form of petition. An exponential power principle is revealed in Leviticus 26:8, Deuteronomy 32:30, and Matthew 18:19. In Leviticus, God told Moses that five faith-filled believers can prevail against a hundred of their enemies and one hundred believers can prevail against ten thousand, a five-fold multiplication of prayer power through faith and *unity*. In Deuteronomy, the Word says one can put a thousand to flight, and two can put ten thousand to flight, a tenfold increase! Finally, Jesus said in Matthew 18:19 that if two of us agree on earth concerning anything we ask, it will be done by our Father in heaven. We may not know the timing,[197]but we can know anytime we pray in agreement, and according to Scripture, our prayers will be much more effective. No wonder the devil constantly attempts to divide the body of Christ! Prayer, especially united prayer, is a powerful tool indeed.

The Power of the Cross

"This is a faithful saying: For if we died with Him, we shall also live with Him" (2 Timothy 2:11). The cross is key to the resurrection power of God, symbolizing Jesus' physical death and our own "death to self," representing God's will for Jesus and for us individually. Romans 6:6–7 says, "…knowing this, that our old man was crucified with Him, that the body of sin might be done away with (rendered inoperative), that we should no longer be slaves of sin. For he who has died has been freed (cleared) from sin." In laying down a life of self-seeking to seek first the kingdom of God and His righteousness, we discover our life in Christ. The Word says to "reckon (consider) ourselves to be dead indeed to sin, but alive to God in Christ Jesus our Lord" (Romans 6:11). This "reckoning"[198] becomes the pivotal position in standing against the demonic; it's where the rubber meets the road.

In the new birth, our spirit instantly received the life of God, but in our soul, the process of sanctification through renewing our mind must be initiated regularly. As we do, the will of God takes shape within our hearts and knowing God's will can make the difference between living a casual, lukewarm life or changing the world. Jesus said in Matthew 16:24, "If anyone desires to come after Me, let him deny himself, and take up his cross, and follow Me."[199] Luke 9:23 says this is "daily." By seeking God's will, endeavoring to follow Him, we are, in effect, dying to self. Reaffirming our death to self through the cross and life in God through Christ positions us to kick demons out and close spiritual doors we or others have opened, doors that will remain open until we close them with Christ's authority.

The first spiritual door is mentioned in Genesis. A situation sparked Cain, the firstborn of Adam and Eve, to resent and kill his brother, Abel. God revealed how He must be approached because of sin. Abel was obedient, bringing a blood sacrifice, but Cain offered fruit from the ground that had been cursed (Genesis 3:17). Abel's offering symbolized Christ's sacrifice and the resulting gift of salvation; Cain's offering symbolized man's works to attain salvation apart from God. When Cain's offering was not respected, he became angry. God said, "Why are you angry? And why has your countenance fallen? If you do well, will you not be accepted? And if you do not do well, sin lies at the door. And its desire is for (toward) you, but you should rule over it" (Genesis 4:6–7).

Sin opens the door and gives legal ground to the enemy, as does deception. Jessie-Penn Lewis, author of *War on the Saints,* wrote,

> It is this matter of ground given which is the crucial point of all. All believers acknowledge known sin to be ground given to the enemy, and even unknown sin in the life, but they do not realize that every thought suggested to the mind by wicked spirits, and accepted, is ground given to them.[200]

From the moment Eve listened to the serpent, mankind's susceptibility to deception and its resulting sin has been proven time and time again.

Because the enemy must obtain legal ground to execute his plans, he looks for doors, which are potential openings or portals. By presenting a thought or suggestion to our mind, he knocks on a door through which he may gain admittance. If it is recognized and refused, we keep the door closed. But if it's not recognized and refused, it creates an "opening" in our souls or spheres. Ground speaks of a literal place in topography (although located in the spirit or soulish realm), where we took the bait, receiving the lie as truth, now having something "in common" with the enemy that will not be removed without the truth of God's Word.

In Luke 4:33, a man possessed with a demon in the synagogue cries loudly to Jesus. In verse 34, he says, "Ah, let us alone! What have You to do with us (what have we in common), Jesus of Nazareth? Have You come to destroy us—I know Who You are—the Holy One of God!" (AMP). Common ground is where strongholds are built in the mind through further lies and deception; places where negative words and ideas have taken root and are strengthened by injected thoughts, feelings, and adverse circumstances. The enemy could never get through a door and claim legal ground in Jesus, but this commonality of agreement is where he *can* claim legal ground in us if he successfully deceives us into opening a door for him.

Christians must take a stand against sin through daily affirmation of the cross regarding our old man. Paul declared in Galatians 2:20, "I have been crucified with Christ; it is no longer I who live, but Christ lives in me; and the life which I now live in the flesh, I live by faith in the Son of God, who loved me and gave Himself for me." The position of death to self and resurrection victory should be affirmed verbally by the believer. Although we are physically alive on Earth (if you are reading this, you are physically alive), according to Colossians 3:3 (NASB), "...you have died, and your life is hidden with Christ in God." In Jesus, we occupy a spiritual seat in heaven, making available every covenant blessing we are given in Christ. And it all begins with repentance and identification with His cross.

In Luke 14:27, Jesus said, "And whoever does not bear his cross and come after Me cannot be My disciple." Our cross isn't sickness or anything Jesus paid for us to be free of, but rather following Him in whatever He reveals as His will. He will never lead us outside the framework of His Word, but He does call us to overcome everything inside us that has exalted itself against the knowledge of God, dealing with obstacles created by our flesh, the world, and the enemy. The cross positions us to "be doers of the Word," putting God first, others second, and ourselves last, releasing blessings and peace that passes understanding. The Holy Spirit leads and reveals when we are in or out of His will, a season is ending or a new one beginning. He prepares and goes before us and confirms us.[201] The amalgamation of knowing the Word and listening to the Spirit is the foundation upon which God discloses His life-giving directives.

Instead of seeking the Lord, many are trying to find themselves. No matter what we achieve, without Christ, it's a dead-end—literally. Now's the time to seek Him and His will for our lives. His purpose and plan are satisfying in this life and more incredible than we can imagine in the next. It's not too late to serve God wherever you are and with what you have been given. It may not be easy, but if He has called you to it, He will see you through it. Just as Jesus did, "…who for the joy that was set before Him endured the cross, despising the shame, and has sat down at the right hand of the throne of God" (Hebrews 12:2).

Revelation 12:11 says, "And they overcame him (Satan) by the blood of the Lamb and by the word of their testimony…" Most people, when quoting this passage, stop at two-thirds of the verse. Yes, there is power in the blood and the word of our testimony, but that power is accelerated when we are positioned for victory. The last third of this verse reveals why: "and they did not love their lives to the death." Although there have been and will be times when Christians must lay down their lives for their faith, in the day-to-day, "loving not our lives to the death" is the position of the cross.

By understanding the power of the cross we are empowered to deal with our carnal and fleshly impulses, and by faith, appropriate what Christ made available to us through His resurrection. By believing and receiving what the Word says regarding our position in Christ through faith and prayer, we can then activate His promises through faith and declaration. The cross is man's legal ground of identification with all Jesus accomplished and ground zero for the devil, the world, and our carnal man.

The Power of Fasting

First Corinthians 8:1b says, "Knowledge puffs up, but love edifies." Puffed up means feeling self-important and arrogant, which boils down to being prideful. God resists the proud but gives grace to the humble,[202] requiring man to walk humbly with Him (Micah 6:8). Psalm 35:13b says, "…I humbled myself with fasting." Fasting helps keep our flesh in check; it does *not* twist God's arm to do our bidding, but it does help us recognize His will, making choices that agree with His Word and purposes. Some fasts, we choose to do; other fasts the Spirit brings us to.

Jesus had no pride problems but fasting was important enough for Him to undertake forty consecutive days and nights' worth before He began His public ministry. In Mark 1:10–12, Jesus came up from the baptismal waters, the heavens parted, the Spirit descended, and His Father spoke an affirmation unparalleled with any other. Then Jesus was immediately driven into the wilderness. God's Spirit was in Jesus, but He needed empowerment by the Holy Spirit for the next forty days and beyond because He faced Satan as a man.[203] What the enemy took from Adam by stealth in the garden, Jesus regained and released into the lives of His followers. The beginning of the end of Satan's tyranny was Jesus' forty-day-fast.

"Then Jesus returned in the power of the Spirit to Galilee," after the fast (Luke 4:14a). Fasting isn't easy or fun, but the benefits are substantial. In Matthew 17:14–21, Jesus, Peter, James, and John approached a multitude after the transfiguration, and a man ran to Jesus begging Him to deliver his son from epilepsy. Jesus rebuked the demon, and it came out of him. When the disciples asked Jesus why they couldn't cast it out, He said,

> Because of your unbelief; for assuredly, I say to you, if you have faith as a mustard seed, you will say to this mountain, "Move from here to there" and it will move; and nothing will be impossible for you. However, this kind does not go out except by prayer and fasting.

The disciple's inability to cast out a demon stemmed from unbelief. The antidote for unbelief is faith. "Faith comes by hearing and hearing by the Word of God" (Romans 10:17). Knowing who we are in Christ, the authority of His Word and name, empowers Christians to cast demons out. But the disciples who walked, talked, and lived with Jesus the entire duration of His ministry were unable to cast this demon out, so Jesus gives a deliverance clue—prayer *and* fasting. In prayer, we draw closer to God and He to us, adding fasting "thins" our flesh for greater sensitivity to the Spirit.

Isaiah 58:6 defines the connection between fasting and freeing those who are bound, "Is this not the fast that I have chosen: to loose the bonds of wickedness, to undo the heavy burdens, to let the oppressed go free, and that you break every yoke?" Verse seven says to share our blessings and resources with those in need, then a promise of a breakthrough in verse eight. Most Old Testament records of fasting were related to repentance, mourning, or an urgent need to seek God for deliverance from impending devastation,[204] but not all, according to Isaiah 58.

Fasting usually entails abstinence from food. If partaking of this discipline, we should do it sensibly. Use wisdom, common sense, and consult your physician regarding health issues. We can also fast TV, computer, social media, etc.; anything we give up temporarily to draw nigh to God in prayer will not go unnoticed by Him, even if it is only one meal. We should fast discreetly if possible (Matthew 6:16–18). If we announce we are fasting, that alone is our reward, but when we fast secretly unto God, He will reward us openly. Jerry Falwell said, "When a person calls attention to his fast, he has missed its point. Fasting is not designed to get the eye of the world but to get the ear of God. It is a private matter between God and the person who is fasting."[205] Fasting realigns our spirit with the Holy Spirit for a static-free reception, at least temporarily. Fasting can be a tool in dealing with fleshly, soulish, or demonic concerns, reinforcing our efforts to humble ourselves in the sight of the Lord.

Years ago, I became painfully aware of a family member's struggles, with no clear-cut solution. I began to fast in small increments over a span of several weeks, praying for God's intervention. He later revealed that during the fast, He readjusted the course of this person's life about one-two degrees, like the vector on a graph. An adjustment in an airplane's flight plan by one degree can make the difference between landing at our chosen destination or Timbuctoo. I just skipped a meal here and there, prayed more, cut out some cokes, etc. But I knew in my spirit when it was done, and eventually, it was apparent God had indeed intervened in this person's life.

At the beginning of 2001, I faced another painful situation. At the onset, the Lord said, "Five days." I knew He was calling me to fast five days on water only. After day one, I went to bed feeling strange; the Holy Spirit said, "You're dehydrated. Go drink some water." I got up and drank as much as I could. The next night, more water. By the third night, I was staying hydrated, so no more "midnight at the oasis." By the end of the fifth day, I was feeling good physically, so I asked, "Lord, do you want me to continue this fast?" A little later, I heard in my spirit, "To obey is better than sacrifice." So, I ate. The crisis was averted because the fast God instructed me to do broke the enemy's power.

In John 4:32, Jesus ministered to a Samaritan woman while His disciples went to buy food. Upon returning, they urged Jesus to eat, and He said, "I have food to eat of which you do not know." Verse 34, "Jesus said to them, 'My food is to do the will of Him who sent Me, and to finish His work.'" The Word doesn't say Jesus was fasting, but a spiritual assignment took priority over His eating lunch that day. When God calls us to participate in this kind of fast, our part is to yield, and we feel little or no desire to eat. When the fast is over (and it's usually short), our appetite returns.

There are no rules on fasting in the New Testament, although it is helpful and needful in certain situations. Jesus indicated an appropriate time to fast in Mark 2:19–20. The disciples of John and the Pharisees asked Jesus why His disciples didn't fast as they did. He said,

> Can the friends of the bridegroom fast while the bridegroom is with them? As long as they have the bridegroom with them, they cannot fast. But the days will come when the bridegroom will be taken away from them, and then they will fast in those days.

Jesus was speaking of His current bodily presence and future earthly departure. However, anytime we are going through a spiritual dry spell, unable to feel God's presence, it's time to fast. When increasing prayer and Bible time is not sufficient, give yourself a spiritual "tune-up" and do some fasting. Skip a meal and pray instead.

In Acts 13:2–3, the Antioch church fasted and "ministered to the Lord," setting time apart to wait on God through prayer, praise, and worship. Kenneth Hagin's book, *A Commonsense Guide to Fasting*, says, "ministering to the Lord is worshipping Him; not wanting anything."[206] When the guys in Antioch fasted and ministered to the Lord, the Holy Spirit spoke to them and gave instructions for Barnabas and Saul, which began Paul's first of three missionary journeys that changed the world.[207] Jesus said, "when you fast" and not "if you fast" in Matthew 6:16, and the Scriptures record it was practiced in the Old Testament as well as the New.[208] Nevertheless, God leaves the choice to fast up to the individual. May the Lord lead and give you wisdom if you decide to fast; it's a "power tool" where less is more!

The Power of Jesus' Name

Throughout Scripture, God revealed His nature through many names describing His provision for mankind. He revealed Himself to Abraham, Isaac, and Jacob as "El Shaddai," meaning, "God, the All-Mighty One."[209] To Moses, He revealed Himself as "YHWH" (pronounced "Yahweh"), meaning "I AM" (Exodus 3:14).[210] Gideon built Him an altar, calling Him "Jehovah Shalom," meaning "The Lord is Peace" (Judges 6:23–24), and there are many more.[211] But God has exalted the name of *Jesus* above every other name. Acts 4:12 says, "Nor is there salvation in any other, for there is no other name under heaven given among men by which we must be saved." The Bible is clear; redemption isn't possible without Jesus. He claimed to be the way, the truth, and the life, and He said no one comes to the Father except *through* Him (John 14:6). If Jesus' words were not 100 percent truthful, He couldn't defeat Satan because Satan is the father of lies. If He couldn't defeat Satan, He couldn't rise from the dead. But He did defeat Satan. The resurrection proves it.

Jesus' legal ground for conquering Satan is found in John 14:30. As the crucifixion drew near, Jesus told His disciples, "I will no longer talk much with you, for the ruler of this world is coming, and he has nothing in Me." Jesus, as the spotless Lamb of God, must be completely sinless to atone for the sins of man. Any sin in His life would have brought Him under Satan's dominion, like Adam, because 2 Peter 2:19b says, "...for by whom a person is overcome, by him is he also brought into bondage." Jesus' word in John 14:30 was confirmed in John 20:16 when He revealed Himself to Mary after His resurrection.

God the Father has limited access to Himself except through the Person and name of His Son.[212] John 1:12 says, "But as many as received Him, to them he gave the right to become children of God, to those who believe in His name." Paul wrote in Galatians 3:26, "For you are all sons of God through faith in Christ Jesus." On the deity of Jesus, Pastor David said, "when you're riding in the car and another car comes out in front of you, or eighteen wheels start to skid in front of you, all you have to do is use the name of *Jesus*. You don't have to (formally) say, 'God the Father, I come to You now in the name of Jesus Christ!!'"[213] It's that simple—there's power in that name! And concerning needs, Jesus said, "...Most assuredly, I say to you, whatever you ask the Father in My name He will give you" (John 16:23), but Jesus also has authority to answer our prayers. "If you ask anything in My name, I will do it" (John 14:14). God is not our sugar-daddy, but He *is* our Father when we become a part of His family through Christ, and He *will* take care of us when we approach His throne through the name of Jesus.

The authority God the Father has bestowed upon His Son, Jesus (Yahweh Saves) Christ (Anointed), is unmatched anywhere in existence. Philippians 2:9–11 says,

> Therefore God also has highly exalted Him and given Him the name which is above every name, that at the name of Jesus every knee should bow, of those in heaven, and of those on earth, and of those under the earth, and that every tongue should confess that Jesus Christ is Lord, to the glory of God the Father.

God has commanded the enemy to bow. The angels in heaven already do, and every person will, too, either voluntarily now or after it's too late to change their eternal address.

Those who have faith in His name have been given the legal right to use that name, including dealing with the forces of darkness. We are ambassadors of the kingdom of God, which is the kingdom of light. Therefore the Father and all of heaven are backing up the name of *Jesus*. He has placed complete authority over His entire creation into Jesus' nail-scarred hands[214] because Jesus overcame and defeated Satan and his cronies, the world's schematic, and the fallen nature of human flesh.

People wonder, "If Jesus has that kind of authority, why is evil still so rampant?" In John 12:31, immediately after the triumphal entry of Jesus into Jerusalem, He said, "Now is the judgment of this world; now the ruler of this world will be cast out." Jesus was not saying the enemy would be cast out of the Earth. He was saying Satan would be cast out of God's presence in the third heaven. This could only be made possible by the blood Jesus was about to shed at Calvary and subsequently applied to the mercy seat in heaven. The enemy is now restricted to our earthly atmosphere and directly above it. Ephesians 2:2 calls him the "prince of the power of the air."

Satan may be running the world systems, but that will end shortly because Jesus is coming soon.[215] In the meantime, we must live and function in the world even though we are not of the world (John 17:16). As born-again Christians, the enemy no longer has any legal authority over our eternal spirit, but he still works to gain influence in our souls and limit the resident power that is contained within our spirit. We must use the name of Jesus to rebuke, break, bind, loose, and cast out anything and everything that opposes His lordship in our hearts and minds. He has given us His name that we may exercise His authority in our sphere and release the kingdom of God here on Earth.

The name of Jesus is God's seal of authority (John 6:27). A seal is something that authenticates, affirms, or attests. Mark 16:17–18 says,

> And these signs will follow those who believe. In My name they will cast out demons, they will speak with new tongues, they will take up serpents, and if they drink anything deadly, it will by no means hurt them, they will lay hands on the sick and they will recover.

Through the name of Jesus, we tell demons to leave, and they must; we believe and receive eternal salvation and the infilling of the Holy Spirit. We have true and genuine fellowship with our heavenly Father, identifying and destroying the works of the enemy. We have been given supernatural protection such as the full armor of God, the holy angels, and the prayers of the saints. We release God's healing power into the bodies and souls of others and ourselves. Through binding, loosing, and prophetic decrees, we move forces that don't and won't budge without our speaking in the authority and power of the Lord Jesus Christ.

May we never forget the majesty and weightiness of who Jesus is and the preeminence His name carries. It is the name above every name; only by that name are we heard on high. God's Son defeated Satan, secured our place in heaven, and commissioned us to go and make disciples of all nations, giving us the legal right to use His name in the process. He gives us the judicial right to exercise and use the spiritual tools, keys, and weapons that enforce His victory over Satan and all power of the enemy. We have been authorized and deputized to use His name for Kingdom building, business, and work. Thank you, Lord Jesus, for the authority and power contained within your matchless name!

The Power of Jesus' Blood

Blood is the life-sustaining substance human and animal bodies depend upon for oxygen and nutrients needed to function and cleanse vital organs. Before we had scientific knowledge, God revealed in Leviticus 17:11, "For the life of the flesh is in the blood, and I have given it to you upon the altar to make atonement for your souls; for it is the blood that makes atonement for the soul." "Atonement" means "reconciliation; agreement" (Dictionary.com). This substantiates the Biblical principle of restitution; but holds infinitely greater meaning when the atoning blood is Christ's. Romans 5:9 says, "Much more then, having now been justified by His blood, we shall be saved from wrath through Him." And Ephesians 1:7, "In Him we have redemption through His blood, the forgiveness of sins, according to the riches of His grace..." One man's sinless blood appeased the righteousness of God for all humanity from the garden to the gates of glory.

A blood sacrifice represents a covenant between two individuals. The Old Testament, or Old Covenant, attests to the covenant God made with Abraham and established through Moses. The New Testament, or New Covenant, God made with all humanity and established through Jesus. Under the Old Covenant, a lamb was sacrificed every morning and evening in the tabernacle and then in the temple for the sins of the people.[216] Under the New Covenant, the Lamb of God was sacrificed for all mankind, offering eternal forgiveness of sin.[217] Jesus' blood is our legal victory over Satan, cleansing sin initially and continually washing us when we walk in Jesus' light (1 John 1:7). The blood destroys Satan's power, protects us, and supplies an entrance to the throne of God! Hebrews 4:16 says, "come boldly to the throne of grace, that we may obtain mercy and find grace to help in time of need." We can come boldly only because of the blood of Jesus (Hebrews 10:19).

Because blood is a vehicle for life, its properties contain spiritual characteristics. In Genesis 4:10, Cain had slain his brother, Abel, and lied to God about it. "And He said, 'What have you done? The voice of your brother's blood cries out to Me from the ground.'" Abel's blood, after his death, still spoke to God. Hebrews 12:24 says Jesus' blood "speaks better things than that of Abel." Jesus' blood speaks mercy, reconciliation, and life, not vengeance, judgment, and death. The movie, *The Passion of the Christ* was a sobering revelation of the enormity of Christ's suffering and sacrifice, required because only sinless blood could be sprinkled upon the mercy seat in heaven. The blood from Immanuel's veins is the most precious, priceless substance in existence; without it, no one could be saved. Hebrews 9:22 says, "and according to the law almost all things are purified with blood, and without shedding of blood there is no remission." The word for "remission" here is "aphesis," meaning freedom, pardon, deliverance, forgiveness, and liberty.

"The blood" has the power to remove our guilt and guilt feelings. Hebrews 9:13 says, if sacrifices under the Old Covenant were useful for spiritual cleansing, "how much more shall the blood of Christ, who through the eternal Spirit offered Himself without spot to God, purge (cleanse) your conscience from dead works to serve the living God?" (Hebrews 9:14, KJV). Jesus' blood is alive and powerful, purifying hearts and paralyzing demons. John & Paula Sandford wrote,

> May every Christian never forget the greatest tool of power God has placed in his hands—the blood of Jesus. The Word of God is given for a mighty tool, for it is "the power of God for salvation" (Romans 1:16). But the blood of Jesus is the foremost power for the cleansing of the heart.[218]

As we "plead the blood" over ourselves, our loved ones, homes, and belongings, we exercise faith in our covenant with God based on Jesus' sacrifice. Mary Bostrom pointed out that to "plead is a legal word. The entire Bible is a legal document with legal phraseology such as testament, covenant, adoption, mediator, judge, pardon, judgment, redemption, etc."[219] Like every covenantal blessing, faith in our heart released through our voice activates the power the blood brings to bear on any situation.

The blood of Jesus is eternal and viable. While serving in Women's Aglow, we had a prayer gathering after attending a retreat. I was experiencing oppression and had not gotten a release at the retreat, so I asked these ladies to pray. When they began, I felt light-headed and fell backward; I was "slain in the spirit." They caught me, but even if they hadn't, I wouldn't have felt a thing. It seemed dreamlike, but I could hear them praying and kept my eyes closed. Someone put their finger on my forehead and rebuked a spirit of pride. After this, I felt something liquid sprinkle on my forehead, and someone drew the sign of the cross on my stomach. I thought, *This group is not Catholic; is that holy water?* Then I saw, in a vision, myself standing before Jesus, and He was looking toward me, but not at me. He fixed His gaze on a short, rotund, person-like thing just over knee-high and hiding behind my right leg. God later revealed that *was* the spirit of pride.

After they prayed, I got up from the floor and asked, "Who touched me?" They said only the one rebuking the spirit of pride. I said, "Y'all (I'm from the south!) didn't sprinkle holy water on my forehead or make the sign of the cross on my stomach?" Again, "No." The fluid sprinkled on my forehead was the blood of Jesus, giving me assurance His blood is sufficient, and the cross on my stomach pointed the way to victory. The oppression I felt lifted momentarily but came back when I sat down in my minivan to go home. However, I did not acknowledge it; I knew I had experienced something immensely powerful, and the enemy is a liar. By the next day, the heaviness began to dissipate and was soon completely gone. The way to keep our healing, deliverance, etc., is to keep our mouth and words in line with God's Word.

Communion recognizes and applies the blood of Jesus. In John 6:53, Jesus said, "Most assuredly, unless you eat the flesh of the Son of Man and drink His blood, you have no life in you." The disciples complained when hearing this; eating *any* flesh with blood was forbidden.[220] Thus, many disciples withdrew from following Him (John 6:66—not a coincidence). But Jesus was prophetically referring to the sacrament of communion, which would be instituted the day before His crucifixion, replacing the Passover meal for those following Him.[221] By partaking of communion, bread symbolizing Jesus' body, and wine (or grape juice) symbolizing Jesus' Blood, we affirm our oneness with Him and each other. Jesus said if we didn't "eat His flesh and drink His Blood," we have no life in us. Every born-again believer should participate in communion corporately and privately, if possible.

Through faith in Jesus' blood, we voice-activate a "power tool" that will move opposing spiritual forces when nothing else will. A spiritual warfare minister once said, "Demons may oppose us when we speak the Word or the name of Jesus, but they will back down when we use Jesus' blood against them." Billye Brim, in her book, *The Blood and The Glory,* said, "One old-timer, Carl Roos, told me before he moved to heaven, 'The Lord told us, 'Make much of the Blood; and the Blood will make much of you.'"[222] In pleading the blood, holding it against the enemy, and singing songs about its power, darkness *will* back off. There is life-giving, demon-busting power in the Blood of Jesus Christ!

The power of Prayer, the Cross, fasting, Jesus' name, and blood are like "neutron bombs" in the spirit realm. Through the Holy Spirit, they "neutralize" enemy power for a moment or a season to bring God's plans and purposes to fruition. These power tools are "mighty in God for the pulling down of strongholds" in our lives and those we pray for. Prayer is our lifeline to God; the cross and fasting help us deal with our flesh. Through the name and Blood of Jesus, we exercise and enforce authority in God. And under Holy Spirit's direction, all of heaven is backing us up. Friends, Jesus has much for us, but the enemy wants to strip us of everything God created for us to be and do. God's plans are good. Satan's bad. Ask the Holy Spirit to help you utilize every power tool freely given in Christ and put the devil on the run and under your feet, where he belongs. Jesus defeated him, but we must contend with him until the Lord takes us home or returns to reclaim this Earth. Either way, we can have the victory God intends for us to have.

Prayer For Utilizing God's Power Tools:

Heavenly Father, I thank you for the vehicle of prayer. Please energize my prayer life with your Word and your Spirit and help me to become consistent in approaching your throne of grace. I recognize the power of the cross and ask you to help me to recognize your perfect will for my life. I know you will not lead me outside of your Word, and I thank you that your plans for me are good. Help me to fast occasionally to put my flesh down and fine-tune my spirit to hear you. I thank you for the matchless name of your Son, the Lord Jesus Christ, the name above every name. Help me to appropriate the power of Jesus' precious blood in my own life and the lives you have called me to pray for. I love you and want my life to be pleasing to you and a powerful instrument—a power tool—in your mighty hand!

~ In Jesus' name, amen!

KINGDOM KEYS

The Bible is God's love letter to mankind. Precious truths are contained within the eternal Word. How sad that many people never investigate what God has offered and promised to those who love and respond to Him: direct access to Himself through His Son, the Word to light our way, the power of His Holy Spirit, fruit, gifts, armor, prayer, the cross, His Blood, and keys. Jesus has given us at least three keys that open doors of blessing and/or revelation, and close doors to unseen forces opposed to our victory in life. Those keys are knowledge, binding and loosing.

Jesus refers to the key of knowledge in Luke 11:52, "Woe to you lawyers! For you have taken away the key of knowledge. You did not enter in yourselves, and those who were entering in you hindered." Lawyers during Jesus' day were current experts in Mosaic Law, not like lawyers of today.[223] Because they interpreted matters of Jewish law, Jesus personally addressed them regarding this key. Soon Jesus would legally retrieve the key of knowledge and give it to His Church, or Ecclesia,[224] the Body of Christ. The Bible is a legal document, unveiling and chronicling truth on crucial matters concerning mankind. The key of knowledge is a crucial key because, without it, we are destroyed (Hosea 4:6). The key of knowledge doesn't save us but opens doors to the truth that will. This knowledge, when breathed upon by the Holy Spirit, becomes a key to understanding the purpose and promised outcome of God's plan to redeem a fallen creation back unto Himself.

The New Testament hadn't been written when Jesus walked the earth; to the Jews alone, the oracles of God had been entrusted.[225] But most religious leaders of Jesus' day utilized their knowledge of

Scripture to promote themselves rather than applying their knowledge and understanding to draw God's people into a loving and personal relationship with the Creator. Books of Scripture that Judaism was based upon consisted of the Torah (Pentateuch), the first five books of Moses, referred to as "the Law:" Genesis, Exodus, Leviticus, Numbers, and Deuteronomy. The books of history: Joshua, Judges, Ruth, First & Second Samuel, First & Second Kings, First & Second Chronicles, Ezra, Nehemiah, and Esther; poetry and wisdom books: Job, Psalms, Proverbs, Ecclesiastes, and Song of Solomon; the Major Prophets: Isaiah, Jeremiah, Lamentations, Ezekiel, and Daniel; and the Minor Prophets: Hosea, Joel, Amos, Obadiah, Jonah, Micah, Nahum, Habakkuk, Zephaniah, Haggai, Zechariah, and Malachi.

Christianity is based upon the finished work of Jesus Christ and New Testament writings. The historical books are the Gospel accounts—Matthew, Mark, Luke, John and also Acts; the Pauline Epistles: Romans, First & Second Corinthians, Galatians, Ephesians, Philippians, Colossians, First & Second Thessalonians, First & Second Timothy, Titus, and Philemon; and the Non-Pauline Epistles: Hebrews; James; First & Second Peter; First, Second & Third John; Jude; and Revelation.

The Bible reveals a myriad of truth to the seeking soul, which coalesces into the essence, purpose, and love given freely by God through His Son. The Holy Spirit oversees and is actively involved in the process of our ingestion and integration of the Word in our minds and hearts. Unlike all other information, the Bible is more than words written on paper. Our life cannot help but be changed and rearranged as we learn and partake of the great exchange. "Knowledge keys" help us understand how amazing and wonderful the Word of God truly is.

Knowledge Key #1: The Word of God is *alive*. Words are used to communicate, but we don't think of them as living organisms such as plants, animals, or human beings. All words possess varying levels of positive or negative influence, but not all words contain life-giving potential that flows from God alone. His words are unique;

they spring from His heart with every syllable saturated with life. Hebrews 4:12 says, "For the Word of God is living and powerful…" God's words are like capsules of living, intrinsic power because they are infused with the DNA of God Himself.

God's Word lives because He is a Person: "In the beginning was the Word, and Word was with God, and the Word was God. He was in the beginning with God. All things were made through Him, and without Him nothing was made that was made," (John 1:1–3). The personification of the Word is the Lord Jesus Christ, and the written Word is the Bible. The Lord unveiled a critical component of truth in John 6:63b: "The words that I speak to you are spirit, and they are life." This is especially true of Jesus' words, but also of all Scripture, which Paul confirmed in 2 Timothy 3:16–17, "All Scripture is given by inspiration of God, and is profitable for doctrine, for reproof, for correction, for instruction in righteousness, that the man of God may be complete, thoroughly equipped for every good work."

Jesus, by the Holy Spirit, speaks to us today through His Word, giving direction, comfort, strength, wisdom, and more. Father God produced everything through His Word in creation and continues to sustain everything by the Word of His power (that is, by Jesus!). One day, that same Word will release judgment, bringing destruction to the ungodly.[226] God isn't willing for any to perish, but He won't strive with man forever.[227] In His mercy, God provided healing through His Word from our own destructions (Psalm 107:20). His Word is alive with creative power.[228] The Almighty speaks through Isaiah 55:11, "So shall My word be that goes forth from My mouth; It shall not return to Me void, but it shall accomplish what I please, and it shall prosper in the thing for which I sent it." His Word doesn't return empty-handed. He and His Word are one; the Word gets it done.

In John 6:63, Jesus said His words were spirit and life. Four verses later, He asks His disciples if they desired to leave Him because of His statement in John 6:53, "unless you eat the flesh of the Son of Man and drink His blood, you have no life in you." Many *did* leave when that was spoken. Nevertheless, Peter, being a Jew, knowing the law of Moses,[229]spoke words of faith in Jesus: "Lord, to whom shall we go? You have the words of eternal life" John 6:68.

Knowledge Key #2: The Word of God *energizes* our inner man. First Thessalonians 2:13 says, "For this reason we also thank God without ceasing, because when you received the word of God which you heard from us, you welcomed it not as the word of men, but as it is in truth, the word of God which also effectively works in you who believe." There is a reverence the Thessalonian believers displayed toward God's Word, which is appropriate. Although all words contain influential potential, God's Word contains the power of miracle transformation for those who receive it in faith. The translation for "works" in this passage is "energeo,"[230] meaning "to be active, efficient, effectual, be mighty in." The translation for the word "believe" is "pisteuo,"[231] meaning to have faith (in, upon, or with respect to a person or thing). Romans 10:17 says, "So then faith comes by hearing, and hearing by the word of God." Living faith is a very potent spiritual mechanism. Jesus said we could move mountains with doubtless faith.[232] Jesus wouldn't have said it if it weren't possible.

In Hebrews 4:2, the writer brings this principle into sharper focus: "For indeed the gospel was preached to us as well as to them, but the word which they heard did not profit them, not being mixed with faith in those who heard it." Exercising faith in God's Word is not possible without first receiving it in our minds and hearts. When we open ourselves to the Lord through hearing and reading His Word, memorizing it, and meditating on it, something happens. There is a divine shift within the very core of our being. We begin to change from the inside out, with fresh comprehension of who we are in God and Who He is in us.

When my girls, Julianne and Gerrah, were growing up, I gave them a Scripture a week to memorize. Before they could receive their allowance, they recited the Scripture verbatim. Every 5th week, we would go over the past four weeks of Scriptures. I couldn't make them love God's Word but wanted them to have exposure to its truth, and hopefully, choose Jesus for themselves, fulfilling God's plan for their lives. The Word works in those who *believe,* which is a pivotal statement. Romans 12:2 says we shouldn't be conformed to this world but transformed by the renewing of our minds that we may prove what is the good, acceptable, and perfect will of God. Without the Word of God to intervene in our thought life, by default, we are pressed into the world's mold of thinking, living, and choosing. Consequently, we must become proactive, making sure the Spirit has something to work with as He leads us into Christlikeness. The Word of God is that transforming agent.

Knowledge Key #3: The Word of God *washes* our minds with the pure water of truth. Ephesians 6:25, 26 says, "Husbands, love your wives, just as Christ also loved the church and gave Himself for it, that He might sanctify and cleanse it with the washing of the water by the word..." In John 15:3, Jesus said to His disciples, "You are already clean because of the word which I have spoken to you." God has given us two spiritual cleansing agents, the blood of Jesus and the Word of God. We are saved by the Blood and regenerated by the Spirit but walking through this fallen world tainted with sin, selfishness, and corruption necessitates daily washing with the water of the Word. Hearing a Sunday sermon is not enough to make up for the 24-7 contamination we are all exposed to.

Psalm 119:9 says, "How can a young man cleanse his way? By taking heed according to Your word." To "take heed" means "to listen and pay attention."[233] When we listen to or read God's Word, carefully considering and meditating upon it, it becomes a cleansing rinse to our soul, enabling genuine faith and trust to develop in God. Once we enter a place of faith, we must endeavor to obey what the Word has revealed. James 1:22 says, "But be doers of the word, and not hearers only, deceiving yourselves." If we don't do what the Word says, we give place to deception, but when we do, we enable a galvanization of the Word in our souls.

John 13:4–9 records Jesus washing His disciples' feet immediately after the Lord's Supper. This incident is twofold. When Jesus came to Simon Peter, in verse 8, Peter said, "You shall never wash my feet!" Jesus answered him, "If I do not wash you, you have no part with Me." Peter changed his mind quick, fast, and in a hurry! The necessity of washing was so important that not allowing Jesus to wash him would jeopardize Peter's position as a disciple. No doubt Peter's thinking was still somewhat carnal, and his spirit had not yet been reborn, but he had enough understanding to take Jesus at His Word and submit to the foot washing, which is a picture of the Lord washing all who follow Him and a simultaneous lesson in humility.

The Lord is still sanctifying and cleansing His Church today through reading and listening to His holy Word. In so doing, we allow Him to cleanse and set us apart, empowering us to stand against the enemy of our immortal soul while His Spirit prepares us as an instrument for His glory. The cleansing power of God's Word is indispensable. When compared to washing in the natural, most people would not think of going one or two days without a bath or shower, and yet go without reading the Word for weeks, years, and sadly, a lifetime. Don't be a spiritual "dirty birdy." Take a Word bath today!

Knowledge Key #4: The Word of God is *food* for our spirit. First Peter 2:2 says, "…as newborn babes, desire the pure milk of the word, that you may grow thereby…" When our spirit is reborn, it must be fed to grow. A mother's milk provides nutrition for her infant, and a steady diet of the basic principles of God's Word supplies our spirit man with needed sustenance. In time, our "feeding" on God's Word, or lack of it, will directly impact our spiritual growth.

The writer in Hebrews 5:12 says to his readers that by now, they should be teachers but must relearn the precepts of God; they need milk, not solid food. "For everyone who partakes only of milk is unskilled in the word of righteousness, for he is a babe. But solid food belongs to those who are of full age, that is, those who by reason of use have their senses exercised to discern both good and evil," verses 13–14. Spiritual growth brings understanding and expertise in utilizing the Scriptures more effectively and continuing in the Word under godly leadership develops skill in managing life's problems and making choices that please God.

Like milk, bread is symbolic of the Word. In Exodus 16:4–31, the children of Israel had been freed from Egyptian bondage for approximately six weeks when they began complaining they had nothing to eat. The Lord heard them and told Moses, "Behold, I will rain bread from heaven for you," and gave instructions on gathering the bread, or manna, from heaven. They could gather a certain quota every morning; except the sixth morning, they could gather twice as much because no manna fell on the seventh day, a day of rest.

Jesus said, "I am the bread of life" twice and, "I am the bread which came down from heaven," twice.[234] The Israelites' manna fell for forty years during their wilderness wanderings and sustained their physical bodies, but they eventually died. Jesus, the Bread of Life, sustains and gives life to our eternal spirit. In John 6:53, Jesus told His listeners they had no life unless they ate His flesh, alluding to reading and meditating on God's Word (which Jesus is).[235] Indeed, the new birth is predicated upon receiving and believing the Word of God! Continued nourishment of our spirit depends upon further receiving, believing, and acting upon the Word.

Years ago, an advertiser referred to their bread as the "staff of life." But bread isn't the staff of life; Jesus is. When Jesus was tempted by Satan to turn stones into bread, He quoted Deuteronomy 8:3, "It is written 'Man shall not live by bread alone, but by every word that proceeds from the mouth of God.'"[236] We are born into the kingdom to fellowship, serve, worship, and love the God who created us; His provision of growth is through His Word—the Bible. To fulfill our purpose, we must grow, and we cannot grow without a steady diet of God's Word.

Knowledge Key #5: The Word of God is the *seed* of His kingdom. Seed, by definition, is a "propagative plant or animal structure,"[237] basically a confined configuration designed to launch reproduction of plant or animal life. Our words are spiritual seeds. In the natural, a seed contains the blueprint to reproduce the plant it came from and everything it possesses. In the spirit, the Word has the power to reproduce the kingdom of God and everything pertaining to it in us.

In the Synoptic Gospels, Jesus teaches on the Parable of the Sower,[238] explaining privately to His disciples the seed sown is God's Word. As the Sower sows, some seeds fall by the wayside, where hearers don't understand it and the enemy quickly steals it from them. Their heart is hardened like a beaten path, leaving no place for the Word to adhere. In the second group, rocky soil prevents the seed from establishing a deep root. This group does fine temporarily, but when persecution over the Word comes, or temptation is dangled in front of them, group two falls away. I identified with this group but asked the Lord to change my heart, and He did. The third group was sown among thorns, where cares of this world and deceitfulness of riches choke the word, producing nothing of eternal value. Finally, the seed sown on good ground is the hearers who receive, understand, and keep the Word, bearing much fruit.

When people have hardened hearts, are ruled by fear, weak to temptation, or their priorities are wrong, the answer is to break up their fallow ground. "Fallow" means uncultivated or untilled soil. Humans have much in common with soil. God used soil to make Adam (Genesis 2:7); the seed is planted in soil. Jeremiah 4:3 says, "For thus says the Lord to the men of Judah and Jerusalem: 'Break up your fallow ground, and do not sow among thorns.'"[239] We must pray, fast if needed, but never leave our hearts in a hardened condition toward God. We cannot change ourselves, but if we prayerfully read the Bible and listen to Holy Spirit, we can become all God created us to be.

Genesis 1:11 states the replication principle: "Then God said, 'Let the earth bring forth grass, the herb that yields seed, and the fruit tree that yields fruit according to its kind, whose seed is in itself on the earth' and it was so." By speaking or sharing God's Word, we release Kingdom seeds into others, creating an opportunity for

God's Spirit to minister to them. The Lord said to me, "Don't stop giving out gospel tracts—you're planting seeds." The Law of Reciprocity[240] is at work here. Our words are seed, whether we speak positively, negatively, spiritually, or carnally, producing crops that affect us and everyone in our sphere.

Besides others, we can speak encouragement to our own souls.[241] We should weed out (fall out of agreement with) words others or we have said or thought about ourselves that don't agree with Scripture. The Church has been given the opportunity to work in tandem with the Spirit of God. To be a fruitful follower of Jesus, we must receive, understand, and share His Word, the seed of His kingdom.

Knowledge Key #6: The Word of God is spiritual *light*. Spiritual light is factual.[242] Just as Jesus used natural elements to illustrate spiritual truth, spiritual light and darkness have their natural counterparts—the presence of light[243] enables our eyes to see, the absence of light prevents our eyes from seeing. In God's Word, Psalm 119:105 says, "Your word is a lamp to my feet and a light to my path." Verse 119:130 reads, "The entrance of Your words gives light; it gives understanding to the simple." Receiving the Word permits spiritual light to influence our thoughts and words, affecting our understanding and decisions in life. People who never crack a Bible or refuse to listen to the Gospel of Jesus Christ are living in spiritual darkness. Just as a blind man cannot see where he has come from or where he is going, are those who turn from or ignore the spiritual light of God's Word.

When God spoke, "Let there be light," in Genesis 1:3, the earth was awash in darkness. Genesis 1:1 says God created the heavens and earth "in the beginning," then Genesis 1:2 says, "The earth was without form and void; and darkness was on the face of the deep." Although darkness enshrouded Earth in Genesis 1:2, with verse 3 came a separation of spiritual light and darkness because our sun, moon, and stars weren't created until the fourth day. The Hebrew word for "darkness" is "choshek,"[244] literally meaning "darkness" and figuratively "misery, destruction, death, ignorance, sorrow, wickedness." The word for "light" is "ore,"[245] meaning "illumination or luminary in every sense including lightening, bright, clear, morning, sun." First John 1:5b says, "God is light and in Him is no darkness at all." John 1:4 says, "In Him was life, and the life was the light of men." Jesus said, "I am the light of the world. He who follows Me shall not walk in darkness, but have the light of life" (John 8:12). Spiritual light and darkness cannot usually be seen, but scripture *does* record instances where they are physically visible.[246]

For born-again believers filled with the Holy Spirit, a discerning of light and darkness realms will become perceptible. While walking in a small East Texas town, I sensed a growing discomfort in my spirit as I approached a store window with items depicting violence and evil. The further I got from the store, the less darkness I felt. On the contrary, at Community Christian School, I walked past a coworker as she prayed with someone. I felt warmth around them grow stronger as I approached and less after I passed by. Years ago, Orange Women's Aglow sponsored a program on KTFA, the local Christian radio station. While someone recorded a segment in the production room, the manager later said the staff could feel the Holy Spirit when they passed by that door.

On another occasion, a friend spent forty-five minutes praising God before driving somewhere in the Golden Triangle. On the way there, she discerned increasing spiritual darkness. Her sensitivity was the residual effect of releasing God's light into her sphere through worship. Proverbs 14:12 and 16:25 both say, "There is a way that seems right to a man, but its end is the way of death." Don't embrace "the way of death," which is swathed in spiritual darkness. Only God's Word, through the illumination of the Holy Spirit, leads us to and in the path of God's glorious light.

Knowledge Key #7: The Word of God is spiritual *fire*. In the Old Testament, God revealed Himself several times through fire.[247] By observing fire, "a state, process, or instance of combustion in which fuel or other material is ignited and combined with oxygen, giving off light, heat, and flame,"[248] we quickly become aware fire is not something to play with! And God was not playing nor burning Himself up in these appearances, but conveying His holiness, purity, and power.

Fire can represent God's judgment: fire rained down on Sodom and Gomorrah, and on soldiers sent to arrest Elijah; fire will rain on the nations gathered against the Lord and His saints.[249] Fire from heaven consumed certain sacrificial offerings: Elijah's sacrifice on Mt. Carmel, David's sacrifice on the threshing floor of Ornan the Jebusite, and Solomon's sacrifices at the dedication of the temple.[250] For Gideon, the Angel of the Lord caused fire to rise "out of the rock and consumed the meat and unleavened bread" (Judges 6:21), all signifying God's acceptance of these offerings.

Fire is symbolic of God's zeal. In Jeremiah 19, the prophet rebuked the leaders of Jerusalem and prophesied their demise because they worshiped foreign gods and sacrificed their children to idols (v.3–5). He was promptly beaten and thrown in jail. But Jeremiah could not prophesy falsely to Judah, so he wrote, "I will not make mention of Him, nor speak anymore in His name. But His word was in my heart like a burning fire shut up in my bones; I was weary of holding it back, and I could not" (verse 20:9). The weeping prophet was faithful to preach truth to the people of Judah, yet they wouldn't hear nor heed, losing sight of their definitive name. Sinking dangerously into apostasy, Jeremiah warned and pleaded with Judah to return to God.

Sharing the Word is sometimes met with hostility. In one incident, I felt the Spirit leading me to share a gospel tract with an acquaintance; she shut the door in my face. Another time someone told me, "This was not the time or place for talking about God." We were at a wedding reception, and my conversation was not with him. A few minutes later, while peeling a shrimp, he accidentally squirted himself in the eye with hot sauce. Years later, though, he asked me to pray for him. While working for KOGT, I gave a book about Jesus to one of my advertisers, who was Jewish. He quickly handed it back and said, "You get to heaven your way, and I'll get to heaven my way." On a positive note, I gave a tract to a friend of my husband who later told me he believed the gospel message in that tract. When he died, I had no doubt our friend James had gone to be with Jesus.

God's Word can feel like a "fire shut up in our bones"! We know we should share something from God with someone but experience fear and uncertainty. Ask the Lord for courage, utterance, and love to share Christ with others. Even when we blow it, or they don't receive, it's better to step out in faith and attempt to obey the Spirit. Lean into Him for guidance because, after all, it is Him working *through* us, not us doing it *for* Him; and one soul is worth pushing past all the devil's objections!

Jesus paid the price of sin for every man and sent us His Holy Spirit; now we have access to the one true God who empowers us to represent Him on Earth. John the Baptist prophesied of Jesus' Holy Spirit baptism and fire.[251] On the day of the Holy Spirit's arrival (Pentecost), His manifest presence was visible divided tongues of fire resting upon the disciples in the upper room (Acts 2:3). The Word's "firepower" is also recorded in Luke 24:32 when Jesus appeared to two followers on the road to Emmaus. When He disappeared, they said, "Did not our heart burn within us while He talked with us on the road, and while He opened the Scriptures to us?" As Jesus explained the Scriptures, they felt an undeniable burning love within their hearts, an unmistakable drawing to God.

Mankind is free to choose the purifying, empowering fire of God's Word and Holy Spirit or face eternity in the fire prepared for the devil and his angels. My granddaughter Tori, getting up from a nap, told me she dreamed that she, Paw Paw Bennie, and I were in space looking at the Earth which was on fire, and we didn't have space suits on. I immediately thought about 2 Peter 3:10, the future judgment of all the sinful works done on the Earth. God's Word produces blessed assurance for those who believe and receive or fearful terror for those who reject and deceive. As the writer of Hebrews stated, "...our God is a consuming fire" (verse 12:29).

The choice of which fire we partake is given by the One who gave, honors, and enforces our free will.

Distractions, diversions, deceptions, dissipation, etc., are only a small portion of an endless list of detours for the soul. If the enemy can keep us occupied on some trivial pursuit, we might ignore the life-giving, energy releasing, soul cleansing, spirit nourishing, seed-bearing, light blazing, fire power in God's Word. Only from Him can we learn the truth, the whole truth, and nothing but the truth! "For the Lord gives wisdom; from His mouth come knowledge and understanding" (Proverbs 2:6). By receiving revelation from God's Word, we receive knowledge keys that possess the potential to further transform us into the likeness of Christ.

Keys of Binding and Loosing: the keys of the kingdom of heaven are given to us by Jesus and are indispensable in putting a stop to the enemy running roughshod over God's people. Understanding our authority in Christ is a prerequisite to operating these keys effectively. Kenneth Hagin shared a story that revolutionized my grasp of Christian authority. In 1952 the Lord appeared to him in a vision, speaking about enemy operations. An evil spirit jumped between Brother Hagin and Jesus, releasing a black cloud and making noise; Jesus was no longer visible or audible. Brother Hagin wondered why Jesus did nothing about this interference. After some time, Brother Hagin spoke to the spirit and told it to "shut up in the Name of Jesus," which it did and fell to the floor "like a sack of salt." The black cloud also cleared, and Jesus told Brother Hagin that if he (Brother Hagin) had not done something about the evil spirit, He (Jesus) couldn't have.[252] Why? Because Jesus has already done all He's going to do regarding the devil until He sends His angel to lock him up in the bottomless pit (Revelation 20:1–3).

Brother Hagin's story is reminiscent of Paul and the apostles being followed by a young woman possessed with a spirit of divination (Acts 16:16–18). Paul was grieved by this woman following and crying out that the apostles were there to show the way of salvation. She spoke the truth, but her occupation involved consulting demon spirits, of which God has no part (Jesus didn't let the demons speak either!). [253] Scripture tells us after many days, "...Paul, greatly annoyed, turned and said to the spirit, 'I command you in the name of Jesus Christ to come out of her.' And he came out that very hour." Paul probably did pray about it, but when Holy Spirit rose in him, Paul did the casting out in Jesus' name. Victory over Satan was solely accomplished by Jesus' sacrificial death, burial, and resurrection, but when something is done regarding enemy activities here on earth, praying is important, but doing it is through the Church in Jesus' name.

In Matthew 16:13–18, Jesus asked His disciples, "Who do men say that I, the Son of Man, am?" After various answers, Jesus asked, "But who do you say that I am?" Peter said, "You are the Christ, the Son of the living God" (verses 15–16). Jesus responded by saying Peter was blessed because this revelation, that Jesus is the Anointed Savior and Son of God, had not come from men but from God. Like Peter's name (Petros[254]), the rock of revelation given him was the rock of revelation on which Jesus would build His church, a church that "the gates of Hades shall not prevail against..."

With this revelation in mind, Jesus says, "And I will give you the keys of the kingdom of heaven, and whatever you bind on earth will be bound in heaven, and whatever you loose on earth will be loosed in heaven" (Matthew 16:19). Jesus says this again in Matthew 18:18 (KJV), adding "verily," which means "surely." The word for "bind" is "deo,"[255] meaning "to bind, be in bonds, knit, tie, wind." The word for "loose" is "luo,"[256] meaning "to loosen, break up, destroy, dissolve, unloose, melt, put off." The word for "heaven" is "ouranos,"[257] meaning "the abode of God" in the spirit realm. These keys of the kingdom are given to stop demonic forces and release their captives.

The prerequisite for receiving and operating the keys of binding and loosing is receiving revelation that Jesus is the Christ, the Son of God. Although there is no record of Jesus' disciples binding and loosing, Jesus used the terms to describe dealing with demonic rulers in three of the gospel accounts. "But if I cast out demons by the Spirit of God, surely the kingdom of God has come upon you. Or how can one enter a strong man's house and plunder his goods unless he first binds the strong man? And then he will plunder his house" (Matthew 12:28–29).[258] In Luke 13:12, Jesus "loosed" a woman from an infirmity. He first spoke it, then He "laid His hands on her, and immediately she was made straight, and glorified God" (verse 13). In verse 16, Jesus said, "So ought not this woman, being a daughter of Abraham, who Satan has bound—think of it—for eighteen years be loosed from this bond on the Sabbath?" Through the Lord Jesus Christ, the tables have turned on the devil for everyone who will believe in Jesus' name, submit to His authority, and by faith, use the keys of the kingdom to bring protection, deliverance, and healing.

The Lord reminded me on several occasions to use these keys. When I sold Home Interiors and Gifts in the '90s, while working in my garage, my car keys fell out of my pocket. The Holy Spirit quickened to me what just happened was a picture of me losing sight of the keys of the kingdom and why Jesus gave them to us. I had been struggling in my prayer life, so I told the enemy to loose my prayer life! I felt more freedom as I loosed myself from the enemy's lies and bound his interference.

While working at CCS preschool, occasionally, children came in with difficulty adjusting to a classroom setting. Very quietly and gently, I would pray for these children, loosing them from fear, binding it, and command fear to leave. I then covered the child with the blood of Jesus, praying God's peace and rest upon my little friend. Nearly every time, within minutes, the child stopped crying and began listening and responding. Soon, he/she would be playing with other children. My friend Kim mentioned it might take a few minutes for binding or loosing to manifest, so we shouldn't become discouraged if results aren't immediate.

Whether dealing with natural emotions or evil spirits, through faith and voice activation of the keys of the kingdom, we release God's peace and power. Remember, Jesus said, "Whatever." Brother

David said when dealing with an issue that needs to be overcome, whatever it may be, "treat it like a demon, and get deliverance."[259] We don't always have full revelation of what we're up against; some things have roots too deep and involved, along with strongholds, for someone other than a bona fide deliverance minister to effectively deal with. But we can use wisdom and the keys of the kingdom to extricate ourselves from enemy bondages and help many within our sphere.

Conversely, keys of binding, loosing, knowledge, and the exercising of our authority in Christ must not be used in attempting to control the hearts and minds of other people. My friend Christine referred to this type of praying as "psychic prayer" and bound powerless its operation in or against our Aglow meetings. Psychic and soulish prayers are not in line with God's Word and are rooted in witchcraft, which is "the exercise or invocation of alleged supernatural powers to control people or events."[260] The Bible declares witchcraft is a work and sin of the flesh,[261] its aim being to control, intimidate or manipulate others for any purpose. It is contrary to the ways and means of God, who works by the power of His Holy Spirit, respecting the free will of mankind to infinity and beyond!

Binding and loosing are mostly directed toward the negative forces of evil. However, these keys can be used in a positive sense. Liberty Savard, in her book, *Shattering Your Strongholds,* shares how we use these keys to bind ourselves to the stable, immoveable, and fixed things of God: the mind of Christ, the will of God, the blood of Jesus, the work of the cross, the truth of His Word, paths of righteousness and God's timing. Through binding and faith, we verbally realign our spirit, soul, and body with the Word and Spirit of God. Loosing releases areas of our lives from spiritual, mental, and emotional strongholds constructed in conjunction with our flesh, the world, and the enemy. Construction materials for building strongholds are wrong attitudes, thinking patterns, mindsets, ideas, desires, beliefs, behaviors, habits, generational curses, bondages and iniquities, and curses spoken to us, by us, or about us.[262] By dismantling strongholds, we make room for the Lord's healing, restoration, and peace. Some strongholds are obvious, others well camouflaged; either way, God, through Christ, has given us keys to help identify and break them.

The enemy came in by stealth to establish sinful beliefs and actions with resulting bondages and strongholds; therefore, God's Word brings enlightenment and empowerment to establish submission to God and resistance to the enemy. If we choose to reject or fail to believe and act on the Word, we cannot break free of the sin, darkness, and deception that is the malady of mankind. And once the enemy has locked onto the human will, he is in the driver's seat of that person's life until someone will intercede for him/her through prayer, fasting (if necessary), binding, and loosing until the person in question can begin to see the light of Jesus Christ. Unlike the enemy, God will never cross the line of our free will. He will accept a person's decision to reject Him even if it separates that person from Him forever, but this is never His will. However, the enemy has no problem crossing the line of free will; and before we come to Christ, we are defenseless to his wiles and schemes, except for the sovereignty of God and the prayers of the saints.

Thank God for Jesus Christ! He alone has given us the authority, power, weapons, tools, and keys to take back what the enemy has stolen. And it is we who must do it because we are free moral agents.[263] Subsequently, we must individually come out of agreement with the enemy, his lies, and deceptions. Because God has given us free will, we each possess primary authority over our own lives. As we identify areas of wrong thinking, believing, speaking, etc., repent (turn), and embrace what God says about the issue, we retake ground the enemy used to influence our decisions.

In the conquest of Canaan, God gave the Israelites the land, but they had to go in and take it. Not by themselves, but under the direction of the Commander of the army of the Lord (Joshua 5:13–15). Likewise, God has given us liberty in Christ, but we must take back "the land" we have given the enemy through sin, deception, and ignorance under the direction of the Holy Spirit.[264] Becoming aware of the enemy's places of access enables us to be on guard, preventing future attacks. As we take authority in our own lives, we are better equipped to help others. Our authority, however, diminishes as our sphere of influence enlarges because other people also possess primary authority over their own lives. Hence, lasting deliverance is only accomplished with their cooperation.

A person must accept God's Word as truth; there is no other way to break deception's power. The Word helps us recognize where we must submit to the Lord so He can forgive, cleanse, and renew, thus initiating healing, deliverance, and healthy change. By ourselves, we cannot change our internal processes; they are rooted in spiritual places. We may modify our behavior, but only God can change us from the inside out. Keys of knowledge unveil revelation and understanding, but keys of binding and loosing are spiritual devices initiating change in the spirit realm. They are faith and voice-activated, but occasionally, I have bound and loosed in my thought processes and experienced success.

Although defeated, our unseen adversaries have a great apprehension of the Church utilizing the keys of the kingdom. A particular visit to a denominational church we attended seemed to have no anointing, just going through the motions. In my mind, I asked the Lord if He was present. He opened my eyes to see Him standing in the corner of the sanctuary. He also let me see the serpentine form of two religious spirits who were also present. The pastor was preaching on Matthew 16. As he moved through the verses, expounding each one, nothing changed until he reached verse 16:19b, "…whatever you bind on earth will be bound in heaven and whatever you loose on earth will be loosed in heaven." The snake-like spirits became extremely agitated and defensive while he taught on this verse but settled down when the pastor moved on to the next verse. Evil spirits understand Christians' authority over them better than most Christians do!

As I pondered this scenario and prayed, the Lord reminded me of John the Baptist, who called the religious leaders of his day a "brood of vipers" (Matthew 3:7). John the Baptist never did any miracles, yet Jesus said he was the greatest prophet born among women (Luke 7:28). One who holds the office of a prophet must have two gifts of revelation operating in his/her life, along with prophecy, on a regular basis. John, through the gift of discerning of spirits and word of knowledge, must have seen the snake-like demons who were controlling the religious leaders and spoke by revelation to them accordingly. Those spirits were granted permission by the religious leaders themselves, so John told them to repent. Repentance begins the uprooting process that can eventually set one free if he/she continues in the truth.

After considering this vision, I marveled at the love and humility of Jesus. He was present because these people had invited Him in, were learning His Word, and growing as Christians. But He was not ruling; something else was. This is a picture of many churches all over the world. Instead of our Lord being enthroned on our praises, worshiping Him in spirit and truth, we have allowed religious spirits to control what is happening in the spirit and natural realm. The spirit controls the natural realm, but the natural gives right-of-way to the spirit realm. If religious spirits have free reign in our churches, our homes, and individual lives, the Lord Jesus may be resident, but He is not President! This is one reason He has given us the keys of binding and loosing. When we submit to Jesus' lordship, we are authorized to loose ourselves from the enemy's grip, bind him powerless and speechless, and command him to leave.

Prayer to Receive Revelation and Activation for Kingdom Keys:

Heavenly Father, thank you for granting me the revelation that Jesus is the Christ, the Son of the Living God. I ask you to release keys of knowledge in my life, giving me a deeper and higher understanding of truth and greater faith in you, your plan, and your purposes. I humbly receive your provision for kingdom building; please anoint me to hear your Spirit and utilize the keys of binding and loosing. As you activate these keys according to your Word and your will, I give thanks that all heaven is backing my words with Almighty God's authority. I thank you, Lord Jesus, for leading and guiding me to use these keys for maximum effectiveness on earth and maximum glory to Your matchless name.

~ In Jesus' name, I pray, amen.

THE PRAISE PRINCIPLE

The Lord in His faithfulness has delivered me from various and numerous enemy attacks. Our adversary is real, but more so God's Spirit, His gifts, armor, weapons, tools, and keys. "For the weapons of our warfare are not carnal (of the flesh) but mighty in God for pulling down strongholds" (2 Corinthians 10:4). However, before learning of God's provision, I felt like "A Boy Named Sue" in the 1969 Johnny Cash song, which described a man's battles in life because of a name he was given. That song somewhat described my feelings, but I didn't know, unlike the song, what happened to put my life in a tailspin. I didn't know what doors I opened (or what a spiritual door was), except possibly when I asked God to use me to help others who were tormented. I even prayed, "Never mind, don't use me for this, Lord. It's too hard!" If it hadn't been for the prayers of the church, the truth of His Word, the power of His Spirit, and His great faithfulness, I wouldn't have made it this far.

For years, I couldn't see how God could bring anything good out of what I was walking through. Although I was learning, when spiritual skirmishes arose, I reverted to self-defense mode, operating in fear, and it drained me. I was becoming more dependent on the weapons themselves and my feeble ability to use them than I was on the Lord Jesus Himself. My focus would become inward instead of upward. But thank God; through His written Word, the prayers of others, and the Rhema teaching I received at the right time, He always pulled me back into a place of Christ-centeredness again. And He still does; we're all a work in progress.

During this time of learning about spiritual warfare, I had a dream where I was standing in the middle of an old house with two doors located on an enclosed front porch, one door facing left, the other facing right. I inspected the doors; the one on the left was freshly painted with bright curtains and clear glass windows; down its side were about ten brass locks—each one different from the others. I thought, *there's no way anyone is coming through this door.* I turned and saw the door on the right was just a broken-down screen door. The screen was torn with no way to secure it. I immediately sensed the vulnerability this door presented and moved back into the house interior. Sure enough, I saw a man through one of the house windows coming toward the screen door. He entered the house, and I fought him with a sword. The sword represented the Word of God. The door on the left represented my efforts to keep the enemy out of my life—the locks being the "weapons of warfare" described in 2 Corinthians, but what did that broken-down screen door on the right represent? At the time, I could only guess. Much time would pass before it would be fully revealed.

After years of struggling, the Lord made known to me the power of a weapon that, up until then, I didn't consider tremendously substantial. In fact, I didn't know this was a weapon and a key to unlock and release God's power in my life. I thought it was only part of a church service, but I have come to believe it's something every believer can and should use every day. We could even call it another secret weapon[265] because it's not aimed at the enemy but greatly disrupts and hinders his operations. It's not about us, not for us, but the residual benefits unto us are astounding. King David discovered this secret early in life, and to this day, it remains a hallmark of his legacy. This weapon, this key, is none other than the power of *praise.*

The paradigm shift began in 2002 when I felt led to attend a weekend retreat at the "Promised Land" near Moss Hill, Texas, also known as Touched by Grace Ministries. Some of my intercessor friends from Community Church planned on going that November, and I felt stirred to go also. Little did I know what was waiting for us at this wonderful place. When we arrived, they put me in the Shoutin' Shanty, giving me an inkling God was up to something.

After a delicious dinner, the Friday evening service began. The dance team joined us, dancing all over the church as we sang praises to the Lord. I don't recall being in a church service before this when people danced in praise and worship, and frankly, it was a little much. I wouldn't look those praise dancers in the eye, hoping they wouldn't come and pull me out into the aisles like my Community comrades.

I was blessed by the speaker's message that Friday evening, but when I went to bed, I couldn't sleep or rest. I spent most of the night rebuking the devil, praying in tongues, choosing to focus on and rest in Jesus, then binding everything I could think of that might keep me from sleeping. To make matters worse, I was on a top bunk (consideration of others in our cabin), the restroom was in *a different* cabin, and it was cold that night—man, was I miserable!

After much spiritual wrestling and several trips to the ladies' room, sometime in the early morning hours, the Lord gave me a vision of the retreat leader holding up my hand like Rocky Balboa when he won his first hard-fought fight with the movie's heavy-weight champion, Apollo Creed. In the vision, she said, "Try Praise!" I thought, *what could it hurt? No one knows me here except the people from Community, and they have already gone ape!* I then resolved the next night to join the worship through praise and dance. Saturday evening, they moved the chairs off the sanctuary floor and up against the wall, and I got with the program. I danced and ran throughout the church, all the while shouting and singing praises unto God. To my surprise, it was exhilarating! Joy welled up within my spirit, giving me greater freedom to praise the Lord. This was a new-found spiritual energy; the more I praised, the better I felt, the better I felt, the more I wanted to praise the Lord!

During this time of worship, the Lord gave me another vision. I saw, from an aerial view, the little church where we were worshiping, and from every orifice, shafts of light were beaming from the building, like high-intensity spotlights piercing the nighttime sky. It was an incredible sight. Two angels flew over this little church, that was exploding with light. They weren't assigned to this meeting;

however, they were drawn to the luminous sight emanating from the building and came down to investigate. Later, I remembered the Scripture, 1 Peter 1:12b, "…things which angels desire to look into." First John 1:5 says, "…God is light and in Him is no darkness at all."[266] That gleaming light bursting forth from the church was the manifest presence of God. In the spirit, the light of God is as discernible as the midday sun in the natural. Just because we don't see it when we are worshiping God doesn't mean it's not there. It's not hidden to those who live in the spiritual realm.

Jesus said in John 8:12, "I am the light of the world. He who follows Me shall not walk in darkness but have the light of life." First Peter 2:9 says, "But you are a chosen generation, a royal priesthood, a holy nation, His own special people, that you may proclaim the praises of Him who called you out of darkness into His marvelous light."[267] For the Christian, the light of Jesus is resident within our spirit continually, but when we praise and worship God, that light is amplified and released into the atmosphere around us. Now consider what's possible when we're in the company of other believers also praising, worshiping, and dancing, glorifying God. Just like agreement in prayer, agreement in worship releases the multiplication principle within the gathering of believers, ushering in a tangible, felt presence of the Holy Spirit and, at times, manifestations of His presence. We may not see the spiritual amps our spirits are generating, but the enemy is well aware of the possibility that any minute, the trillion-watt light of God could break forth, and he isn't going to hang around for that. Praising God is not the only way, but it is one of the best ways to put the enemy on the run!

On Sunday morning at the Promised Land retreat, testimonies were given, and I shared my joy and vision with the congregation. Several women began to shout praises unto God, giving me the feeling that what I shared was something they had prayed specifically for. The retreat leader took my hand, raised it up like the "Rocky" vision, only she said, "Lord, make her a wild woman!" The battle was about to become an adventure.

Some people have a problem with people dancing in the church. I sort of did, not minding others dancing, but I wasn't comfortable stepping out in that myself. Nevertheless, when the Lord revealed what transpires in the spirit, I changed my mind. It's not unscriptural to dance in worship services. Psalm 149:3 says, "Let them praise His name with the dance." Psalm 150:4 says, "Praise Him with the timbrel and dance." Dance can and should be incorporated into the praise and worship portion of our church services. Nevertheless, in churches where this is not recognized or encouraged, we must not dishonor our leadership. I usually dance unto the Lord mostly in my home, privately. When we have danced privately unto the Lord, dancing in corporate worship is easier because the enemy can't condemn us for being hypocritical. We aren't dancing to be seen by others according to Satan's accusation. We are dancing as David did with all his might (2 Samuel 6:14).

We can know if dancing is appropriate at a particular time in service by watching and following the leader. Of course, there are times when excesses, errors, and attention-seeking spirits attempt to negatively affect a gathering. First Corinthians 14:33 and 40 say, "For God is not the author of confusion, but of peace…" and, "Let all things be done decently and in order." When it's genuine and Spirit-led, praise dancing, along with other forms of exuberant worship, is beautiful, liberating, and inspiring. Taking measures against fleshly exhibitions is done through intercession for the meeting beforehand, using Christ's authority and the keys of the kingdom to block enemy efforts to disrupt and derail what God intended. If we do our part in the preparation, we won't "throw the baby out with the bathwater" in our efforts to keep order in a meeting.

After this encounter with extravagant praise, worship, and revelation of God's magnificent glory, I should have dug in, acquiring more understanding of the power of praise and worship, but I didn't. Not everyone around me had the same revelation (even in a spirit-filled church) and didn't see the applied importance of it, although they agreed in doctrine. I have no one to blame but myself for not pressing in, although life was busy with one daughter going through her junior and senior high school years, graduation, and starting college while my other daughter was adjusting to marriage and motherhood. Things were hectic, but they almost always are. But God is good—He grants us countless second chances! And it's a good thing because, over the next two years, the enemy siphoned this truth from my thinking, so God sent me back to the Promised Land in November of 2004.

This time, our large group wasn't going, but two precious friends, Debbie D. (who has gone home to be with the Lord), and Vicki S. wanted to go. The night before we left, while drying dishes, I accidentally pulled a knife off the counter. It hit my foot and glanced off. I felt a little sting, then saw the blood. Remember the opening song of the 1960's sitcom, *The Beverly Hillbillies?* "And then one day he was shootin' at some food, and up through the ground come a bubblin' crude."[268] Well, maybe not that dramatic, but close. The knife hadn't gone too deeply into my foot, possibly just nipped a vein.

Right after it happened, I called Bennie and told him of my dilemma while sitting on the floor holding a towel on my bleeding foot. He was at least fifteen minutes away, and I became concerned if the bleeding didn't stop soon, I might pass out, so I called our good friends and next-door neighbors, Hammon and Glenda. They came over to help while we waited for Bennie to get home. I pulled the towel away; the bleeding appeared to stop, so I stood up and thanked them for coming. While talking, Glenda said, "Uh, Patrice…" and pointed down. My foot was bleeding again. Shortly after that, I remembered the first aid training we received at CCS and elevated it (thank you, Mrs. Lee, for all those CPR courses!)

Being accidentally stabbed in the foot didn't stop us from heading to the Promised Land the next day to sing, praise, and dance unto the Lord (a little gingerly, perhaps). The enemy is determined to keep us from praising and dancing in the spirit; he doesn't want us praising God with our whole being because of how powerful it is. Consequently, I determined to worship and dance privately before the Lord on a regular basis, and revelation began pouring into my life. When I shared with the ladies attending the retreat about the knife-in-foot incident, there was quite a bit of laughter. Not so funny when it happened, but it helped me see the necessity for Christians to engage in this unique form of spiritual warfare. Unique because none of our attention is focused on the enemy, as in traditional spiritual warfare, but entirely on the Lord.

Daniel 12:4 says in the last days, "knowledge shall increase." This is true in the natural world and in the spirit realm. The revelation of radical praise isn't new to everyone, but it was a game-changer for me. The church is the only entity on Earth possessing the authority to activate the key that releases God's presence and power. When the light of God's presence is released and our full-throttle praise and worship engaged, darkness must flee. We need only flip the switch of a lightbulb or light a candle in a dark room to understand this principle. The enemy must have darkness to work, so we greatly hinder his attempts to infiltrate our lives when we praise and worship the Lord regularly and passionately. In Psalm 119:164, the psalmist says, "Seven times a day I praise You, because of Your righteous judgments." The Lord is worthy of all our praises—be it one, seven, or a hundred and eleven—and each time we do, we glorify God and shun the enemy.

There are many forms of praise: singing, speaking of His wonderful acts and holy attributes, dancing, lifting our hands, etc. All or any of which may activate the "praise principle"—when praises go up, His presence comes down. Psalm 22:3 reveals a pivotal, powerful truth. It says, "You are holy, who inhabit the praises of Israel." The word "inhabit" is "yashab,"[269] meaning "to sit down (as judge, in ambush, in quiet), to dwell, to remain, to settle." As the Lord's praises leave our heart and mouth, we are, in effect, creating a place for God's rule, authority, and presence in our sphere. Although God is everywhere (omnipresent),[270] the tangible, manifest presence of God is usually not recognized until we remove the veil of concealment through our praise. The following are Biblical accounts of praise being a vehicle for God's intervention and revelation unto His people:

The praise principle is evident in various places throughout Scripture, playing an important role in the lives of people like Abraham, the father of faith. He was given a tremendous promise from God, yet the time factor before the promise came forth was considerable. Abram (his original name) was seventy-five years old when God first spoke the promise: "Now the Lord had said to Abram: Get out of your country, from your family and from your father's house, to a land that I will show you. I will make you a great nation; I will bless you and make your name great; and you shall be a blessing" (Genesis 12:1–2). Before Abram could become a great nation, he must first become a father. Isaac, the promised son, wasn't born until Abraham (God changed his name in Genesis 17:5) was one hundred years old and Sarah, his wife, was ninety! For twenty-five years, Abraham's faith in God didn't diminish but was strengthened as he steadfastly gave God glory (Romans 4:20). Consistently praising the Lord strengthens our faith and stabilizes our hearts and minds.

When standing on God's promises, we must be faithful to praise Him in our season of waiting that we may grow stronger in faith as time passes. In Genesis 17, God revealed Himself as El Shaddai to Abram, meaning, "God Almighty," Abram's All-Sufficient Supplier.[271] God has given everyone a measure of faith (Romans 12:3); He also gives increase (1 Corinthians 3:6). Instead of complaining or worrying about what God appears to not be doing, we should give Him glory while waiting for His promise to manifest. Praise is one of the most important ways we reinforce and fortify the faith He has given us while waiting for His answer or promise to come forth.

We can use our mouths to give God glory due to His name like Abraham did, producing blessing and life for us and others, or we can use our mouths to bring forth destruction and death issuing from our old man, the world, and the enemy's lies. We must intentionally choose, just as Moses decreed to the Israelites as they were about to enter Canaan over 430[272] years later,

I call heaven and earth as witnesses today against you, that I have set before you life and death, blessing and cursing; therefore, choose life, that both you and your descendants may live; that you may love the Lord your God, that you may obey His voice and that you may cling to Him, for He is your life and the length of your days; and that you may dwell in the land which the Lord swore to your fathers, to Abraham, Isaac, and Jacob, to give them,

Deuteronomy 30:19–20

The Israelites were encouraged to choose life by holding fast to an attitude of gratitude, obeying God's commandments, and avoiding anything that usurped His place in their lives. Although Jesus is the only one who completely fulfilled the law, Moses words are still a target of our behavior if we love God. By thanking, praising, and worshiping our Lord, honoring His Word, and cooperating with Holy Spirit, we bring our attitudes, utterances, and actions into submission to Christ,[273] who is life.

A question many people wrestle with was answered in Cindy Jacobs' book, *Possessing the Gates of the Enemy.* Cindy was mulling over the question of why we tell God how good He is. She said she knew He was worthy of our praise, but right in the middle of her thoughts came the words, *Am I selfish?* She sensed this question was from the Lord and responded, "No Lord, you are never selfish. It is impossible for you to be selfish." "Then why do you think I desire to be praised?" She thought about it, but before she could answer, the Lord said: "I want you to praise me because when you do, I become what you have praised me for. When you have a financial need, for instance, and worship me for being Jehovah Jireh, I come into your situation and meet your needs. I want you to praise me for your good, not mine."[274] Cindy's testimony reaffirms God's provision as El Shaddai to us, just as He was to Abraham. Through our worship, the Lord can release His unfathomable provision to meet every need. He desires to be intimately involved in our lives that He may protect and bless us because He is good.

An example of how lifting hands is significant in activating the praise principle was at work in Moses' life during the Israelites' battle with Amalek at Rephidim (Exodus 17:8–16). Moses told Joshua to take men and go fight with the opposing Amalekites while he stood on top of the hill with the rod of God in his hand. Exodus 17:11, "And so it was, when Moses held up his hand, that Israel prevailed; and when he let down his hand, Amalek prevailed." Lifted hands=victory. Lowered hands=defeat. Moses's hands became physically tired. Aaron and Hur sat Moses on a rock and helped hold up his hands until the sun set, and Joshua defeated Amalek. The Amalekites were descendants of Esau, who was a type of flesh nature. Sometimes our flesh does not feel like praising God, but this battle exposes the ongoing importance of keeping a stance of praise in spiritual combat. Although it was a group effort, the lifted hands made the difference between Joshua capturing a victory or suffering a crushing defeat.

After the battle, Exodus 17:15–16 says, "And Moses built an altar and called its name, The-Lord-Is-My-Banner (Jehovah Nissi), for he said, 'Because the Lord has sworn: the Lord will have war with Amalek from generation to generation." In verse 14, the Lord said He would utterly blot out the remembrance of Amalek from under heaven, which He did many years later, under the reign of King Hezekiah and through supernatural intervention in Queen Esther's life, protecting the Jews as recorded in the book that bears her name.[275] However, spiritually speaking, the generation to generation war with Amalek spoken of in verse 16 is a war that will be fought until Christ returns (because of our flesh), and we receive our resurrection bodies; bodies in which our flesh nature has been annihilated through the transformation of our physical being.[276]All humans deal with fleshly issues, but the born-again child of God has the ability to recognize this battle and do something about it by choosing to be led by the Spirit rather than the dictates of his flesh.[277] Praise is an antidote to our flesh nature!

The lifting of hands to the Lord has a place in praise, worship, and warfare. Moses, Aaron, Hur, and Joshua demonstrated the dynamics of this concept. The physical battle they experienced then typifies many spiritual battles we face now. Moses' raised hands represented the banner, or flag, of the Lord, just as ours do, too. King David wrote in Psalm 60:4–5: "You have given a banner to those who fear You, that it may be displayed because of the truth. Selah. That Your beloved may be delivered, save with Your right hand, and hear me." And Psalm 141:2, "Let my prayer be set before You as incense, the lifting up of my hands as the evening sacrifice." Various authors in various Scriptures also write concerning lifting hands to God.[278]

From another aspect, raised hands in a battle indicate one of the opponents is surrendering. When we raise our hands in worship, we are surrendering to the Eternal God, releasing Him to do our fighting for us. Spiritual battles are won by spiritual means, and the raising of our hands to the Almighty is more powerful than we know. A friend once said the Lord revealed that when we raise our hands in worship, we are like a lightning rod with which God's power may connect; power which enables us to live and walk in victory over the forces of evil.

Another incident involving Moses in Numbers 13 and 14 reveals a thought-provoking perspective of how faith and positive confession can make or break divine directives. God had commanded Moses to send scouts, one from each of the tribes of Israel, with Joshua into the land of Canaan for exploration. According to Numbers 13:6, the scout from the tribe of Judah was a man named Caleb, who said, "Let us go up at once and take possession, for we are well able to overcome it" (Numbers 13:30b). After forty days of spying out the land (forty, the number of testing), ten scouts came back with a report frightening the Israelites, saying, "the land truly flowed with milk and honey," but the inhabitants were huge and much stronger than they. Of all the men who spoke of what would be their Promised

Land, only the man from Judah (which means "praise") and Joshua (a type of the Messiah) gave a faith-full report of the land which the Lord intended to *give* Israel.[279]

God saw Caleb's faithfulness and said, "But My servant Caleb, because he had another spirit with him, and hath followed Me fully, him will I bring into the land whereinto he went; and his seed shall possess it" (Numbers 14:24, KJV). The difference between Caleb and the other ten spies was choosing to believe God (like Abraham) and speaking faith to encourage and strengthen his brethren. The ten scouts that brought a fearful report, causing Israel to complain and grumble, never entered the Promised Land. Numbers 14:37–38 says, "those very men who brought the evil report about the land, died by the plague before the Lord. But Joshua the son of Nun and Caleb the son of Jephunneh remained alive of the men who went to spy out the land." Only Caleb and Joshua, with their families, entered Canaan, out of six hundred thousand men who listened to the ten fearful scouts (Exodus 12:37–38).

In Numbers 14:7–9, Caleb (and Joshua) spoke again to encourage the people, declaring their faith in God:

> The land we passed through to spy out is an exceeding-
> ly good land. If the Lord delights in us, then He will
> bring us into this land and give it to us, a land which
> flows with milk and honey. Only do not rebel against
> the Lord, nor fear the people of the land, for they are
> our bread; their protection has departed from them,
> and the Lord is with us. Do not fear them.

Caleb believed, and therefore he spoke; without faith, it is im-possible to please God. When we verbally affirm our heart's faith and trust in God's integrity and Word, we can face even what appears to be insurmountable odds. It's a declaration to the natural and spiritual realms regarding God's character, nature, and goodness, affecting the very course of our existence. Caleb and Joshua believed God, proclaimed their faith, and courageously obeyed His Word. They made it to the Promised Land; God made sure of it.

Joshua was also a man of faith, obedience, and praise. He is probably best remembered for the victory God gave him and the Israelites at the battle of Jericho—the first of many cities in Canaan they were called to conquer. Their instructions from the Lord were to:

> March around the city, all you men of war; you shall go all around the city once. This you shall do six days. And seven priests shall bear seven trumpets of rams' horns before the ark. But the seventh day you shall march around the city seven times, and the priests shall blow the trumpets.
>
> Joshua 6:3–4

Verse 5: "…when they make a long blast with the ram's horn, and when you hear the sound of the trumpet, all the people shall shout with a great shout; then the wall of the city will fall down flat." Only God could cause the fortified walls of Jericho to fall with only a shout from the mouths of mere men, and He had sent the Commander of the armies of the Lord with countless angelic troops to enforce His word to Joshua and through him break every idolatrous stronghold in the land of Canaan (Joshua 5:14).

The ark of the Lord, which represented the presence of God, went with them to encircle the city of Jericho once a day for six (the number of man) days and seven (the number of spiritual perfection)[280] times on the seventh day. The ram's horns[281] the priests blew represented power. In Joshua 6:10, Joshua commanded the people to be quiet and not speak during these processions until he told them to shout. At the end of the seventh day, the seventh procession of that day, Joshua said, "Shout, for the Lord has given you the city!" Verse 20 says, "So the people shouted when the priests blew the trumpets. And it happened when the people heard the sound of the trumpet, and the people shouted with a great shout, that the wall fell down flat." The word for the verb "shout"[282] means to mar (especially by breaking); figuratively *to split* the ears (with sound).

Did God amplify the sound of their shout, like sonic weapons developed by modern man, where soundwaves literally broke the walls into pieces? Or did their obedience to follow God's instructions implicitly release His "angelic jackhammer" on the walls? Whatever happened, the point is this: The Israelites' shout removed the protection of the people of Jericho. In the previous story, Caleb and Joshua said, "their protection has departed from them and the Lord is with us." When the Israelites encircling Jericho followed the Lord's instructions and came into alignment with His Word, their shout dealt a lethal blow to the enemy's natural *and* spiritual fortress. Likewise, when we are walking in line with the Word and obedient to the Spirit of God, our shout comes against strongholds of the enemy we may not even be aware of!

This was a shout of obedience, praise, and pent-up excitement, a culmination of specific instructions given by God to people He appointed to inherit land He promised to Abraham's descendants. Shouting in Scripture is many times connected to God's presence. First Chronicles 15:28 describes the transportation of the ark: "Thus all Israel brought up the ark of the covenant of the Lord with shouting and with the sound of the horn, with trumpets and with cymbals, making music with stringed instruments and harps." Isaiah 12:6 says, "Cry out and shout, O inhabitant of Zion, for great is the Holy One of Israel in your midst!" Shouting, at the appropriate time, should have a place in our worship. Zephaniah 3:14–15 says,

> Sing, O daughter of Zion! Shout, O Israel! Be glad and rejoice with all your heart, O daughter of Jerusalem! The Lord has taken away your judgments, He has cast out your enemy. The King of Israel, the Lord, is in your midst; you shall see disaster no more.

We shout at pep rallies, demonstrations, and almost every kind of sporting event. Many people think it irreverent to shout in church but shouting has its place when done in the right spirit at the right time; when exuberant praise has broken out in our midst, and we feel prompted in our heart to join in with the hosts of heaven glorifying the One True God. He is worthy of shouts of praise and adoration, for He is the King of Kings and Lord of Lords! May the Holy Spirit free us to release our shouts of praise when He is moving in this vein in our midst and give us the joy of His strength so that no rock will out-shout us, child of God![283]

When praises go up, His presence comes down, and His presence is life changing. One of the most profound examples of the manifestation of God's presence is in 2 Chronicles 5:11–14:

> And it came to pass when the priests came out of the Most Holy Place (for all the priests who were present had sanctified themselves, with keeping to their divisions), and the Levites who were the singers, all those of Asaph and Heman and Jeduthun, with their sons and their brethren, stood at the east end of the altar, clothed in white linen, having cymbals, stringed instruments and harps, and with them one hundred and twenty priests sounding with trumpets—indeed it came to pass, when the trumpeters and singers were as one, to make one sound to be heard in praising and thanking the Lord, and when they lifted up their voice with the trumpets and cymbals and instruments of music, and praised the Lord, saying: "For He is good, for His mercy endures forever," that the house, the house of the Lord, was filled with a cloud, so that the priests could not continue ministering because of the cloud; for the glory of the Lord filled the house of God.

Note in these verses, the Levites were singing, Asaph's group was playing cymbals (which are loud!), stringed instruments, and harps, with another 120 priests sounding trumpets (also loud!). When they were unified, making one sound of praise and thanksgiving to the Lord, God showed up. Many people today refer to this manifestation of God's presence as "the glory cloud." Kenneth E. Hagin calls it "the corporate anointing." In his book entitled, *Understanding the Anointing,* he states:

> I'm thoroughly convinced—although you can neither prove nor disprove it by the Bible—that we as the Body of Christ as a whole have the same measure of the Holy Spirit that Jesus did—but we as individual members of the Body of Christ do not. The greatest anointing of all is the corporate anointing.[284]

Just as unity in prayer has tremendous potential, the power of unity in worship cannot be overstated. What the Lord showed me at the Promised Land in Moss Hill, Texas—the explosion of the light of His presence—is available to all! Brother Hagin described what he saw concerning the glory cloud, saying, "I was laying hands on people in the healing line, and I saw the glory cloud roll in. It's like waves of the sea, but it's a cloud."[285] People, we need this because we need more of God. None of us walk in the corporate anointing alone; God has placed us in the body of Christ that we may strengthen, encourage, and bless one another,[286] and He is the one who receives the glory because it is *Him* working through His body!

The peace, power, and potential of unity in God's people are seen in Psalm 133, where God commands the blessing of life evermore. We must put aside our differences and humble ourselves before the King of Glory, worshiping Him in spirit and truth, becoming one with each other and with the Spirit of God. When we do, the power of God will be released in our midst to do the "greater things" Jesus spoke of (John 14:12). But unity can be a powerful thing even among those who don't serve God. Remember the tower of Babel in Genesis 11:1–9, where the people's motive was to "make a name for ourselves" (verse 4). The truth we must now see in this incident is best summed up in the words of John Piper, "God's will for all mankind is not that we find joy in being praised, but that we find joy in praising Him." Amen. Many times, no one will see the glory cloud, but people may be "slain in the spirit," or "fall under the power," which is what happened to the priests at the dedication of Solomon's temple. People I know have been "slain in the spirit," and I have fallen under the power myself.[287]

My cousin Terry experienced the Lord's manifest presence in a mall here in the Golden Triangle. The last place you would expect to sense the presence of God, Terry felt it immediately when he stepped inside. It was not until he approached a church group singing God's praises in a presentation that he understood why. The more time we spend in the Word, prayer, praise, and worship, the more sensitive we become to God's manifest presence. And while corporate gatherings of believers in unity may create the greatest potential for God's power to manifest and be released, we should never discount small gatherings of two or more (Matthew 18:20) or just us and God. In fact, our time alone with Him is critical to our spiritual growth, preparing, sensitizing, and helping us understand the moving of the Holy Spirit in deeper and greater measures.

When God's presence manifests, sometimes the gifts of His Spirit will also begin to operate. These occurrences happened in the Old Testament as well as the New. In 2 Kings 3:15, the prophet Elisha said, "'But now, bring me a musician.' Then it happened, when the musician played that the hand of the Lord came upon him." When the hand of the Lord came upon Elisha, he delivered a prophetic utterance to King Jehoram of Israel, King Jehoshaphat of Judah, and the King of Edom what God's answer was to meet their need for water. When praises go up, His presence comes down, and the right atmosphere determines whether the Spirit of prophecy or any of the gifts of the Spirit will operate in our midst. Songs of music and praise unto God "rolls out the red carpet," extending a loving welcome to the Holy Spirit.

The praises of God can protect us in the natural and unseen realm as King Jehoshaphat would testify if he were here today. His story of protection in 2 Chronicles chapter 20 describes when the Moabites, Ammonites, and Meunites came against Jerusalem, greatly alarming the king. He called a fast in all Judah and set his face to seek the Lord for what he should do. When an assembly had gathered, Jehoshaphat prayed to acknowledge the preeminence of God, His faithfulness to the people of Israel, and the covenantal promises established through Israel's King Solomon when he dedicated the temple he had built to the Lord,[288] approximately sixty-one years earlier.

And God responded. The spirit of the Lord came upon Jahaziel, a descendent of the sons of Asaph, giving the people of Jerusalem instructions for victory against the opposing forces who had arrayed themselves against Judah. In his prophetic word, Jahaziel spoke plainly that the people of Judah were not to be afraid or dismayed because this encroaching conflict was God's battle—not theirs. They wouldn't need to fight but were to position themselves, stand still and see the salvation of the Lord; the Lord was with them. The next morning, they rose early and went out to meet the opposing armies, and Jehoshaphat encouraged his people. After consulting with them, Jehoshaphat demonstrated he was indeed a man of faith—he believed the word which had been spoken by Jahaziel the day before and did not put his finest warriors on the front lines, "just in case" things went south. Instead, he sent the choir out first, ahead of his fighting men! Yes, the choir. "Now when they began to sing and to praise, the Lord set ambushes against the people of Ammon, Moab, and Mount Seir, who had come against Judah; and they were defeated" (2 Chronicles 20:22).

How would you like to be sent to the front lines to sing a tune of praise to God when three hostile armies are poised to strike just a hill or two away? It's a sobering thought, but seeking the Lord, hearing what He says, and doing what He has spoken will activate a supernatural faith in which praise is the only appropriate response.[289] There is power in praising the Living God! The praise principle will work for anyone who has faith in Yahweh, the covenant-keeping God, who has revealed Himself through His Son, the Lord Jesus Christ, the mediator of a better covenant, established on better promises.[290] Now Jesus, Son of the Highest, has sent His Holy Spirit to testify of Himself and what He has provided for all men. God's promises reveal His unwavering commitment to all who sincerely put their faith and trust in Him.[291]

The praise principle is woven throughout Scripture and partially described in Psalm 100:4, "Enter into His gates with thanksgiving, and into His courts with praise. Be thankful to Him and bless His name."[292] This Scripture is a prophetic picture of the believer crossing the thresholds of the outer and inner courts of the heavenly Temple of God, a spiritual progression into His presence. When we verbalize our thankfulness for everything God has done for us and blessed us with, we step into the outer court, or gate, of His dwelling. As we move into praising Him for His righteous acts and holy character, we come into His inner court, enclosed by His presence. The way into the Holy of Holies, a place of intimacy with the Father made possible through Jesus' atoning sacrifice, is through worship and becomes a *spirit-to-spirit* exchange.

The worship I give to the Father, only I can give. The worship you give Him, only you can give. He won't compel us, but He does invite us; He is searching for those who will worship Him in spirit and truth—those who will discover a divine satisfaction, fulfillment, and completeness. The result is a perfect harmony likened to the marriage relationship between man and wife. Isaiah 60:18b says, "…But you shall call your walls Salvation, and your gates Praise." Praise propels us into spiritual places nothing else will and gives us understanding that true salvation is only found in the Lord of life, Jesus Christ. Because of Jesus' precious atoning blood, we may enter the presence of God anywhere, anytime, a presence that is life-giving and life changing. And it is our praise that can bridge the gap between Christendom's denominational divisions, bringing us together regardless of our varying religious views.

Worship is a correct and due response to our Creator, Savior, deliverer, and healer who alone is worthy to receive all blessing, honor, glory, and exaltation. Offering thanksgiving and praise regularly and faithfully to the Lord of Life is a life-altering decision.

Although the Bible tells of many committed worshipers of our great God, one person epitomized and established the principle of praise as a premier and defining quality in his relationship with the Lord. That person is David, son of Jesse, shepherd boy, musician, warrior, leader, and the most powerful and influential king of Israel except for Jesus Christ Himself. David, the worshipper. David, the man after God's own heart.

THE KEY OF DAVID

King David is best known for his confrontation with and defeat of Goliath, the Philistine champion, when he was a youth. David wasn't perfect; he sinned grievously,[293] but his unfeigned love for God always pointed him toward genuine repentance. He received God's mercy and forgiveness, although he reaped what he had sown. Most notably, David's thankful, praise-filled lifestyle distinguishes him in Scripture. His stance on worship positioned him to receive great blessings and favor from the Lord. Next to Jesus, David's name is mentioned more than anyone in Scripture, and the "sweet Psalmist of Israel"[294] eventually discovered his destiny through fulfilling the purpose for which we all were created: praising, worshiping, and loving our holy, infinite, and sovereign God.

While teaching preschool at Community Christian School in Orange, Texas, the Lord taught me more about life through children than I taught them. They hadn't learned to put on the mask adults have been unconsciously trained to do. The dichotomy of flesh and spirit within a carbon vessel is readily seen with spiritual eyes; incredibly impressionable are they. How greatly accountable are we who oversee them. Without a doubt, the greatest honor and responsibility of teaching is sharing God's Word with little ones, who receive it like parched earth drinks in the rain.

Music effectively captures preschoolers' attention; singing, moving to music, and learning to sign the current memory verse is kinesthetically stimulating while planting seeds of truth in little hearts. We covered numerous Bible stories throughout the year, but while studying David, my appreciation congealed regarding the importance of praise and worship; my two trips to the Promised Land totally groundbreaking. And God kept adding to my understanding of this "key" that was there all along, shifting my focus from warfare to worship. Although many Bible heroes had favor, protection, and God's anointing to fulfill their callings, David stands out. This teenager[295] moved in confidence and positivity of God's faithfulness and protection; he didn't tuck tail and run from life-threatening danger but ran toward it, as evidenced by his slaying a lion, a bear, and ultimately a giant.

In 1 Samuel 13:14, the prophet Samuel announced to Israel's first king, Saul, that God had chosen "a man after His own heart" to replace him, who was David, the eighth son of Jesse the Bethlehemite. Saul began well as king, but in time disobeyed in crucial matters, including God's command to destroy the Amalekites. Saul's obedience would have fulfilled a vow God made to Moses regarding the destruction of Amalek in Exodus 17:14. Saul's disobedience revealed his heart's condition: he leaned on his own understanding rather than God's wisdom; he was afflicted with the fear of man and reluctant to face the truth. He believed in God but lacked depth in his relationship with Him, experiencing a disconnect between his head and heart, something everyone wrestles with until coming to God on His terms, acknowledging our sin and inadequacy.

David made mistakes that cost him dearly, but God still chose him over Saul and took him from tending sheep to ruling Israel. David sought, valued, and stood in awe of God; when he sinned, he repented and returned to the Lord with his whole heart. And David was a worshipper; his focus was upon God and what God could do rather than upon himself. His faith helped him overcome fear, and although he walked in denial for a season, when confronted with truth from God's voice of authority, David didn't try to justify himself but repented and sought the Lord's mercy (2 Samuel 12:13–23).

When he was secretly anointed by Samuel as Israel's next king, "the Spirit of the Lord came upon David from that day forward" (1 Samuel 16:13). In time, Israel was challenged by the Philistines, whose champion stood six cubits and a span (approximately nine feet, six inches[296]). In 1 Samuel 17:34–36, David volunteers to fight Goliath, explaining to Saul he had killed a lion and a bear attempting to swipe a sheep from his father's flock and will also kill this oversized Philistine. David prevailed over the giant with only a sling and one of five smooth stones he retrieved from a brook, but not before informing Goliath who he had really come against—Jehovah Sabaoth, the God of the armies of Israel.

David cultivated courage and developed proficiency on the harp. During the hours of solitude, while shepherding sheep, he must have used his time praying, playing his harp, and singing to God. And God noticed. Psalm 50:23 says, "Whoever offers praise glorifies Me; and to him who orders his conduct aright I will show the salvation of God." To glorify means to give glory, praise, and honor. David's sincere worship of God, complimented by his growing proficiency in musical skills, was also noticed by others, who brought him before Saul to refresh the king's soul[297]when a distressing spirit was upon him. Many of the psalms are evidence of the depth and devotion David consistently offered unto God, eventually authoring almost half of them, seventy-three.[298]

Through praise and worship, David demonstrated his love for God. To praise means speaking or singing words that set forth God's glory and goodness, and David descended from the tribe of Judah, meaning "praise." Judah was the fourth son borne to Leah, Jacob's first wife (Genesis 29:35). Judah's life wasn't as colorful as his younger brother, Joseph's, who was Jacob's eleventh son and first borne to Rachel, Jacob's second wife. In Genesis 49, Jacob spoke blessings over his twelve sons, whose descendants became the twelve tribes of Israel. What he spoke over Judah and Joseph was messianic, but Judah's prophecy gives valuable insight into the resident power released through praise.

Jacob's words to Judah begin in Genesis 49:8a, "Judah, you are he whom your brothers shall praise..." Just as wisdom is justified by her children[299] or the outcome of choices made, bear witness to wisdom (or lack thereof) used in making those choices, so shall those who praise the Lord see His involvement in their lives in greater measure. The anointing is unmistakably enhanced in those who consistently and faithfully praise and worship the Lord. Matthew Henry's Commentary says, "Those that are to God for praise shall be the praise of their brethren."[300]

Not only David, but Jesus Christ, the Messiah, made His entrance into humanity through this ancestral line. Genesis 49:8b says of Judah, "Your hand shall be on the neck of your enemies;" praise gives us spiritual leverage. There are moments, occasions, and seasons when we need spiritual leverage, and it's better for our hand to be on the enemy's neck than vice versa! Praise will move forces bigger than we are because praise lines us up with heaven itself. In Psalm 69, David petitions God to draw near, saying, "I will praise the name of God with a song and will magnify Him with thanksgiving" (verse 30). When we offer thanksgiving for all God is, has done, and promised, our perception of Him will grow. He doesn't get bigger, but faith increases in our hearts, much like David, when he encouraged himself in the Lord (1 Samuel 30:1–8). When faith grows, problems and worries shrink. H.A. Ironside, Bible theologian, said, "We would worry less if we praised more. Thanksgiving is the enemy of discontent and dissatisfaction."

Pastor David Berkheimer once said, "We're looking at God through a telescope backward, making God look really little and us really big."[301] When we turn that contraption around with singing and thanksgiving, our perspective changes. Psalm 34:3 says, "Oh, magnify the Lord with me, and let us exalt His name together." To "magnify" means "to be made large."[302] We also magnify God through tongues. Acts 10:46 says, "For they heard them speak with tongues and magnify God."[303] We're in covenant with the Eternal God who made everything and redeemed mankind from sin and hell through His Son, and breathes life into us through His Spirit, enforcing Christ's finished work. Jeremiah 32:27 says, "Behold, I am the Lord, the God of all flesh. Is there anything too hard for Me?" Absolutely not, but we must first believe. Praise, vocally recognizing and attributing the holy characteristics that are intrinsically God's, is a catalyst bringing our mind, mouth, and heart into alignment with the Word and Spirit of truth.

The prophecy spoken over Judah in Genesis 49 can be attributed to the coming Messiah, Jesus Christ. Jesus truly deserves our praise; He undeniably defeated the enemies of God. We, His followers, are blessed to partake of and appropriate His victories, victories He alone secured. Genesis 49:8c says, "your father's children shall bow down before you." Although it was Joseph who prophetically saw and subsequently experienced his family bowing down to him, it is Jesus to whom every knee will bow, and every tongue will confess He is Lord, including His own nation, Israel.[304]

Genesis 49:9a says, "Judah is a lion's whelp; from the prey, my son, you have gone up." The Amplified Bible says, "With the prey, my son, you have gone high up (the mountain)." Genesis 49:9b says, "He bows down; he lies down as a lion; and as a lion, who shall rouse him?" Jesus humbled Himself, or "bowed down," to become human; He "went up" to Calvary, a skull-shaped hill of execution outside of Jerusalem.[305] There He "laid down" His life. In John 10:18, Jesus said, "No one takes it (life) from Me, but I lay it down of Myself. I have power to lay it down, and I have power to take it again. This command I have received from My Father." Laying down his life in a sinless condition and taking it up again was the devil's doom. It appeared Satan won when Jesus died, but Jesus destroyed the power and works of Satan. Truly, "with the prey, He did go up" to Calvary because there Jesus rendered sin and Satan powerless for all who believe and follow Him. In Genesis 49, Judah was compared to a lion cub, a small, vulnerable creature, but possesses the DNA to become king of the jungle. Similarly, what began with praise and naming a man child eventually revealed itself as the human vehicle through which Yeshua[306] would arrive to deliver us from evil once and for all.

Jacob's prophetic word to Judah continues in Genesis 49:10a, "The scepter shall not depart from Judah, nor a lawgiver from between his feet until Shiloh comes; and to Him shall be the obedience of the people." Scepters are symbolic of kingly rule, and kings decree laws of the land (although Levi's descendants eventually oversaw the law in the Torah). "Shiloh"[307] is an epithet for the Ruler of Judah, who is Christ. Jacob prophesied the Messiah will come from Judah's descendants. Jesus' ancestral line, including an assortment of patriarchs, kings, and leaders, is listed in Matthew 1:1–16 with a summation in verse 17, "So all the generations from Abraham to David are fourteen generations, from David until the captivity of Babylon are fourteen generations, from the captivity in Babylon until Christ are fourteen generations."[308] The numbers of generations reflect God's sovereign administration over Christ's birth; fourteen is double seven and seven is the number of spiritual perfection.[309] The "scepter" of authority remained within Judah's tribe until the arrival of God's Son. Now that He has come, the obedience of many Jews and also Gentiles is to Jesus, their King, Savior, and Lord.

Two animals in Scripture symbolize the Person and ministry of Jesus Christ; a lamb, representative of sacrificial offering, cited in Isaiah, John, Acts, 1 Peter,[310]and in Revelation twenty-six times. The other is Revelation 5:5, "But one of the elders said to me, 'Do not weep. Behold, the Lion of the tribe of Judah, the Root of David, has prevailed to open the scroll and to loose its seven seals.'" Jesus is the Lamb of God *and* the Lion of Judah. His sacrifice was sufficient to appease the wrath of God; now, our praises release the power of God. The "Lion of the tribe of Judah" is used only once in Scripture; a recollection and fulfillment of Jacob's prophecy to his son, Judah, the tribe that would arise from his name, and the energy of the Messiah ignited when His people speak forth His praise.

The numeral reference for the Lion of Judah is Revelation 5:5, "revelation" meaning "disclosure,"[311] and five, the number of grace.[312] This Scripture is earmarked with double grace! The Lamb has overcome and released God's glorious grace to undeserving people wherever and whenever they respond to His invitation of eternal salvation through Christ. Jesus has won! He lives! When faced with circumstances seeking to rob us of peace, we aren't slaves to anxiety, confusion, or heaviness; we invite the presence of God by praising the Lamb of God and release the power of the Lion of Judah through faith in our heart and the words of our mouths!

In Revelation 5:5, the Lion of Judah is also the Root of David, another reference to God's sovereignty regarding Jesus' birth, with David occupying a pivotal position. During the years before David's ascension to the throne, he traversed a labyrinth of successes and persecutions, which developed character and prepared him for the immense responsibility God would entrust to him. He was anointed with oil, symbolic of the consecration and empowerment of the Holy Spirit, three times before becoming king of all Israel.[313] First, by the prophet Samuel, second by the men of Judah in Hebron, and finally, by the elders of Israel, culminating God's faithfulness to fulfill His Word. David experienced many trials but never lost sight of who God was and consistently verified his love for Him through extravagant praise and worship, which sensitized him to God's manifest presence. Subsequently, God's manifest involvement in David's life was phenomenal. When we understand the power of praise and ask Holy Spirit to help us adopt a lifestyle of worship, we, too, are on the threshold of something illuminating, liberating, and life-changing because…

Praise pleases God. Psalm 51:15–16 says, "O Lord, open my lips and my mouth shall show forth Your praise. For You do not desire sacrifice, or else I would give it; You do not delight in burnt offering." Animal sacrifices were necessary until God's only Son, the Lamb of God, was offered on the cross. Jesus' sacrifice made it possible for us to be given responsive hearts unto God via His shed blood and indwelling Holy Spirit. Our Lord deserves an eternity of "thank you's" and is worthy of all praise and worship that we, His Body and bride, can give; a fitting response from those redeemed from the pit of hell and invited to come and live with the Father, Son, and Holy Spirit for all eternity. While Psalm 69:30 speaks of praising and magnifying the Lord, verse 31 says our praise "… shall please the Lord better than an ox or bull, which has horns and hooves." Although David lived under Old Testament law, he recognized that praising God yielded enlightenment, understanding, and peace. Psalm 78:67–68 says, "Moreover He rejected the tent of Joseph, and did not choose the tribe of Ephraim, but chose the tribe of Judah, Mount Zion which He loved." Praise and love for God guided David into His manifest presence, the definitive place of peace while producing surprising and substantial benefits.

David's worship made him fit for victorious warfare. Psalm 144:1 says, "Blessed be the Lord my Rock, who trains my hands for war, and my fingers for battle." David's military accomplishments were extraordinary because he faithfully sought the counsel and strategy of God. Biblical accounts provide a roadmap and pattern for personal and corporate spiritual victories today. Chuck Pierce with John Dickson wrote, "Whatever the issue in your life, the key is to worship a holy God who created you and knows everything about you—your failures, shortcomings, insecurities, besetting sins and fears." They go on to write God is saying something like this, "If you'll worship Me, I will visit with you. I can tell you how to get untangled from the snares in your path and… even reveal to you things to come that are pertinent to your life and world."[314] When we "ascend" in worship, the Lord will release needed peace, discernment, or revelation that we may "descend" into our earthly spheres with strength, understanding, or angelic assistance to successfully navigate life.

The seraphim flying above God's throne are continually shouting, "Holy, holy, holy, Lord God Almighty, Who was and is and is to come!"[315] Dr. Jesse Duplantis, in his book, *Heaven, Close Encounters of the God Kind,* wrote, "Every time they (the angels) circled the Throne they praised God because they saw a new facet of Him they had never seen before."[316] He also writes this has been going on since the beginning of their existence. Like the angels, we have been called to faithfully praise the Lord. Isaiah 43:20b–21 (AMP) says, "…I give waters in the wilderness and rivers in the desert, to give drink to My people, My chosen, the people I formed for Myself that they may set forth My praise (and they shall do it)." Will you touch the heart of God through your praise?

Praise, like forgiveness, is a choice. Sometimes we must push through feelings to praise. Isaiah 61:3 says the Messiah's ministry is, "to console those who mourn in Zion, to give them beauty for ashes, the oil of joy for mourning, the garment of praise for the spirit of heaviness; that they may be called trees of righteousness, the planting of the Lord, that He may be glorified." Praise is an antidote to our flesh nature *and* to depression. When we don't feel like praising God, we nonetheless affect the spirit realm by choosing to offer praise anyway. We walk by faith and not by sight, or rather, by what the Word reveals and not how our soul man feels. Hebrews 13:15 says, "Therefore by Him let us continually offer the sacrifice of praise to God, that is, the fruit of our lips, giving thanks to His name." God always deserves praise, regardless of circumstances, and remarkably, praise possesses the power to change those circumstances.

The enemy is envious of God's worship and glory; he covets something belonging solely to God. Angels dare not allow men to worship them.[317] When we choose to worship God during trials and temptations, we glorify and invite Him into our situation. Years ago, I began experiencing an ache in my left arm, hurting for days. I asked the Lord frequently for healing or deliverance—whichever I needed. Being familiar with 1 John 5:14–15, I began thanking God for deliverance. The pain got worse, but I was determined to continue thanking God instead of begging Him to deliver or heal my arm again. I moved to the living room and sat in our recliner, resting my arm on a pillow; every so often thanking God for deliverance. The pain became excruciating, feeling like my arm was clamped in a burning vice. About 3 a.m., it completely lifted, and my arm felt normal. To this day, if I feel that pain trying to come back, I resist it in Jesus' name and use the keys of the kingdom. If I encounter opposition, I ask my husband, Bennie, to pray for me because he is my spiritual covering in our marriage. Then repeat the above steps.

Thanksgiving, praise, and worship produce a shift in the spirit realm nothing else will because our focus is off ourselves and on the Lord. But if He never answered another prayer, God is still worthy of praise, and we are wise to give it. Habakkuk 3:17–18 says,

> Though the fig tree may not blossom, nor fruit be on the vines; Though the labor of the olive may fail, and the fields yield no food; though the flock may be cut off from the fold, and there be no herd in the stalls, yet I will rejoice in the LORD, I will joy in the God of my salvation.

This life is temporary; God is eternal. Praise helps us look beyond our limitations unto the Lord, who is everlasting and limitless. In keeping an eternal perspective through praise, God will strengthen and empower us from within our spirit, His dwelling place.

Praise precedes and ushers in the manifest presence of God. Second Samuel 6:12–16 and 1 Chronicles 15:25–29 describe David dancing before the ark (representing God's presence) as it was carried into the City of David. Michal, Saul's daughter, saw and despised him for it. In the New Testament, during Jesus' triumphal entry into Jerusalem, people rejoiced and praised loudly before the Lord, who is God's manifest presence. Both Michal and the Pharisees were angered at these expressions of worship. David told Michal,

> It was before the Lord, who chose me instead of your father and all his house, to appoint me ruler over the people of the Lord, over Israel. Therefore, I will play music before the Lord. And I will be even more undignified than this, and I will be humble in my own sight...
>
> 2 Samuel 6:21–22a

In other words, David was saying, "My worship is unto and for the Lord, and not for those who may look unfavorable upon how I choose to worship Him."

The Pharisees told Jesus to rebuke the people crying out during His triumphal entry into Jerusalem. He responded with, "I tell you that if these should keep silent, the stones would immediately cry out" (Luke 19:40). The blood speaks,[318]the heavens declare,[319]and the stones cry out if men do not praise their Creator, Redeemer, and King. Our unfettered worship of God releases His mighty presence in our midst, which the enemy dreads, so he uses whoever and whatever available to stop us from praising God. Of course, sometimes people get out of order. Our cues come from our leaders. When they are praising, worshiping, dancing, etc., we should "follow the leader!" Let us purpose to be Spirit-led in our meetings, removing restrictions we ourselves have put on God. "Now the Lord is the Spirit; and where the Spirit of the Lord is, there is liberty" (2 Corinthians 3:17).

In Mathew 21:15, after Jesus cleansed the temple, the chief priests and scribes became indignant upon hearing people praise Him. Jesus responds by quoting a portion of Psalm 8:2, "Have you never read, 'Out of the mouth of babes and nursing infants You have perfected praise?'" But Psalm 8:2 contains more concerning praise, "Out of the mouth of babes and nursing infants You have ordained strength, because of Your enemies, that You may silence the enemy and the avenger." Praising God becomes "fingernails on the chalkboard" to demons; our praises can also stop enemy backlash when he attacks in retribution. Overcoming power is released in and through those who praise Him.

Most of the sanctimonious Jewish leaders of Jesus' day were ruled by religious and prideful spirits that influenced and persuaded them to resist God's Son. JB Phillips, in his treatise on the New Testament, said, "Those who think they know God always persecute those who really do."[320] Do not let a rock out-praise you, and never be too dignified to worship the Lord! However, the same principle applies to enthusiastic praise in our house of worship as it does to dancing in the church. Honor your headship but find a group where high-spirited praise is welcome or cut loose when you are at home. Experiencing God's manifest presence for ourselves, ushered in through sincere praise and worship, is exhilarating and life-changing (2 Corinthians 3:18).

Praise is a portal into the tangible presence of God; it is the nucleus of the praise principle.[321] Psalm 118:19–20 says, "Open to me the gates of righteousness; I will go through them, and I will praise the Lord. This is the gate of the Lord, through which the righteous shall enter." Gates, like doors, are openings allowing or barring entrance into an area or enclosure. The righteous are justified by their faith in God, not by their works.[322] Before the gospel of Christ was preached, the Spirit of God revealed this truth to those whose heart was in tune with the Almighty. Isaiah wrote, "Open the gates, that the righteous nation which keeps the truth may enter in" (verse 26:2). Thanksgiving and praise are the only viable responses to God's benevolent goodness. David experienced this, but so did Jacob, his ancestor, who prophesied the Messiah would come through the praise tribe of Judah.

Originally a trickster, Jacob's name means "heel-catcher" or "supplanter," and he lived up to it until God intervened, bringing a change in his heart and name.[323] In Genesis 28, Jacob's father, Isaac, sent him to Padan Aram to find a wife among his mother's kinfolks. On his journey, after sunset, Jacob used a stone for a pillow and lay down to sleep. Verse 12, "Then he dreamed, and behold a ladder was set up on the earth, and its top reached to heaven; and there the angels of God were ascending and descending on it." The Lord stood above this ladder and spoke to him, confirming His promise to his grandfather, Abraham. Then Jacob awoke from the dream and said, "How awesome is this place! This is none other than the house of God, and this is the gate of heaven!" (Verse 17).

David wrote in Psalm 24:7–8, "Lift up your heads, O you gates! And be lifted up, you everlasting doors! And the King of glory shall come in. Who is this King of glory? The Lord strong and mighty, the Lord mighty in battle." The gates of God are opened, and the everlasting doors are lifted up through our worship of the King of Glory. Only entering the pearly gates of heaven and opening our heart's door to Jesus is more vital than these spiritual entrances God has provided. The sobering realization is that doors can also be opened to sin. Proverbs 8 discusses the praise of wisdom, who, personified, "…cries out by the gates, at the entry of the city, at the entrance of the doors" (verse 3). We must recognize and guard the gates and doors that block or allow access to our souls.

It is fitting for those who have received the righteousness of God through faith to give Him cheerful and genuine thanksgiving and praise while entering His presence. The opposite state of mind is deceitful and dangerous. Romans 1:21 describes man's initial descent into darkness, "…because, although they knew God, they did not glorify Him as God, nor were thankful, but became futile in their thoughts, and their foolish hearts were darkened." Don't go there. Turn your eyes upon Jesus and take the first step of thanksgiving into God's glorious gateway.

Praise provides protection and opens the heavens. In Numbers 22–24, the prophet Balaam was contacted by King Balak of Moab and asked to come and curse the Israelites because, "Moab was exceedingly afraid of the people because they were many, and Moab was sick with dread because of the children of Israel," (Numbers 22:3). Balak's expectations of Balaam cursing Israel, thus weakening them, embodied his hope of victory against this ominous Israeli threat. Ironically, every time Balaam opened his mouth, he blessed Israel, irritating Balak to the max and giving us key insight into God's response to our praise. Verse 23:21b, "…The Lord his God is with him, and the shout of a King is among them." The Lord inhabits the praise of His people; when they praised, it was as if the King, the Lion of Judah roared! Balaam could not curse Israel because God had blessed them, and blessing moved Israel to praise and worship God. Many years later, King David would write in Psalm 5:11a, "But let all those rejoice who put their trust in You; let them ever shout for joy, because You defend (protect) them.…"

When Jesus began unveiling the power of praise, it streamed into my life over several years. One summer day, after my second visit to the Promised Land, I was taking a bite of turtle cake when a vision unfolded. I saw myself dancing and praising God in my living room and a clear dome expanding outward, encompassing most of my house. This was startling, for I was not in a spiritual frame of mind but afterward began seeing it in other places as well, with similar and differing characteristics. When I shared this with my friend and co-worker, Debbie S., she said, "Oh, the praise bubble!" Praise bubble? I was encouraged knowing others have seen this phenomenon and believe it provides protection for worshipers only thanksgiving and praise can create: a spiritual force field! Psalm 5:12 says, "For You, O Lord, will bless the righteous; with favor You will surround him as with a shield." Psalm 32:7 says, "You are my hiding place; You shall preserve me from trouble; You shall surround me with songs (and shouts) of deliverance." Whose songs and shouts of deliverance? Ours!

Ephesians 4:27 says don't "give place to the devil." When we neglect to enforce Jesus' victory through praise, we allow enemy influence in certain areas of our lives by default. Through praise, God has given us protection from the enemy and a weapon of assault upon spiritual darkness. Isaiah 30:32 (AMP) says, "And every passing stroke of the staff of punishment and doom which the Lord lays upon them shall be to the sound of (Israel's) timbrels and lyres, when in battle He attacks (Assyria) with swinging and menacing arms." Psalm 149:5–9 reveals that praise executes vengeance, punishments, God's written judgment, and binds the "kings and nobles" of the nations. These kings and nobles are principalities and powers who oppose the kingdom of God on Earth. *Praise unlocks, pushes back, and opens the heavens!*

British inspirational writer, poet, and author Euginia Herlihy wrote, "Praise and worship is such a powerful device; able to dismantle every shackle and it's able to break down every wall." Praise and worship of our Lord are not just for Sunday but every day and anytime. Acts 16:25–26 says,

> But at midnight Paul and Silas were praying and singing
> hymns to God, and the prisoners were listening to them.

> Suddenly there was a great earthquake, so the foundations of the prison were shaken; and immediately all the doors were opened, and everyone's chains were loosed.

Paul and Silas didn't complain about their situation or allow fear to take hold. They prayed and sang to God, never mind who might be annoyed by the late-night serenade these two jailbirds were emitting. God heard them and sent a confirmation earthquake at midnight, opening every door of captivity and loosing every chain of confinement. Their faith in and worship of God impacted everyone in the prison including the prison guard. Paul and Silas fulfilled their purpose, regardless of their circumstances. We should too. Prayer and the Word are indispensable in the believer's life, and as we grow in Christ, spiritual warfare will inevitably become part of dealing with challenges pertaining to the enemy. Praise contains power most of the church has overlooked. Our warfare will lessen or cease if we imitate Paul and Silas in the place of our greatest need. Praise should be part of our daily walk with Christ but especially when dealing with our flesh, overwhelming circumstances, or enemy confrontations. One morning, while listening to Eagle Mountain Church in Dallas, Texas, on a video, Kenneth Copeland said we should be offensive to the enemy—not defensive. Praying is good, binding & loosing is good, the Word is good, but we bring out the *big guns* when we praise. He said when we pray, we go to God; when we praise, He comes to us![324]

Extravagant praise and worship are appropriate for the advent of the King of Kings' presence and are prophesied in the Bible. In Acts 15:13–17, James, the half-brother of the Lord, refers to Amos 9:11 and the reinstitution of the Tabernacle of David. This was a tent set up in Jerusalem and prepared by King David in 1 Chronicles 15 for the successful relocation of the ark from Kirjath Jearim, its resting place for nearly twenty years after the Philistines captured it and promptly brought it back after they experienced a series of "unfortunate events" (1 Samuel 5). In 1 Chronicles 16, right after the praising and dancing incident with Michal, the ark was placed inside the tent, the only animal sacrifices were made by the priests, and Levites were appointed to minister "before the ark of the Lord to commemorate, to thank, and to praise the Lord God of Israel" (verse 4).

The central idea in Amos 9:11–15 speaks of rebuilding the nation of Israel[325] and heralds the return of Gentiles belonging to the Lord. But also important is the inference regarding worship in the last days. Pastor David wrote,

> In Amos 9:11, it was prophesied that God would again raise up the Tabernacle of David. In Acts 15:16, as James affirmed what God was doing among the Gentiles, he referred to it as the Lord raising up the Tabernacle of David. These passages, no doubt, refer to the restoration of the *Davidic type of worship*.[326]

Referring to the Tabernacle of David, Acts 15:17 says, "So that the rest of mankind may seek the Lord, even all the Gentiles who are called by My name." The worship continually flowing from the Tabernacle of David was lavish, celebratory, and joyful. First Chronicles 16:5–6 describes those who played musical instruments such as harps, cymbals, and trumpets before the ark of the covenant. David wrote a psalm commemorating the occasion (verses 8–36); a litany of thanksgiving, praise, exhortation to sing to the Lord, tell of His wondrous works and declare His glory to the nations. David had discovered the praise principle.

It is this Davidic type of worship that invites the presence of God which releases the power of God, changing lives and drawing people unto God. Consequently, heartfelt praise and worship are essential elements activating Jesus' usage of the key of David. First mentioned in Isaiah 22:22, "The key of the house of David I will lay on his shoulder, so he shall open, and no one shall shut; and he shall shut, and no one shall open;" it is one of three keys our Savior now holds.[327] When Isaiah penned these words, he describes the imminent replacement of Shebna, a steward over King Hezekiah's treasuries, with Eliakim, a man whose heart pleased God. It spoke of current events but also foretold of one who would eventually come, fulfilling all prophecy concerning the House of David.

Keys open doors creating access, or lock doors, denying access. They represent authority, position, and power. When someone is given a key to a lockbox, a vehicle, or a house, he/she has legal admission to everything contained within. Jesus words in Revelation 3:7–8:

> And to the angel (messenger) of the church of Philadelphia, write, 'These things says He who is holy, He who is true, "He who has the key of David, He who opens and no one shuts, and shuts and no one opens." I know your works. See, I have set before you an open door and no one can shut it; for you have a little strength, have kept My word, and have not denied My name.

Christ now holds this key, symbolizing His absolute authority in all aspects regarding the House of David, the Church, and everything pertaining to heaven and Earth. But remember it was David's heart that initially pleased the Lord,[328] exemplified through obeying, honoring, praising, and worshipping God. Because Christ is the root and offspring of David, and David served and praised wholeheartedly, worship helps us understand God's reason in choosing David and naming this key after him.

When first reading Revelation 3:7–8, I assumed an open door from the Lord was a lateral spiritual opening, a "green light" from God, to go and preach the gospel. In 1 Corinthians 16:5–9, Paul says he will come to the Corinthian church when he passes through Macedonia but was staying in Ephesus until Pentecost because "a great and effective door has opened to me and there are many adversaries." God opens and closes doors in any direction or dimension regarding physical or spiritual locales, but the praise principle points to a vertical door. This portal, accessed through heartfelt praise and worship, opens to the very throne of God, granting the church unhindered access, bypassing interference of principalities and powers in the second heaven.

Jesus set an open door before the Philadelphia Church. Revelation 3:9 reveals why this door is open, "Indeed, I will make those of the synagogue of Satan, who say they are Jews and are not, but lie—indeed I will make them come and worship before your feet, and to know that I have loved you." Why would Jesus have the "synagogue of Satan" come and worship before the feet of the Philadelphia[329] Church? "Philadelphia" means "brotherly love, kindness." Through their worship of God and love for others, they fulfill God's two primary commandments (Matthew 22:37–40), but persecution arises regarding their worship. Like David and Michal, Jesus and the Pharisees, a religious spirit will persecute those who worship God with their whole heart.

Of the seven churches addressed in Revelation, only to Philadelphia Jesus says, "Because you have kept my command to persevere, I will also keep you from the hour of trial, which shall come upon the whole world, to test those who dwell on the earth," (Revelation 3:10). One of several Scriptures supporting the doctrine of the Rapture of the Church,[330] perseverance is noted by Jesus. Their worship of God in spirit and truth (John 4:23) has designated them for a heavenly departure only Enoch and Elijah have experienced. However, an open heaven is available to all who serve the Lord in the same vein, but only those represented by the Philadelphia believers in Revelation 3:7–13 and are alive on earth at the commencement of the hour of trial will be raptured or preserved. The "hour of trial" is the seven-year Tribulation, also referred to as the time of Jacob's trouble and Daniel's seventieth week.[331]

The seven churches addressed were historic churches located in Asia Minor, which is currently modern-day Turkey; the original writings addressed each of them in particular. Some teach that each of the seven churches represents a succeeding segment of Church history from inception until Christ's return. Others teach the seven churches represent different church types within the Body of Christ at any given moment from the inception of the Church[332] until Christ's return.

Although many groups of people have worshiped and served God like the Philadelphia Church and experienced an open heaven, at some point, this open heaven may prove to be a heavenly "escape hatch" for those faithfully looking for Jesus, walking in obedience, and worshiping God wholeheartedly, as David did. The most important thing we can do in life is prepare for the day we will stand before the Lord. Jesus' sacrifice is sufficient for all of us for all time, but we are still called to watch and pray for His imminent return.[333] If we are born again, and our heart is right, thanksgiving, praise, and worship will be a big part of that preparation.

My purpose in writing this book was to share the revelation God has given regarding praise, but before that, He taught me to fight spiritually. Holy Spirit was then insistent I learn the veracity of praise and worship—and talk about a paradigm shift! He even used a kiddie computer game to reinforce His point. In the game, a piece of treasure map was hidden that my granddaughter Tori needed to finish. I began playing the game myself to help her find it because the missing key was starting to eat my lunch. After quite some time, we finally found it, enabling her to finish the game. Finding the key was significant because the Lord was regularly revealing truths about worship at the time, and worship is key to establishing an overcoming lifestyle and finishing our own race well.

In the previous chapter, I wrote about a dream where I found myself in an old house with two front doors located on either side of an enclosed front porch. The door on the left side was secured with locks, but the door on the right was not secure and broken. For years I surmised what the useless door meant. Around eighteen years later, Holy Spirit brought me back to this same house in another dream. I recognized my surroundings and went into the porch area, turning to face the screen door once again. Extrapolation and human reasoning had failed; it would take God and God alone to interpret what was this broken door's significance. Astoundingly, the Spirit, waking me up, spoke plainly and undeniably to my heart: *"This is the praise-less life!"*

From the moment we are born, our spirit, soul, and body crave attention. The elements of the world are calibrated to continually turn our focus back onto ourselves while the enemy strategizes how to access our fleshly faults, wounded souls, and generational curses. Enlightenment, the new birth, the baptism of the Holy Spirit, growing in God's Word, and experiencing supernatural spiritual giftings are all part of our growth in Christ, but there are many temptations and trials along the way. Nevertheless, we are not helpless against the wiles of the devil. We have been given tools, weapons, and keys mighty in God to the pulling down of strongholds—in us and in others. But it is the power of praise that invites the presence of our heavenly Father, our Lord Jesus Christ, and His sweet Holy Spirit into our sphere.

Praise isn't just a church thing or a religious thing. It's a heart-for-God thing. Christians, if we aren't cultivating a lifestyle of thanksgiving and praise, we are missing the boat, missing the point, missing the reason for which we were created. When praises go up, His presence comes down. Because of the blood of Jesus, heaven has established an open-door policy for those who will love and worship God with their whole heart and love their neighbor as themselves. This was David's key, and it touched the heart of Almighty God. Through Jesus our Lord, we can too.

Prayer of Activation for the Key of David:

Heavenly Father, forgive me for allowing my flesh, the world, and the enemy to stop me from thanking, praising, and worshiping you. Wash me in Jesus' precious blood and fill me with your Holy Spirit, that I may give you all my heart in worship, obedience, and fulfill my purpose in life. By the authority I have been given by your Son, Jesus Christ, I loose myself from every claim, hindrance, and obstacle of the enemy, binding my mind to the mind of Christ and my will to your perfect will. Anoint and empower me to release thanksgiving, praise, and worship that reaches your throne, joining the heavenly chorus of all who know and love you with their entire being. I do love you and desire to worship you in Spirit and truth all the days of my life. ~ In Jesus' matchless name, amen!

ENDNOTES

1 Mayo Clinic, *Obsession symptoms*; www.mayoclinic.org

2 International OCD Foundation; en.wikipedia.org

3 Strong's Concordance is referenced using the King James Bible Version giving English renderings from original Hebrew (Old Testament) and Greek (New Testament) languages; kingjamesbibleonline. org, biblegateway.com or biblehub.com. Access Strong's Exhaustive Concordance online at biblestudytools.com.

4 Strong's, Greek, #1018 & 1017

5 Judges 6:22–24; John 14:27; Hebrews 13:20, 21

6 John 6:1–14, 22–27, 31–35, 41, 42, 48–63, 67–69

7 John 8:31, 32, 36; Romans 8:2; 2 Corinthians 3:17, 10:4, 5

8 Matthew 10:1; Mark 3:13–15

9 *Kenneth Hagin Ministries*, www.rhema.org

10 John 3:27; James 1:17

11 Plural: the term used in the King James version of the Bible; interchangeable with the word "demons" or "unclean spirits"

12 Satan is mentioned eighteen times in the Old Testament, forteen of those in the Job chapters 1 & 2; he is mentioned thirty-four times in the New Testament.

13 Strong's; Greek, #4487, meaning: *utterance*

14 John 6:63; Ephesians 6:17; Hebrews 4:12

15 Exodus 40:34; Leviticus 9:6; 1 Kings 8:10, 11; 2 Chronicles 5:13, 14; Matthew 17:5; 2 Peter 1:17

16 Daniel 10; 2 Corinthians 4:18; Ephesians 6:12; 1 Thessalonians 2:18

17 Genesis 9:16, 17:7; 1 Samuel 18:3; 2 Samuel 9:1, 6–7; Isaiah 55:3; Hebrews 13:20

18 Acts 2:3, 4, 11; 10:46; 19:6

19 1 Corinthians 12:10, 28; 14:5, 39

20 Matthew 10:1, 13:19; Mark 4:15; Luke 8:12; 1st Peter 5:8; Revelation 3:11

21 John 1:12, 13; 14:23; Revelation 3:20

22 Strong's, Greek, #5545—the Greek word for anointing is chrisma; from whence we get the term "charismatic"

23 Isaiah 14:12–15; Ezekiel 28:12–17

24 Jude 9; Revelation 12:7–9

25 Exodus 22:18; Leviticus 20:27; 1 Chronicles 10:13

26 Matthew 25:46; Luke 16:19–31; John 10:28, 11:25, 26; Hebrews 5:9; Revelation 20:10

27 John 3:36, 14:6; 1st John 2:23, 5:12

28 Philippians 4:3; Revelation 20:11–15

29 1 Corinthians 15:51,52; 1 Thessalonians 4:17; Revelation 3:10

30 Romans 5:15, 16; 6:23; Ephesians 2:8, 9; Hebrews 10:19, 20

31 Joel 2:32; Matthew 10:32; Romans 10:13

32 John 8:24; Acts 4:12; Hebrews 5:9; 1 John 5:12

33 John 1:29; Hebrews 9:12–14; 1 Peter 1:18–21

34 Romans 5:14–19; 1 Corinthians 15:45

35 John 1:1–3; Colossians 1:15–17, Revelation 19:13

36 Strong's, Hebrew, #5397

37 Numbers 23:19; 1 Samuel 15:29; Titus 1:2; Hebrews 6:18

38 World Book Dictionary

39 Leviticus 11:14, 19:2, 20:26, 21:8; 1 Samuel 2:2; Job 6:10; Psalm 71:22

40 Daniel 12:2; Romans 5:12; Colossians 2:13; Ephesians 2:1–3

41 Leviticus 24:20, Deuteronomy 19:21

42 Genesis 4:1–5; 8:20; 12:7, 8; 13:18; 26:25; 33:20; 31:54; 35:1–7; 46:1; Exodus 17:15

43 See Leviticus chapters 1–7

44 Strong's, Hebrew, #6491

45 Strong's, Hebrew, #3045

46 A good resource on this issue: *There Were Two Trees in the Garden* by Rick Joyner, available online.

47 John 4:10; Romans 5:8, 15, 16, 10:3; Galatians 3:22

48 Matthew 4:8–10; Luke 4:5–8; 2 Corinthians 4:4; Ephesians 2:2

49 1 Corinthians 4:4; Ephesians 2:2

50 John 12:31; 16:11; Matthew 28:18; Colossians 2:15; Hebrews 2:14, 15

51 Genesis 3:6; Matthew 4:1–11; Luke 4:1–13; 1 John 2:16; Hebrews 2:18, 4:15

52 Strong's, Greek, #5055

53 Romans 5:10; 2 Corinthians 5:18, 19; Ephesians 2:16; Colossians 1:20

54 Matthew 27:50, 51; Mark 15:37, 38: Hebrews 9:6–9

55 Strong's, Greek, #1357

56 Exodus 25:10–22; Leviticus 16:2, 3; Hebrews 9:1–5, 12–15, 23

57 Strong's, Greek, #2784

58 Genesis 5:24; 2 Kings 2:1, 11; Hebrews 11:5

59 2 Corinthians 5:8; Philippians 1:23; Acts 2:32, 33; 7:55, 56; Mark 16:19

60 Psalm 14:3; Psalm 51:1; Isaiah 53:6; Romans 3:23; Galatians 3:22

61 Matthew 4:1; Mark 1:12; Luke 4:1

62 Ephesians 6:11–17; Philippians 2:25; 2 Timothy 2:3, 4

63 John 1: 1, 2; Philippians 2:9–11; Revelation 1:7,8; 19:11–16: 22:12, 13

64 "Restoring the Foundations; An Integrated Approach to Healing Ministry," Second Edition; p. 101

65 Strong's, Greek, # 5117

66 Matthew 28:18; 1 Corinthians 15:27, 28; Hebrews 1:2; Revelation 1:18

67 Luke 9:23; John 12:24; 1 Corinthians 11:31; Galatians 2:20

68 Strong's, Hebrew, #3820 and #3824, respectively

69 Romans 8:29; 2 Corinthians 3:18

70 For more on the discipline of fasting, see chapter 7, *Power Tools*.

71 Matthew 7:21–23; Luke 6:46; 1 Corinthians 3:11–15

72 Romans 3:22; 2 Corinthians 5:21

73 Romans 6:3, 12:1; 1 Corinthians 15:31; Galatians 2:20; Colossians 1:24

74 Philippians 4:3; Revelation 3:5, 20:12

75 Isaiah 9:2; John 1:4, 5, 8:12, 9:5, 12:35, 36; 2 Timothy 1:10

76 John 3:3,5,7; 20:22; Acts 8:12; 2 Corinthians 5:17

77 John 15:5; Galatians 5:22, 23

78 Matthew 3:11; Luke 3:16; John 7:37, 38; Acts 2:38, 8:14–17

79 Page 63

80 The 9 manifestation gifts of the Spirit are listed in these passages. Other gifts of the Spirit are listed in Romans 12:6–8, which are the motivational gifts; and Ephesians 4:7–13, the five-fold ministry gifts.

81 Matthew 10:1; Mark 6:7; Luke 9:1—in each of these references, the words authority and power are used interchangeably, but the Greek word is the same: exousia,

82 Strong's, Greek, #1849

83 Page 8

84 Page 9

85 Pat Robertson Answers to 200 of Life's Most Probing Questions, p. 102

86 Mark 6:5, 6:13, 16:17, 18; Luke 4:40; Acts 28:8; James 5:14

87 Mark 16:20; John 2:11; Acts 14:3; 19:11; Hebrews 2:4

88 Acts 2:1–4, 11, 38, 39; 10:44–46; 11:15–17; 19:6. In Acts 8:14–18 and 9:17, 18 it is implied.

89 Isaiah 28:11, 12; Jude 1:20, respectively

90 According to Wikipedia, the online dictionary

91 According to Ethnologue (published by SIL international) whose detailed classified list as of 2009 included 6,909 distinct languages. Linguistic Society of America, linguisticsociety.org. Also 1 Corinthians 13:1; 14:10.

92 Goodnewsdispatch.org; Probability of Jesus Christ Fulfilling Prophecy.

93 Page 11

94 2 Samuel 23: 1, 2; 2 Peter 1:19–21

95 *The Ministry of a Prophet,* by Kenneth E. Hagin, p. 10

96 Amos 3:7; 2 Peter 1:21; 1 Corinthians 14:24, 25

97 Strong's, Greek, #3618

98 Acts 17:11; Isaiah 34:16; John 5:39

99 To "appropriate" means to take possession of or to set apart or assign to a particular purpose or use, Merriam-Webster online dictionary.

100 Strong's, Greek, #1463

101 Isaiah 40:31; Ephesians 4:32, 6:18: James 1:22, respectively

102 January 4, 2017

103 John 14:17, 15:26, 16:13; 1 John 4:6

104 Matthew 7:1; Luke 6:37; Romans 14:3, 4

105 Romans 15:1; Galatians 6:2; James 5:16

106 Psalm 86:11, 143:8; Ephesians 6:5, 6: James 4:8

107 John 15:3, 17:17, 19; 1 Corinthians 6:11; Ephesians 5:26

108 John 8:47, 10:27, 18:37; 1st John 3:18, 19

109 Proverbs 23:7; Matthew 12:34–37; Luke 6:45

110 Proverbs 6:2; 13:3; 18:21; Isaiah 55:10, 11; James 1:26; 3:2–12

111 David Berkheimer sermon, *"Obedience Righteousness,"* January 6, 2002

112 Romans 3:21–26, 5:17; 2 Corinthians 5:21

113 Isaiah 59:17; 1 Thessalonians 5:8

114 Psalm 34:9, 10, 84:11, Isaiah 60:19, 20; Malachi 4:2

115 Genesis 8:22; Psalm 62:12; Proverbs 24:12; Romans 2:6; Galatians 6:7, 8

116 Psalm 32:5; Proverbs 28:13; 1 John 1:9

117 Philippians 2:14; 1 Peter 4:9

118 Galatians 5:16–21; Romans 6:12, 7:15–17; 1 Corinthians 6:9–11; Ephesians 5:3–5; Colossians 3:5–11

119 There are an estimated 146,357 deaths each day, with 6098 people dying each hour; Ask.com

120 Ezekiel 33:11; 1 Timothy 2:3, 4; 2 Peter 3:9

121 1 Corinthians 3:6–9; 2 Corinthians 3:5

122 Job 28:28; Psalm 111:10; Proverbs 8:13, 9:10, 10:27, 14:26

123 Daniel 7:13, 14; Matthew 28:18; John 3:35, 36; Acts 4:12; Hebrews 1:1, 2

124 Deuteronomy 32:20; Habakkuk 2:4

125 Strong's, Greek, #4102

126 Parable of the Soils: Matthew 13:3–23; Mark 4:1–20; Luke 8:4–15

127 Genesis 15:6; Romans 4:3; Galatians 3:6

128 Strong's, Greek #2375

129 Isaiah 59:17; Ephesians 6:17; 1 Thessalonians 5:8

130 *Number in Scripture,* by E.W. Bullinger, p. 107.

131 1 Chronicles 22:19a; Colossians 3:2; 1 John 2:15

132 Genesis 1; John 1:3; Colossians 1:16, 17; Hebrews 1:3, 10–12

133 Matthew 4:1–11; Mark 1:12, 13; Luke 4:1–13

134 Genesis 3:6; 1 John 2:16

135 Matthew 3:10a; 1 Timothy 6:10a; Hebrews 12:15

136 Strong's Concordance, Greek, #3056—*A word (as embodying an idea) a statement or a speech*

137 The apostle Paul, of course; wiki.answers.com

138 Ephesians 6:11; 1 Peter 5:8; James 4:7

139 John 14:16, 26; 16:13; Isaiah 11:2

140 Strong's, Greek, #2032

141 Job 1:6; Zechariah 3:1; John 12:31, 16:11

142 Strong's, Greek, #746

143 Merriam—Webster online dictionary, 2 rendering

144 Rick Renner—Principalities, Powers, Rulers of Darkness and Spiritual Wickedness; YouTube

145 Exousia—Ephesians 3:10; 6:12; Colossians 1:16; 2:15. Dunamis—Matthew 24:29; Mark 13:25; Luke 21:26;1 Peter 3:22

146 Strong's, Greek, #1849

147 Rick Renner—Principalities, Powers, Rulers of Darkness and Spiritual Wickedness; YouTube

148 Romans 8:38; Ephesians 3:10; 6:12; Colossians 1:16; 2:15

149 Strong's, Greek, #2888

150 Page 15

151 Matthew 12:29; Mark 3:27; Luke 11:21, 22

152 Page 96

153 Kenneth E. Hagin, The Origin and Operations of Demons, Page 16

154 The NAS Greek New Testament Lexicon, "kosmos;" definition #1

155 The KJV Greek New Testament Lexicon, "kratos;" definition #1; Rick Renner—Principalities, Powers, Rulers of Darkness and Spiritual Wickedness; YouTube

156 Strong's, Greek, #4152

157 Strong's Greek, #4189

158 Page 113–115

159 Kenneth E. Hagin, *The Origin and Operation of Demons*, p. 5; Derek Prince, *1001 How Conflict Began, the Pre-Adamic Period*, YouTube; Billye Brim, *Pre-Adamic Civilization*, YouTube

160 Luke 22:3; John 13:27

161 Daniel 10:13, 20; Luke 10:18; Ephesians 2:2; 3:10; 6:12

162 Matthew 12:43–45; Mark 3:11; 5:12, 13; Luke 11:24–26; Acts 16:16–18, 19:13–16

163 About.com Chemistry; *How much of Your Body Is Water?*

164 Romans 8:13; 1 Corinthians 6:9, 10; Revelation 22:15

165 Matthew 18:21, 22; Luke 17:4; 1 John 1:9

166 December 13, 1991 newsletter, Community Church

167 1 Corinthians 8:7–12, Romans 14:23

168 Strong's, Greek, #3900

169 Matthew 4:1–11; Luke 4:1–13

170 Romans 7:17; 1 John 5:18

171 Anatomy of a Scorpion by Ira Milligan, pages 21–24

172 Original sin is the condition or state of sin into which each human being is born. The origin of this state has been ascribed to the sin of Adam; Britannica.com

173 Romans 8:1; Galatians 5:16

174 Page 20

175 Matthew 6:24; Luke 16:13

176 John 5:19, 20; 8:28; 12:49; 14:10

177 Page 15

178 According to the Barna Research group, nearly half of all Americans who accept Jesus Christ as their Savior do so before the age of thirteen (43 percent), http://www.barna.org/barna-update/article/5-barna-up-date/196-evangelism-is-most-effective-among-kids?q=age+salvation

179 Ephesians 5:26; Romans 12:2

180 Dictionary.com, definition #1; this definition also includes "or an object of worship."

181 Ephesians 1:20, 2:6; Colossians 3:1

182 Mark 16:17, 18: Luke 10:17; Acts 5:12

183 John 5:19, 30, 6:38, 8:28, 12:49, 14:10

184 Raising Lazarus from the dead (John 11:41), the Lord's Supper (Matthew 26:26). For a more extensive list of Jesus' prayers, please see Jesusalive.cc

185 Matthew 6:9–13; Luke 11:2–4

186 Matthew 21:13; Mark 11:17

187 Matthew 26:40; Mark 14:37

188 Psalm 119:89, 152; Matthew 5:18, 24:34, 35; 1 Peter 1:25

189 Psalm 84:11; James 5:16

190 Psalm 66:18; Isaiah 59:2

191 Matthew 6:14, 15; Mark 11:25, 26; Luke 6:37

192 Matthew 7:7, 8; Luke 11:9, 10: James 4:1–4

193 Mark 11:24; John 14:13, 14, 16:24; James 1:5, 6

194 Exodus 20:3; Ezekiel 14:3; Ephesians 5:5

195 Daniel 10:13; 2 Corinthians 4:3, 4

196 Ephesians 5:33; 1 Peter 3:7; 1 Corinthians 11:3–5

197 Matthew 24:36; Acts 1:7

198 Ephesians 4:22; Colossians 3:9

199 Matthew 10:38; Mark 8:34

200 Page 69

201 Deuteronomy 31:8; Psalm 139:5; Isaiah 52:12

202 Proverbs 3:34; James 4:6; 1 Peter 5:5

203 Philippians 2:7, 8; Galatians 4:4; Hebrews 2:17

204 2 Samuel 1:12; 2 Chronicles 20:3; Ezra 8:21–23; Nehemiah 1:4; Esther 4:16; Daniel 10:3; Joel 2:12; Jonah 3:5–9

205 Fasting—What the Bible Teaches, page 29, 30

206 Page 30

207 Acts 13–14, Acts 15:36–18:22, and Acts 18:23–20:38

208 Old Testament examples of fasting: Esther 4:16, Ezra 8:21–23; Nehemiah 1:4; Daniel 9:3–5; Joel 2:12. Examples of New Testament fasting: Luke 2:37; Acts 14:23

209 Genesis 17:1, 28:3, 35:11; El-Shaddai.org

210 Agapebiblestudy.com; The Many Names of God

211 Blueletterbible.org, the Names of God in the Old Testament

212 1 Corinthians 15:27, 28: Ephesians 1:22; 1 John 2:23, 4:15, 5:11,12

213 April 29, 1990 sermon, *The Deity of Jesus*

214 Matthew 28:18; Luke 10:22; Colossians 2:10; 1 Peter 3:22

215 Mark 13:26: Luke 21:27; Acts 1:11; Revelation 1:7; 22:7, 12

216 Exodus 29:38–42; 2 Chronicles 2:4; also see Got questions.org; *What does it mean that Jesus is the Lamb of God?*

217 Isaiah 53; John 1:29, 36; 1 Peter 1:18, 19; Revelation 5:6

218 *Transforming the InnerMan*, p. 102

219 *The Power of the Blood* by Ken & Mary Bostrom; What to Do When There Is Judgment in the Land, part 5

220 Genesis 9:3; Leviticus 3:17, 17:10–12, 17:14, 19:26; Deuteronomy 12:16, 23, 25, 15:23

221 Matthew 26:26–28; Mark 14:22–24; Luke 22:19–20; 1 Corinthians 11:23–26

222 *The Blood and The Glory* by Billye Brimm, page 22

223 gotquestions.org; "What does the Bible say about lawyers?"

224 Strong's, Greek #1577—"A calling out; esp. a religious congregation (Jewish synagogue, or Christian community of members on
earth or saints in heaven or both—assembly, church."

225 Acts 7:38; Romans 3:2

226 Genesis 1:3–31; Hebrews 1:3; 2 Peter 3:7

227 Genesis 6:3; Jude 1:14, 15; 2 Peter 3:10

228 Exodus 15:26; 2 Kings 20:5; Psalm 107:20: Jeremiah 30:17; Malachi 4:2; Matthew 15:21–28

229 Leviticus 3:17, 17:10, 14; Deuteronomy 12:23

230 Strong's, Greek, #1754

231 Strong's Greek #4100

232 Matthew 17:20; Mark 11:23

233 Definition of "take heed" by the Free Dictionary

234 John 6:35, 41, 48, 51

235 Also, a prophetic reference to Communion

236 Matthew 4:4, Luke 4:4

237 Definition of "seed" by Merriam-Webster

238 Matthew 13:1–23; Mark 4:1–20; Luke 8:4–15

239 See also Hosea 10:12

240 Pat Robertson ANSWERS to 200 of Life's Most Probing Questions,
page 264: the law of reciprocity is exemplified in the Golden Rule—
Matthew 7:12; also, Luke 6:38, 2 Corinthians 9:6

241 1 Samuel 30:6; Psalm 56:3

242 God's clothing is light, Psalm 104:2; God is the Father of lights, James
1:17; Christians called to be light and salt, Matt. 5:13–16; the armor of
light, Romans 13:12; Christians exhorted to walk in light, 1 John 1:7

243 The visible light spectrum is the segment of the electromagnetic spectrum that the human eye can view; this range of wavelengths is called
visible light—science.nasa.gov—Tour of the Electromagnetic Spectrum

244 Strong's, #2822

245 Strong's, Hebrew #216

246 Manifest spiritual light—Exodus 34:30; Matthew 17:1–8; Acts
6:15; manifest spiritual darkness—Exodus 10:21–23; Mark 15:33

247 Genesis 15:17; Exodus 3:2; 13:21; 19:18

248 Dictionary.com

249 Genesis 19:24; 2 Kings 1:10, 12; Revelation 20:9

250 1 Kings 18:38; 1 Chronicles 21:25, 26; 2 Chronicles 7:1—please see Gotquestions.org; "How many times has God sent fire from heaven?"

251 Matthew 3:11, Luke 3:16

252 *Demons & How to Deal with Them* by Kenneth E. Hagin; page 24. Scriptural references: Mark 16:17, James 4:7, Ephesians 4:27

253 Mark 3:11, 12; Luke 4:35, 41

254 Strong's Greek #4074—"a piece of rock"

255 Strong's Greek #1210

256 Strong's Greek #3089

257 Strong's Greek #3772

258 Mark 3:27, Luke 11:21, 22

259 Community Church's January 10, 1991 newsletter

260 britannica.com

261 1 Samuel 15:23; Galatians 5:20

262 Pages 82, 85, 86–95

263 Deuteronomy 30:19; Joshua 24:14, 15; Ezekiel 18:30–32; Luke 21:19

264 Numbers 33:55; Deuteronomy 7:25, 26

265 Tongues could also be considered a "secret weapon;" discussed in greater detail in Chapter 4.

266 Some of the scriptures that refer to the light of God are: Psalm 27:1, 119:105, 130; John 1:5, 9:5, 12:36; James 1:17.

267 Proverbs 6:23; Matthew 4:16, 5:16; Ephesians 5:14; 1 John 1:7; Revelation 21:23

268 "The Ballad of Jed Clampett," composed by Paul Henning and performed by Lester Flatt and Earl Scruggs

269 KJV "inhabitest," Strong's Exhaustive Concordance, Hebrew, #3427

270 1 Kings 8:27; Psalm 139:7–10; Proverbs 15:3; Isaiah 66:1; Jeremiah 23:24; Acts 17:24; Colossians 1:17

271 Names of God, El Shaddai, peacecw.org

272 *Chronology of the Bible*—Wikipedia

273 Proverbs 13:2; Philippians 2:14, 15; James 1:26, 3:2

274 *Possessing the Gates of the Enemy* by Cindy Jacobs, pages 189, 190

275 1 Chronicles 4:42, 43; Esther 9:5–10

276 1 Corinthians 15:51–53; Philippians 3:20, 21; 1 John 3:2

277 Romans 7:18, 8:12–14: Galatians 5:17–24

278 Lamentations 3:41; Ezra 9:5; Nehemiah 8:6; 1 Timothy 2:8

279 Genesis 15:18–21, 26:3, 28:13; Numbers 13:2

280 Number in Scripture by E.W. Bullinger—#6, page 150; #7, page 158

281 Strong's Hebrew #7161, qeren, which figuratively means "power"

282 Strong's Hebrew #7321

283 Habakkuk 2:11; Luke 19:40

284 Page 149

285 Understanding the Anointing, p. 162.

286 Ephesians 4:16; 1 Corinthians 12:12

287 My testimony concerning this is in "Power Tools"

288 1 Kings 8; 2 Chronicles 7

289 Other examples: Genesis 14:20; Exodus 15; 1 Kings 8:56: Isaiah 63:7; Daniel 2:20–23; Jeremiah 20:13

290 John 14:6; Hebrews 8:6

291 Psalm 1:1–3; Proverbs 1:33; Isaiah 40:29–31; Jeremiah 17:7–8 29:11, 33:3; Malachi 3:10–11; Matthew 11:28–29; John 14:27; Romans 6:23, 8:37–39, 10:9–10; 2 Corinthians 2:14; Philippians 4:19: 2 Peter 1:4, 1 John 1:9 and many, many more!

292 2 Chronicles 31:2; Psalm 24:7–10: Jeremiah 7:2

293 2 Samuel 11, 1 Chronicles 21

294 2 Samuel 23:1

295 Gotquestions.org, *How old was David when he fought Goliath?* Probably sixteen-nineteen years old

296 gotquestions.org; *How tall was Goliath?*

297 1 Samuel 16:14–23; Proverbs 22:29

298 Study.com; How many Psalms did King David write?

299 Proverbs 9:10; Matthew 7:24, 11:19; Luke 7:35

300 Matthew Henry's Commentary, Genesis—Deuteronomy, p. 261

301 April 16, 2003 sermon, *He is Holy,* Community Church, Orange, TX

302 Strong's, Hebrew, #1431, "gadal;" which can mean advance, boast, bring up, exceed; become, make, or wax great, etc.

303 Strong's, Greek, #3170, "megaluno;" which means to make (or declare) great, i.e., increase, extol, enlarge

304 Philippians 2:10, 11; Zechariah 12:10

305 Britannica.com, Golgotha hill, Jerusalem

306 The original Hebraic name for Jesus; Christianity.com

307 Strong's Hebrew, #7886—meaning "tranquil" and is an epithet of the Messiah

308 Luke 3:23–38 is also an account of Christ's lineage. Traditional Christian scholars hold that Matthew's account follows the lineage of Joseph, while Luke's follows the lineage of Mary, which explains the differences, Genealogy of Jesus, Wikipedia

309 *Number in Scripture* by E.W. Bullinger, page 158

310 Isaiah 53:7; John 1:29, 36; Acts 8:32; 1 Peter 1:19

311 "Apokalupsis." Strong's Greek #602

312 E.W. Bullinger, *Number in Scripture,* page 135

313 1 Samuel 16:13; 2 Samuel 2:4, and 5:3

314 The Worship Warrior, page 38, 39

315 Isaiah 6:2, 3; Revelation 4:8

316 Page 114

317 Revelation 19:10, 22:9

318 Genesis 4:10; Hebrews 12:24

319 Psalm 19:1; Romans 1:19, 20

320 *Ten Laws for Success,* the Law of Change by Pat Robertson

321 Details in Chapter 9; Psalm 22:3; 100:4

322 Habakkuk 2:4; Romans 1:17; Galatians 3:11; Ephesians 2:8, 9; Hebrews 10:38

323 Genesis 32:28, 35:10; 1 Kings 18:31; 2 Kings 17:34

324 January 27, 2019 broadcast

325 On May 14, 1948, David Ben-Gurion, the chairman of the Jewish Agency for Palestine, announced the formation of the new state of Israel; oneforisrael.org

326 Community Church September 14, 1990 newsletter, Orange, TX

327 Jesus holds the Key of David and the Keys of Hades and Death, Revelation 1:18

328 1 Samuel 13:14; Acts 13:22

329 Strong's Greek, 5359, 5360, 5361

330 Luke 17:34–37; 1 Corinthians 15:51, 52; 1 Thessalonians 4:16, 17; 5:9; 2 Thessalonians 2:7, 8

331 Matthew 24:21; Revelation 7:14; Jeremiah 30:7; Daniel 9:27

332 Biblestudytools.com, *What is the Significance of the Seven Churches in Revelation?*

333 Matthew 24:42–44; Luke 21:36

CPSIA information can be obtained
at www.ICGtesting.com
Printed in the USA
LVHW080355260422
717166LV00015B/590